DANCING THE SELF

DANCING THE SELF

Personhood and Performance in the Pāṇḍav Līlā of Garhwal

William S. Sax

OXFORD
UNIVERSITY PRESS

2002

OXFORD
UNIVERSITY PRESS

Oxford New York
Athens Auckland Bangkok Bogotá Buenos Aires Cape Town
Chennai Dar es Salaam Delhi Florence Hong Kong Istanbul Karachi
Kolkata Kuala Lumpur Madrid Melbourne Mexico City Mumbai
Nairobi Paris São Paulo Shanghai Singapore Taipei Tokyo Toronto Warsaw
and associated companies in
Berlin Ibadan

Published by Oxford University Press, Inc.,
198 Madison Avenue, New York, New York 10016

Library of Congress Cataloging-in-Publication Data
Sax, William Sturman, 1957–
Dancing the self : parenthood and performance in the Pāṇḍava līlā of Garhwal /
William S. Sax.
p. cm.
Includes bibliographical references and index.
ISBN 0-19-513914-3; 0-19-513915-1 (pbk.)
1. Pāṇḍava Līlā. 2. Self presentation in literature. 3. Folk
drama—India—Garhwal—History and criticism. I. Title.
PN2884.5.P36 S29 2001
398.2'0954'2—dc21 00-050183

1 3 5 7 9 8 6 4 2

Printed in the United States of America
on acid-free paper

FOR SYLVIA

Acknowledgments

Over many years researching *pāṇḍav līlā*, I have been fed and housed in dozens of Garhwali homes. I never cease to be amazed, and absolutely delighted, by the kindness and hospitality shown me. Doing fieldwork in Garhwal is a delightful experience, and I must have done something very good indeed in a previous birth to have earned the privilege of working among these good people. There are too many of them to thank individually, but I must mention the bard Bachan Singh from Toli Village; Vishnu Singh from Kaphalori, who was my first host for a *pāṇḍav līlā* performance; Surendra Singh Negi, son of Man Singh Negi of Kaphalori Village in Malla Chandpur; Shambhu Pal Singh Panvar, Gajendra Prasad Gairola, and Darshan Singh Bisht of Jakh Village in Talla Chandpur; Gusain Singh Negi of Taintura, who looked after me at a difficult time; my dear friends Kunvar Singh Negi and Padam Singh Negi from Sutol; Kula Singh, who invited me to Jakhol for the first time; and Bachan Singh of Jabari Village and his son Yogambar Singh. Very special thanks go to the families of Rajendra Prasad Nautiyal, Rajmohan Singh Rangad, Dabar Singh Negi, and Bhuli Das "Dhaki," whose trust and affection mean more to me than all the academic honors in the world.

Previous versions of these chapters were read at the Center for the Study of World Religions, Harvard University; the Centre for South Asian Studies (Melbourne); the Department of Anthropology at Hemwati Nandan Bahuguna Garhwal University in Srinagar, Garhwal; the Indira Gandhi National Centre for the Arts; the Institut für Religionswissenschaft at the University of Bern, Switzerland; the Melbourne South Asia Group; the Religious Studies Society at the University of Canterbury; the South Asia Institute at the University of Heidelberg, Germany; the South Asia Seminars at the University of Chicago and the University of Washington; and at Auckland University, Emory University, Williams College, and the

Universities of Arizona, Iowa, North Carolina, Rochester, Virginia, and Wisconsin. Some of the material was presented as part of the Macmillan Brown Lectures in 1995, supported by the Macmillan Brown Centre for Pacific Studies at the University of Canterbury.

I would also like to thank my friends and colleagues Terri Austrin, Ian Catanach, Steven Columbus, Frank Conlon, Jay Garfield, Ed Gerow, Bob Goldman, Paul Harrison, Alf Hiltebeitel, Nabila Jaber, M. C. Joshi, P. C. Joshi, Julia Leslie, McKim Marriott, Axel Michaels, Paul Morris, Ralph Nicholas, David Novitz, Jim Ockey, Atul Saklani, Paul Titus, Margaret Trawick, and Claus-Peter Zoller for their comments on earlier drafts of various chapters.

The research upon which this book is based was funded by grants from the American Institute of Indian Studies, the National Endowment for the Humanities, and the University of Canterbury.

Chapter 3 first appeared in 1997 as "Fathers, Sons, and Rhinoceroses: Masculinity and Violence in the Pāṇḍav Līlā" which appeared in the *Journal of the American Oriental Society* 117 (2): 278–94.

Chapter 5 is adapted from my 1996 publication. "Draupadi and Kunti in the *Pāṇḍav līlā*," in *The Wild Goddess in South Asia*, edited by Axel Michaels and Cornelia Vogelsanger, and published in Zurich by Studia Religiosa Helvetica, vol. 1, pp. 355–81.

Chapter 6 is adapted from my 2000 publication "In Karna's Realm: An Ontology of Action," which appeared in the *Journal of Indian Philosophy* 28 (3): 295–324.

Chapter 7 first appeared in 1998 as "The Hall of Mirrors: Orientalism, Anthropology, and the Other," in *American Anthropologist* 100 (2): 22–31.

I would like to thank the publishers for permission to reprint all or part of these essays.

Contents

NĀYAKASYA KAVEḤ ŚROTUḤ SĀMĀNONUBHAVAS TATAḤ

ACTOR, PLAYWRIGHT, AND AUDIENCE
HAVE BUT ONE EXPERIENCE.

DANCING THE SELF

Introduction

The Performative Construction of the Self

In 1978, when I was a student at Banaras Hindu University, Richard Schechner and Linda Hess asked me to contribute to their ongoing study of the Ramnagar *rām līlā*, a spectacular annual dramatization of Tulasi Das's Hindu epic *Śrīrāmacaritamānasa* (the Hindi *Rāmāyaṇa*) by interviewing members of the audience.[1] That work introduced me to a kind of performance that was not merely entertaining but also "efficacious," to use Schechner's term. In their respective historical and cultural contexts, various kinds of performance are efficacious in all sorts of ways: shamanic performances heal, legal performances bind, political performances ratify, religious performances sanctify. Performance studies, exemplified by the work of Schechner and Turner,[2] raised a whole set of questions that have intrigued me ever since, the most important of which concerns the issue of efficacy: How do such performances achieve their ends? The topic is made more complex by the fact that many such performances can be and have been analyzed as rituals.[3] Moreover, in India, both folk and classical performances of epic literature seem, almost without exception, to take a ritual form (see later discussion). And yet, in the anthropological literature there are few categories as vexed as that of "ritual," for which a

1. For more on Ramlila, see Awasthi 1979; Hein 1959, 1972; Lutgendorf 1991; Schechner 1983; and Schechner and Hess 1977. My research for Schechner and Hess became my M.A. thesis and was published as Sax 1990a.

2. See especially Schechner 1977, 1983, 1990, 1993; and Turner 1974, 1982, 1986.

3. See, for example, Atkinson 1987; Good 1994; Höfer 1992; Kapferer 1983, 1997; Köpping and Rao 2000; Schieffelin 1985, 1998; Tambiah 1979; and Turner 1981 [1968] for healing rituals; Aronoff 1977; Kertzer 1988; and Turner 1974, 1986 for political ones; and Gluckman 1965 for legal ones.

large number of competing, and often opposed, definitions have been advanced.[4]

One of the most useful resources for thinking about the relationship of ritual to efficacious performance is Tambiah's (1979) essay on performative approaches to ritual, in which he advocates the integration of cultural accounts of rituals with attention to their performative and contextual features. Tambiah argues that, although it is evident that many rituals seek to convey cosmological information (by which he means not only religious cosmologies but also legal codes, political conventions, social class relations, etc.), it is also true that the performance of ritual is always linked to the status claims of participants, in other words, to relations of power and to the various contexts—social, political, religious, and so on—of the performance. Through various performative media, such as dance, music, and drama, a heightened experience is produced in the ritual, thereby indexing (and often altering) social relations while simultaneously legitimating them via cosmological paradigms. Cognitive content and sociological efficacy—meaning and function—are thus linked via the media of performance. In this book, I follow Tambiah's lead and attempt to illustrate how a particular genre of public performance achieves the cognitive task of constructing (at least in part) personal "selves" as part of a nexus of social relations while legitimating them in terms of an overarching cosmology.

Tambiah based much of his argument on the seminal work of the English philosopher J. L. Austin (1962) regarding "performativity" in language. Austin is perhaps best remembered for his demonstration of the way in which certain kinds of linguistic utterances should be regarded not merely as propositional statements that can be subject to rational judgments of truth or falsity but also and more important as efficacious "speech acts" that are subject to normative judgments of felicity or legitimacy. For example, if a wedding officiant says, "I now pronounce you husband and wife," this utterance is in fact the doing of an action (i.e., the marrying of a man and a woman), and the proper question to ask of it is not "Is it true?" but rather "Is it efficacious?" (in Austin's terms, "Is it felicitous?"), that is, did it accomplish its intended task? Judgments of felicity or infelicity will in turn depend on a whole set of ancillary social conditions: Did both persons intend to marry each other? Was the officiant legally empowered to perform weddings? and so on. Such actions as greeting, promising, baptizing, naming ships, sentencing criminals, celebrating Mass, exorcizing demons, and installing chiefs have been subject to Austinian and quasi-Austinian performative analyses by Tambiah and others, in what has become a rich and extensive literature. The great value of this approach lies in the way in which it shifts the terms of analysis of ritual away from judgments of truth or falsity, according to which ritual and its practitioners must inevitably be

4. See the useful summaries of ritual theory by Bell 1992; Humphrey and Laidlaw 1994; and Tambiah 1979. Bell skirts the definitional problem by writing of "ritualization" rather than ritual, while Goody (1977) suggests that the category be rejected outright.

regarded as mystified, irrational, or downright foolish,[5] to judgments of felicity, according to which ritual is seen as one of many human devices for ensuring an ordered social existence.

Many social scientists persist in viewing ritual, rather like laughing or crying, as expressive of inner states and not directed toward concrete ends.[6] "Expressive" action is contrasted with "instrumental" action, defined as a purposive and effective means toward a conscious end: building a machine, for example, or scratching an itch. The expressive-instrumental dichotomy associates such activities as ritual and drama with an internal psychological realm of feeling and sentiment, while instrumental action is associated with an external, and more powerful, realm of economics and politics. Such a dichotomy is inconsistent with—even opposed to—the kind of model I want to advance, in which ritual is seen as helping to shape the world rather than being passively shaped by it. Following Inden, I seek to leave behind talk of actions "expressing" or "symbolizing" some underlying and essential reality and instead to show how actions—in this case, the actions of public ritual performance—"*make* what order there is in the human world" (1990, 26). In particular, I want to show how *pāṇḍav līlā* does not merely reflect the "selves" of those who participate in it but actively creates them.

Unfortunately, the view of ritual as (merely) expressive is persistent, partly because it reflects common wisdom, being rooted in a dualism of matter and spirit that is a recurrent feature of Western thought. Tambiah and Austin provide useful theoretical resources for challenging this dichotomy, Tambiah because his analysis focuses attention on the mutual constitution of meaning and function, Austin because he exposes the way in which instrumentality often hides, as it were, behind expressivity, and vice versa.[7] A third resource for criticizing the expressive-instrumental dichotomy is

5. This is an inevitable consequence of the "intellectualist" approach to religious belief and practice, as exemplified by the work of Tylor and Frazer and summarized by Skorupski (1976). Cf. Bloch 1974, 1986, 1987; Staal 1975.

6. See, for example, Cannadine 1984; Stallybrass and White 1986, 14. In his useful discussion of the epistemological difficulties that Western social scientists can get into by an unreflective extension to other cultures of their own ideas about (theatrical) performance as "illusion" or "deceit," Schieffelin (1998) also fails to realize that these difficulties are at least partly due to the very dichotomy of expressive versus instrumental that he employs. To the extent that we can learn to stop trying to reduce performances to a set of propositional statements and begin to evaluate them as performances (e.g., Austinian "felicity"), then the difficulties discussed by Schieffelin will disappear.

7. Cf. O'Hanlon's criticism of the expressive-instrumental dichotomy within the subaltern studies movement in South Asian historiography, as one example of the "habitual dichotomizing of conventional social science, and its tendency to obscure the real ambiguity and contingency of the fixed identities for which we continually search." Such a model "fails adequately to displace familiar classifications of activity—the economic, the political and the cultural—from their familiar and respected roles: roles which, in their insistence on a clear distinction between the material and the ideal, the instrumental and the symbolic, have themselves been a formidable ally in elite historiography's denial of a political significance to a whole range of subaltern activity" (1988, 213–14).

Pierre Bourdieu's writing about the various forms of capital: not only accumulated (i.e., conventional economic) capital but also educational capital embodied in qualifications, cultural capital acquired through one's class and upbringing, and symbolic capital, which often takes the form of public rituals, dramas, parades, and other forms of display, such as the ritual performances described in this book. The crucial point about these forms of capital is that they are interconvertible, so that educational capital can be converted into economic capital in the form of a high-paying job, and an expenditure of symbolic capital in a ritual performance can be recaptured as cultural capital in the form of enhanced marriage alliances. Some philosophers and social scientists regard public ritual displays as irrational expenditures of time, effort, and money: as Hocart would put it, they may know (conventional) economics, but they do not know people. However, Bourdieu's theory of symbolic capital shows how these apparently "irrational" events do indeed exhibit a kind of implicit rationality, how they serve the real interests of specifiable persons and groups—in short, how apparently "expressive" action is often at the same time deeply "instrumental"—and in chapter 4, I apply this idea to performances of *pāṇḍav līlā*.

In sum, my contention is that performance theory is a valuable resource for understanding how performances—and especially public ritual performances—serve to create, reaffirm, and alter collective worlds of meaning and relationship. However, one question has rarely been asked by performance theorists: How is the self constructed in and through performance?[8] Before beginning to address this question, it is necessary to review the recent literature on self, person, and identity.

Anthropology and the Disappearance of the Self

Within the human sciences generally, the "self" has recently been declared dead. A battalion of poststructuralists, postmodernists, social constructionists, deconstructionists, feminists, and others have killed it, claiming that the notion of a permanent, bounded, autonomous self residing at the human core—a notion that is said to be central to the "Western tradition"—cannot withstand critical scrutiny. Derrida, for example, employing his master concept of *differance*, claimed to deconstruct the "classical subject" of Western metaphysics, revealing it to be nothing more than a nexus of relations.[9] Similarly, Foucault's aim was to create a history of the ways in which Western culture makes human beings into subjects, and in emphasizing in his later work the role of power in the social construction

8. Three important exceptions are Goffman's *The Presentation of Self in Everyday Life* (1959), which is in many respects foundational for performance studies, Judith Butler's (1993) analysis of the construction of gender in and through performance, and Schechner's "The Restoration of Behavior" (in Schechner 1985).

9. Derrida 1978; cf. Buck-Morss 1977; Johnson 1981; Sampson 1989.

of the subject, he argued that the modern, "Western" self is not the agent of its own life story but the transient result of a set of policing processes set in motion by various discourses of power (1980, 115). Foucault contends that the self "is no more than a congeries of theories about its nature," and that theories of the self "are a kind of currency through which power over the mind is defined and extended" (Hutton 1988, 135).

Contemporary anthropologists have not been slow to apply such ideas to non-Western cultures.[10] Geertz's (1983) discussion of Javanese personhood has become a classic of the genre, and a more recent, outstanding example is Dorrine Kondo, who in her analysis of female Japanese factory workers contends (following Derrida) that "selves which are coherent, seamless, bounded, and whole are indeed illusions," and that "[t]he unitary subject is no longer unified" because, like all signifieds, it exists only relationally, as a play of differences (1990, 14, 36). Kondo asserts that in mainstream anthropological studies of the self, "[t]his 'self' is almost never contradictory or multiple, and traits of the "self" are held to be equally characteristic of all members of a society" (1990, 36–37).

I have a number of reservations about this approach. To begin with, numerous anthropologists, philosophers, and psychologists have pointed out that discussions regarding self, personhood, and identity are often clouded by inconsistent and imprecise terminology.[11] Spiro, for example, discerns no fewer than seven distinct ways in which the concept of "self" is employed in this literature (1993, 113–14). Rather more cautiously, Harris argues that anthropologists should distinguish between the "individual" as a biological member of humankind, the "self" as a locus of reflexive self-awareness, and the "person" as a "human being publicly considered as an agent" (1989, 600–602). That the self as a locus of subjectivity (Mauss's *moi*) is a human universal, a viewpoint in the geometric sense, logically prior to and necessary for the development of culturally variable forms of subjectivity and/or personhood, has been argued persuasively by Harré on philosophical grounds (1998; cf. Spiro 1993, 111). At the same time, it seems indisputable that the whole person, as understood in and constituted by a particular cultural and historical context, varies enormously from culture to culture. We are thus left with a large—and largely indeterminate—gray area lying between the poles of biological and existential universals on the one hand and cultural particulars on the other. As I note later, there is simply not enough empirical work, in India or anywhere else, to draw final conclusions about the degree to which concepts of self and person vary among cultures. Therefore, along with Foley (1997, 263), I remain agnostic about claims regarding either the universality or the absolute cultural relativity of notions of

10. See, for example, Carrithers, Collins, and Lukes 1985; Daniel 1984; Lutz 1988; Lutz and Abu-Lughod 1990; Marsella, DeVos, and Hsu 1985; Rosaldo 1984; and Shweder and Bourne 1984.

11. See Carrithers, Collins, and Lukes 1985; Fogelson 1982; Harrè 1998; Harris 1989; Murray 1993; Spiro 1993.

self, personhood, individual, and the like. In what follows, I deal primarily with cultural constructs relating to personhood. Whereas these constructs have mostly to do with self-representation,[12] it is important to note that they are not simply concepts or texts or cognitive facts: they are public, embodied performances. This makes all the difference, as I shall argue later.

Another reason for my skepticism about the supposed "challenge" to conventional Western theories of the self is my growing doubt about whether this challenge is as radically new as it claims to be. As we have seen, Kondo asserts that decentered or multiple "selves" are nearly absent in mainstream anthropology. However, she provides no examples of such writing, and it seems to me that, on the contrary, anthropology anticipated many of the claims of the poststructuralists. Louis Dumont's contrast between Western individualism and Indian holism is an obvious case from the anthropology of India, but there are many older examples as well. For over a century, anthropologists have maintained that the Western concept of the "individual" is a particular historical and cultural product. According to Durkheim, for example, individualism is "itself a social product, like all moralities and all religions. The individual receives from society even the moral beliefs which deify him. This is what Kant and Rousseau did not understand. They wished to deduce their individualistic ethics not from society, but from the notion of the isolated individual" (1898, 12n.).

Continuing in the Durkheimian tradition, contemporary anthropology has retained a theory of relative, "decentered" identity as one of its core theoretical concepts. Werbner has put this nicely:

> A guiding truth of anthropological theory, at least since the publication of *The Nuer* (Evans-Pritchard 1940), has been that group membership is always relative. If social agents bear multiple (and sometimes contradictory) identities, these are typically highlighted or foregrounded situationally and selectively, in opposition. The further important insight contained in Evans-Pritchard's analysis, and one which bears directly upon current debates about identity and social movements, is that these sited identities are valorised in the last instance not by simple material interests or ecological exigencies, but by the moral values of sociality which constitute these interests and constraints within given contexts. (1996, 82)

In his provocative summary of the relations between psychology and postmodernism, Sampson (1989) lists six challenges to the psychological notion of the self or subject as a unique, integrated whole that is a center of awareness, and anthropology, or "cross-cultural investigation," is first on the list.[13] This should come as no surprise because anthropology, at its heart, is the study

12. Spiro (1993, 114) would say that they have to do primarily with self-presentation.

13. The others are feminism, social constructionism, systems theory (because it gives primacy to relations rather than entities), critical theory (which maintains that such a no

of cultural difference, and thus it is only to be expected that, as connoisseurs of the exotic, anthropologists should take particular delight in savoring the variety of cultural constructions of the person, just as they savor differences in language, social structure, costume—even cuisine. Mainstream anthropological thought thus unites with poststructuralism and postmodernism by calling into question any theory that posits an autonomous self as either an elementary or a universal ontological category.[14] On the contrary, the self is generally viewed by anthropology as a contingent sociocultural construction.[15]

It may well be that the coherent, seamless, bounded, male subject that has been so heavily criticized is something of a straw man. Influential Western theorists such as Erikson, James, and Mead insisted long ago that "the self is relational through and through" (Spiro 1993, 139). Fogelson (1982) has raised some provocative questions about the intellectual pedigree of the recurring image of a non-Western native whose individuality is subsumed in society. Both Murray and Spiro have been especially critical of the tendency to reduce the great diversity in conceptions of self and person to a simplistic opposition between "the West" and "the rest," in which the former conceives the self/person as "*essentialist*, *autonomous*, *bounded*, *stable*, *perduring*, *continuous*, *impermeable*, or *unitary*," while the rest conceive of it as "*pluralist*, *fragmented*, *emergent*, *dialogic*, *relational*, *inconsistent*, and *culturally determined*" (Murray 1993, 6, 3–4, italics in original). Spiro is at pains to insist on the diversity of cultural conceptions worldwide, while Murray discusses the internal diversity of the "Western" tradition.

Finally, I am bothered by the way in which postmodernists like Gergen (1991) or Grodin and Lindlof (1996) breathlessly announce the "new" discovery that the self is "decentered," in apparent ignorance of the fact that Indian psychologists made this point centuries and even millennia ago.[16]

Hinduism and the "Dividual" Self

Hindu theories of the self, both learned and popular, are remarkably similar to the ruminations of postmodernists and social constructionists, and

---

tion of self is merely an ideology contributing to reproduction of relations of production), and deconstructionism (which challenges the primacy of the subject [or author]). Note that Sampson relies for his definition of the "North American version of psychology's subject" on anthropologist Clifford Geertz.

14. Gerholm (1988) lists a number of features—plurality of perspectives, fragmented cultural systems, shaping of different private experiences, "hard surface," the ruling, and reinvention of tradition—that he regards as characteristic of postmodernism, and one is struck by the degree to which they are characteristic of mainstream anthropology as well.

15. Indeed, at the moment, the discipline seems to have rejected its old search for the universal bases of human subjectivity, such a search being regarded not only as quixotic but also—even worse—as "essentialist."

16. It could also be argued that Derrida's ideas about relationality were also anticipated by the *sphoṭa* theorists among the Indian grammarians.

it is nothing short of scandalous that this similarity has been so little noticed in the West. The irony has been nicely captured by Bharati, who points out that whereas conventional Indian social scientists have consistently attempted to assimilate Western ideas, Western social scientists have equally consistently failed to take Indian ideas seriously, except perhaps for a few stray Jungians and other cultists (1985, 190). Hindus have generally distinguished between the eternal Self (here spelled with a capital S), or *ātman*, as a locus of awareness, and the ephemeral person (*manuṣya, log, ādamī*, and so forth in the vernaculars of the north) whose caste, class, gender, personality, and subjectivity are transient, contingent effects of antecedent, karmic causes. A late and influential model of this sort is found in the *Vedāntasāra* of the fifteenth-century monk-scholar Sadananda (1968; see esp. verses 61ff.; Cf. Staal 1983–84). According to the philosopher Gerald Larson, one of the five postulates of a "protean *Urphilosophie* of South Asia" is that "the self or soul (*purūṣa* or *ātman*) is clearly distinguished from the psychic apparatus so that the notion of 'self' or 'soul' has nothing to do with notions of mind, ego, intellect, personal identity, and so forth" (1993, 112).

The valorized Western "individual," the self as a locus of creativity, moral value, and so on, is not merely ignored in Indian texts; it is positively disparaged.[17] As Bharati puts it, "All Hindu traditions talk about the self either in order to reject its ontological status (as in Advaita Vedānta just quoted, and in Buddhism), or to assimilate it to a theological and metaphysical construct, which is a self with a capital 'S.' When any of the Hindu traditions speak about what might look like the individual, like an empirical self, it is not to analyze but to denigrate it" (1985, 189).

According to Bharati, the average Hindu's intuition is "thoroughly informed by these seemingly recondite concepts." But this assertion is called into doubt by Spiro, who has argued that "one cannot validly infer actors' conception of the self, let alone their mental representations of their own self, from the normative cultural conception" (1993, 120). Similarly, Lukes

17. The denigration of the ego in South Asian religions and spiritual disciplines is well known and need not be elaborated here. But since this is a book on ritual drama, it should perhaps be noted that the theme repeats itself in classical Indian aesthetic theory as well, particularly in one of its central concepts, that of "generalization" (*sādhāraṇīkaraṇa*), originally propounded by Bhatta Nayaka and later developed by the great aesthetic and tantric philosopher Abhinavagupta: "During the aesthetic experience, the consciousness of the spectator is free from all practical desires. The spectacle is no longer felt in connexion with the empirical 'I' of the spectator nor in connexion with any other particular individual; it has the power of abolishing the limited personality of the spectator, who regains, momentarily, his immaculate being not yet overshadowed by *māyā*" (Gnoli 1985, xxi).

One can compare this doctrine with the heavily aestheticized, devotional theology of the Bengali Vaishnava movement of the sixteenth and seventeenth centuries, which it influenced. The latter movement was among the most influential forms of Indian religiosity, and many contemporary Hindu sects are direct descendants of it. Although the Vaishnavas' goal—to unite with God—was quite different from the goals of classical aesthetics, nevertheless the basic techniques for doing so involved effacement of the individual ego (Haberman 1988; Wulff 1984).

argues that Mauss himself, as well as "most of" the contributors to the volume of which Lukes was coeditor, understand the category of the person "as a *structure of beliefs*."

> They discern an underlying structure of belief beneath the varying cultural forms; and they interpret these forms as expressing or representing that structure, more or less adequately. Indeed, they allow (and this is partly what makes such interpretation appear "deep") that some forms misrepresent and distort the underlying structure (for explicable reasons) and can be interpreted as such misrepresentations and distortions. (Lukes 1985, 285–86)

Ultimately we must face the question: How can we get from cultural conception to experience of the self? Can we get there at all? It is certainly true that there is a lack of studies, anthropological or otherwise, of the relation between normative cultural conceptions of the self, and the lives of actual persons in South Asia. If we search the literature for answers to the question of how religious ideas concerning the ephemerality of the small self and the permanence of the big Self relate to the cultural praxis of contemporary Hindus, we are likely to be disappointed. Answers to such questions would have to be based on sustained research, both ethnographic (to understand how empirical persons and selves are manifest in daily life) and historical (to see how such selves might have changed in response to particular historical conditions). No such study has yet been done, though the work of McKim Marriott constitutes an initial attempt to address the relevant issues.[18] Drawing upon a variety of sources, from Indian sciences such as medicine, astronomy, and law, as well as from literature, philosophy, soteriology, and especially ethnographic reports from India's diverse regions, Marriott has constructed an "ethnosociological" model (i.e., a formal model based on indigenous rather than Western categories) of the Hindu person as a "dividual" composed of shifting and inherently unstable substance, while his students and colleagues have provided a number of focused ethnographic accounts of these dividuals' lives, deaths, exchanges, and other transformations. What is important for present purposes is that Marriott's model (based on an unrivaled knowledge of Indian ethnography) confirms that Hindu thought, both learned and popular, also anticipates postmodern and poststructuralist "deconstructions" of the person/self in the sense that it accords no ontological primacy to the phenomenal "person" or "individual," regarding it as a mere appearance, the temporary effect of a variety of underlying causes.

Another way of bridging the gap between normative cultural conception and lived experience is by focusing, as I have done in this book, not simply on ideas as found in prescriptive texts but rather on ideas that are performed and texts that are embodied. Indeed, one of my central conten-

18. See Marriott 1990 and the essays therein; also Marriott 1988.

tions is that public ritual performances are an especially powerful means for creating (and sometimes undermining) selves, relationships, and communities, precisely because they inscribe cultural concepts on the whole person, the body as well as the mind, and they do so by requiring of their participants a public, embodied assent to those concepts. Spiro's criticism implies that culture is something in the head, a set of "beliefs" that can be reduced to propositions and then logically evaluated.[19] But that is not the case. As Bourdieu puts it, "Practical belief is not a 'state of mind,' still less a kind of arbitrary adherence to a set of instituted dogmas and doctrines ('beliefs'), but rather a state of the body" (1990, 68). Spiro argues that we "cannot validly infer actors' conception of the self" from cultural concepts and symbols. Perhaps that is true, but surely the concepts and symbols are a good place to start. And surely, too, valid inferences can be made regarding the degree of "fit" between cultural conception and embodied experience, especially in those cases where informants' words and actions are at odds with the cultural conception; hence the "misrepresentations and distortions" of which Lukes (and Spiro!) write. In chapter 4, I discuss one such lack of "fit" between imagined and empirical selves.

The application of performance theory to *pāṇḍav līlā* is especially appropriate because over the last few years there have been a number of first-rate studies of oral epic performance in South Asia.[20] Most or all of these performances, which are spread throughout the subcontinent, involve performance in the full sense of the term: the public, reflexive "assumption of responsibility to an audience for a display of communicative competence" (Bauman 1977, 11). And nearly all of them are associated with particular communities. Indeed, Blackburn and Flueckiger have argued that oral epics in India can be defined in terms of "the extent and intensity of a folklore community's identification with them; they help to shape a community's self-identity," and that they "have that special ability to tell a community's own story and thus help create and maintain that community's self-identity."[21] Clearly this has to do with the performative creation of communities and *thereby* of selves—something that no anthropologist should ever forget.[22]

19. The best discussions of the problems attendant upon understanding religion and ritual in terms of "belief" are still W. C. Smith 1964 [1962] and J. Z. Smith 1987. See also Schieffelin's study of the Kalulu séance as "an emergent social construction" rather than "a text or structure of meanings" (1985, 721).

20. Beck 1982; Blackburn et al. 1989; de Bruin 1998; Flueckiger 1996; Frasca 1990; Gold 1992; Hiltebeitel 1988, 1991, 1995a, 1999; Leavitt 1991; Malik 1999; Purohit 1993; Richman 1991; Roghair 1982; Sax 1991b, 1995b, 1996, 1997, forthcoming a, forthcoming b, forthcoming c; Schechner 1985; Schechner and Hess 1977; Smith 1990, 1991; Sullivan 1995; Zoller 1997.

21. Blackburn et al. 1989, 6, 11. Further evidence for this sort of link can also be found in the recent works of Beck 1982; Blackburn 1988; Blackburn and Ramanujan 1986; and Richman 1991.

22. I am reminded of Werbner's (1996) lucid discussion of ethnic communities as threefold: moral communities, aesthetic/interpretive communities, and communities of suffering. The crucial point is that all three communities are created/actualized in public performance.

It could be objected that my thesis is merely an elaboration of the Durkheimian notion that collective rituals serve to create and foster solidarity among groups of various kinds. In a sense this is true: in its concern with the social origins and function of collective representations (performances), my argument does have strong Durkheimian roots. But whereas Durkheim elaborated his model with reference to societies that he considered to be internally undifferentiated, my material is drawn from a local culture that is not only internally differentiated by caste and gender but also peripheral with respect to the larger Indian culture from which the narrative core of the drama—the *Mahābhārata* story[23]—is taken. The collective identity forged in public dramas is internally differentiated, not monolithic, and the burden of my ethnography is to show the complex, gendered, and historically situated ways in which that identity is constructed. Thus, following an introductory description of a *pāṇḍav līlā* performance, subsequent chapters proceed to describe and analyze the relationship of *pāṇḍav līlā* performances to caste, gender, regional, and finally interpersonal identities. I have attempted, in other words, to implement Lukes's useful suggestion that we should analyze political rituals "within a class-structured, conflictual and pluralistic model of society" (1975, 301),[24] and my attempt has also been influenced by Kertzer's lucid demonstration (1988) of the salience of ritual in political life. Kertzer convincingly shows that the Durkheimian solidarity engendered by public ritual does not always or necessarily depend on its specific ideological content, which may after all be understood differently by different participants, but rather on the sheer fact of physical participation in collective ritual activity.

All of which leads us directly to a consideration of power. This study has to do with a particularly powerful set of representations that are narrated, enacted, and ritualized in public performance. Currently there is said to be a "crisis of representation," which is just another way of saying that linguistic and other symbols are ambiguous, with shifting meanings that are not fixed and immutable but rather subject to diverse interpretations according to multiple perspectives and interests. However, the ambiguity of representations does not obviate the fact that some of them are more powerful and authoritative than others. How and why do they achieve this power and authority? In the case at hand, they do so through public enactment/

23. Throughout this book, I intentionally refer to "*Mahābhārata*" or "the *Mahābhārata* story" rather then to "the *Mahābhārata*," as is usually done. I do this to emphasize the fact that there is no single *Mahābhārata*. See chapter 2 for an extended discussion of this matter.

24. Davies (1998, 142) approvingly summarizes Bauman's argument "that ritual in plural societies is often far removed from the Durkheimian expectations either that it unites a community or that its performance is primarily inward directed toward community members. On the contrary, ritual may express conflict and desire for cultural change rather than any celebration of the community as currently imagined or constituted, and in so doing it may involve outsiders, either actually present or as absent categorical referents (Bauman 1992, 102–105)."

embodiment/performance. But if such performances always (at least partly) create power relations, if they do not simply reflect them, then it is important to situate them "in a world of hegemony and struggle in which representation itself is one of the most contested resources" (Dirks 1992b, 219, citing the work of Jean Comaroff).

In other words, one can analyze systems of oppression in terms of a currency of representations. In recent years, anthropologists have tended to focus on the representations of the oppressed, seeking to "give voice" to the marginal, to examine their counterhegemonic discourse. Such an approach runs the justifiable risk of minimizing the real oppression they suffer by attributing too much power to a currency that may, in fact, be hopelessly debased. This book concerns itself with the same issues, but in this case the representative currency is clearly controlled by the dominant group (see especially chapter 4).

Relations of power are themselves unstable, and therefore, because the identities constructed in performances of *pāṇḍav līlā* are implicated in relations of power, they are always changing. Traditionally hegemonic Brahmans have lost their virtual monopoly of educational capital, while the Rajputs are increasingy successful in politics (chapter 4). Performers who formerly referred to themselves as indigenous people now shun the term and claim to be Rajputs (chapter 4). Deities such as Karna and Duryodhana are constantly altering their practices so as to appeal to a sanitized, Sanskritized Hinduism (chapter 7). These changes are partly reflected in the performance, and partly created by the performance: political context, notions of self, and dramatic representation are all constantly changing in relation to each other.

I have said that I wish to investigate the way in which public ritual performances "serve to create, reaffirm, and alter collective worlds of meaning and relationship." To say that humans create their own worlds of meaning is not to lapse into a philosophically naive idealism, nor to deny that human worlds of meaning are conditioned by their environments.[25] Derrida notwithstanding, all of human life is not a text: there are all sorts of extralinguistic contextual elements that influence human cultural constructs, from the phases of the moon to the structure of our brains and bodies to the unequal division of power between men and women to the social relations of production. History, environment, economy, class relations, and so forth must be considered in any account of human agency; they struc-

25. "It may well be true that we all understand our lives in our own terms, but we certainly do not live them as such. The world constantly resists our categories, leaving us to close the gap—instrumentally as well as symbolically—between our terms and its own. A history that would attend only to the visible efforts of mind, however materially envehicled, and not to those resistances, ultimately impoverishes our understanding. 'As more than one real Gloucester has discovered,' Geertz writes, 'sometimes people get life precisely as they most deeply do not want it' (Agnew 1990, 46–47). Note how Agnew uncritically invokes the dichotomy of "instrumental" versus "symbolic." The reference is to Geertz 1973, 45.

ture actions in ways of which agents are often unaware.[26] The challenge, then, is to specify the links between symbolic representations and relations of power without reducing the former to the latter, and the performative approach provides a useful tool for doing so.

While we can say that performance theory provides us with the resources for understanding how the self is created in performance (even though none of the major theorists has applied it in quite this way), it is important to remember that the self that is created in such performances is transitory and devalued—devalued precisely because it is transitory. Which brings us back to the postmodern "discovery" of the "decentered self" and all the existential angst associated with that discovery. However, the difference between postmodernists and Hindus is that, for the postmodernists, nothing is left when the phenomenal self is dissolved—leading to irony and nihilism; Hindus, by contrast, know that this dissolution or deconstruction of the phenomenal self is only a necessary step toward coming to know the real Self, which is not to be confused with the phenomenal personality or ego.

In the following chapters, I will show how *pāṇḍav līlā* constructs a regional self, a gendered self, a caste self, a generational self, and so on. One by one, we peel away these layers, like the skins of an onion. And when the last layer is gone, and we finally ask, "Who is the self that is dancing this dance?" the answer is that the self of the dancer is no one and nothing. And it is everyone and everything.

26. "Most symbolic anthropologists, in the name of cultural relativism or interpretive detachment, have been strangely blind to the political consequences of cultures as ideologies, their situatedness as justifications and mystifications of a local historically cumulated status quo. Where feminists and Marxists find oppression, symbolists find meaning" (Keesing 1987, 166).

Prologue

The Mahābhārata *Story*

It has often been said that the Sanskrit *Mahābhārata* is the world's longest poem. In Garhwal in the central Himalayas of north India, oral versions of the *Mahābhārata* story are also lengthy, taking days and sometimes weeks to recite. The following, highly condensed summary indicates the main points of divergence between the Sanskrit and the oral Garhwali versions of the story.

In ancient India, a king named Shantanu rules over the land of the Kurus at the foot of the Himalayas. He falls in love with the Ganges River after she takes the form of a beautiful maiden, and they have a son named Devavrata. After Devavrata grows up, King Shantanu falls in love again, this time with a maiden named Satyavati, who is the daughter of the chief of the fishermen. Devavrata learns of his father's infatuation and goes to seek the hand of the chief's daughter in marriage for his father. But the girl's father refuses, saying that the sons of such a union will have nothing, since Devavrata himself is the king's designated heir. The father will give his consent only if Devavrata renounces any claim to the throne, for both himself and his descendants. Devavrata agrees to these conditions and goes even further, swearing lifelong celibacy. This is such an awesome vow that henceforth he is known as Bhishma, "the awesome one."

Shantanu and Satyavati have two sons, Chitrangada and Vichitravirya, but they die young and childless, leaving the widows Ambika and Ambalika. Because of his vow, Bhishma cannot father children on them, and so this duty must be performed by a Brahman. Satyavati summons her own illegitimate child, the sage Vyasa (who is believed to have later written the Sanskrit *Mahābhārata*), and two sons are born, Dhritarashtra and Pandu. Although Dhritarashtra is born first, he is blind and cannot succeed to the throne. Therefore, the kingship is taken up by Pandu.

Pandu's first wife, Kunti, is the aunt of Lord Krishna. Years before, she had been taught by the sage Durvasa how to call the gods down from heaven to obtain offspring. She experimented while living as an unmarried girl in her father's home, became pregnant by Surya, the sun god, and gave birth to a son named Karna. She abandoned him at birth, and he was raised by a charioteer. Pandu had been cursed to die if he made love to a woman, and so Kunti's special knowledge is very useful because it enables her to become pregnant by various deities, who are the fathers of her five sons, Yudhisthira, Bhima, Arjuna, Nakula, and Sahadeva. According to Sanskrit versions of the story, Nakula and Sahadeva were twins, but according to the Garhwalis, Nakula was Pandu's only biological son, born of his (fatal) union with his second wife, Madri. Meanwhile, blind Dhritarashtra is married to Gandhari, the daughter of the king of Gandhara (in present-day Afghanistan). Since her husband is blind, Gandhari ties a blindfold around her own eyes for the rest of her life. She gives birth to a hundred sons, of whom Duryodhana, the eldest, is the archvillain of the story.

After Pandu's early death, blind old Dhritarashtra assumes the regency, and the two sets of cousins—the hundred Kauravas and the five Pandavas—grow up together in the capital city of Hastinapura in an atmosphere of increasing rivalry. After they complete their military training under the great archer Drona, they put on a grand display of their martial skills. In the course of this display, Karna arrives and challenges Arjuna to a duel, in which he proves himself Arjuna's equal. When Arjuna's friend Krishna points out that Karna, being the lowly son of a charioteer, is ineligible to participate, Duryodhana makes him a king on the spot. After that, Karna and Duryodhana are the closest of allies.

Duryodhana's hostility toward the Pandavas is implacable, and he resolves to have them assassinated in a fire. They are saved by the intervention of their wise uncle, Vidura, and after many adventures they reach the court of Drupada, who is searching for a husband for his daughter, Draupadi. Arjuna wins her hand by performing various feats of strength and skill, and Draupadi becomes the common wife of all five brothers.

Unable or unwilling to put a stop to the enmity between his sons and his nephews, Dhritarashtra divides the kingdom in two, and the Pandavas establish their capital at Indraprastha (known in Garhwal as Jayanti, or "the city of victory"). During this time, Arjuna goes on a great pilgrimage. According to Garhwalis, it was during this period that he lived with Nagarjuni and she became pregnant with Nagarjuna (although Arjuna did not find out about it until later). With the aid of the architect Maya, the Pandavas build a great palace at Indraprastha and perform a huge, royal sacrifice as a prelude to installing Yudhisthira as king. (In Garhwali versions of the story, the royal sacrifice could not be completed until Pandu's last rites had been completed. These required, among other things, the hide of a rhinoceros, and it was in the course of his search for the rhinoceros hide that Arjuna encountered his long-lost son, Nagarjuna.) A splendid royal sacrifice is ultimately completed, and this provokes Duryodhana's jealousy, so he once more resorts to subterfuge in order to dispose of his rivals.

Duryodhana is aware that his mother's wicked brother Shakuni knows "the secret of the dice," and so he challenges Yudhisthira to a game of dice, asking Shakuni to play on his own behalf. This challenge is a point of honor, and so Yudhisthira cannot refuse, even though he knows of Shakuni's secret knowledge. In one of the story's most agonizing scenes, Yudhisthira gambles and loses everything to Duryodhana: his servants, his armies, his wealth, his lands, his kingdom, even his own freedom. When all is lost, Yudhisthira stakes the freedom of his four brothers one after another, and one after another they, too, become Duryodhana's slaves. Yudhisthira thinks he has lost everything, but Duryodhana tells him that he does in fact have one more treasure: his beautiful and virtuous wife, Draupadi. So Yudhisthira stakes her and loses her, and the despicable Kauravas drag her by the hair into their assembly hall. There, in front of the assembled kings and princes, they humiliate Draupadi. They abuse her and try to strip her naked, as her defeated husbands watch. But she prays to the divine Krishna, who provides her with an endless sari, thus frustrating the Kauravas' attempts to humiliate her. The violence done to the virtuous Draupadi is matched by the violence of the language employed: Draupadi vows that she will put up her hair only after she has washed it in the blood of her enemies. Bhima, the third of the Pandava brothers, swears that he will rip out the guts of Duhshasana, who dragged Draupadi into the assembly hall, and drink his blood, and that he will break Duryodhana's thigh, which he had disrespectfully shown to Draupadi. Blind old Dhritarashtra can bear it no longer. He calls a halt to these shameful proceedings and restores to the Pandavas everything they had lost: their rank, their wealth, their half of the kingdom. It seems a happy ending until Duryodhana challenges Yudhisthira to one last roll of the dice, with fearsome stakes. The losers must renounce their half of the kingdom and wander in the wilderness for twelve years. They must pass the thirteenth year in disguise, and if anyone recognizes them, they must go into exile again. The wager is made, the dice are rolled, and again Yudhisthira loses. The five Pandavas and their wife, Draupadi, are exiled to the forest.

The Pandavas have many adventures during their twelve years of wandering in the forest, and several of these are told by the bards of Garhwal. In the Garhwali version of the story, they are accompanied by both Draupadi and their mother, Kunti, although in Sanskrit versions it is only Draupadi who goes along. They spend their thirteenth year living unrecognized in the court of King Virata, thus fulfilling the terms of their vow. However, Duryodhana is unwilling to return their half of the kingdom to them, and war appears to be inevitable. Embassies are exchanged, and the Pandavas seek some sort of compromise, but Duryodhana is adamant. Finally, both sides prepare for war.

The great battle takes place at Kurukshetra and lasts for eighteen days. Duryodhana and his forces, including Bhishma and Drona, are arrayed against the five Pandava brothers and their allies. Just as battle is about to be joined, Arjuna looks at his friends and relatives, his teachers and playmates, whom he must now try to kill. He cannot bear it; it seems to him that nothing is worth this fratricidal war, not even lordship over the whole earth. He turns to his best friend and charioteer, Krishna, for guidance, and Krishna's answer is the famous *Bhagavad Gītā*.

Like the world wars of our own century, the battle is cataclysmic in scope. All the kings and princes, the great heroes of the age, are slaughtered like animals on the field of Kurukshetra. Arjuna's son Abhimanyu is slain, and so are all the Kauravas with the exception of Duryodhana. On the tenth day, the Kauravas' commander, Bhishma, allows himself to be mortally wounded. On the fifteenth day, Drona is killed because of an untruth told by Yudhisthira. On the seventeenth day, Bhima fulfills his savage vow by ripping open Duhshasana's chest and drinking his blood, in which Draupadi washes her beautiful long hair, and Karna is unchivalrously slain by Arjuna while he stands unarmed on the battlefield, attempting to free his chariot wheel. On the final day, Bhima and Duryodhana have a mace duel, which Bhima wins by ignoring the rules of fair play and breaking Duryodhana's thigh. After the battle, while the Pandavas sleep, three of Duryodhana's surviving supporters creep into their camp and massacre what remains of their forces, including their children, so that none is left alive. So ghastly and tragic was this war that, according to the Hindus, it brought to a close the third age of the world and ushered in the present age in which we live, the final and most decadent of all.

Yudhisthira now performs the great royal horse sacrifice, during which, according to Sanskrit versions of the story, he encounters his son Babhruvahana. Dhritarashtra eventually renounces the world and is accompanied to the forest by Kunti and Gandhari. Thirty-six years after the great battle, Krishna dies when he is mistakenly shot by a hunter. Upon hearing of the death of Krishna, the Pandavas also decide to renounce the world. They wander into the Himalayas, but one by one they drop dead along the way, until only Yudhisthira remains. He reaches heaven and sees that Duryodhana and his supporters are living there. When he asks to see his brothers and Draupadi, he is given an illusory vision of them suffering the torments of hell. He asks to renounce heaven and join them, whereupon the illusion is withdrawn. After bathing in the heavenly Ganges River, Yudhisthira enters heaven and passes beyond this world of anger, enmity, and grief.

I

The Sutol Pāṇḍav Līlā

I was excited. For two years I had been waiting for a chance to see the ritual drama called *pāṇḍav līlā*,[1] and now my friend Kunvar Singh Negi told me that his village had decided to sponsor one. He invited me to come and meet him in the town of Ghat in late November 1986, and together we would walk to Sutol village and see it. The chance to visit Sutol was an added inducement. I had been there once before while trekking in the Himalayas, and it had struck me as the loveliest village I had ever seen in Garhwal, an old kingdom in the central Himalayas of north India.

However, my excitement soon turned to frustration as one day passed, and then another, with no sign of movement toward Sutol. And Ghat was not exactly pleasant. It was a typical market town, located where the Nandakini River, flowing down from Rupkund, joins the road to Deval in the Pindar basin. In the 1950s and early 1960s, it consisted simply of a few wooden shops dominated by shepherds come down for the winter and muleteers taking supplies to the high mountain villages, but following Chinese hostilities along the Tibetan border in the early 1960s, the Indian army hastily constructed a number of roads into the area, and now the shep-

1. *Pāṇḍav nṛtya*, the "dance of the Pandavas," that is, the five Pandava brothers who are the protagonists of *Mahābhārata* (see prologue for the *Mahābhārata* story). This performance genre is also known as *pāṇḍav līlā*, "the play of the Pandavas"; is referred to idiomatically as *paṇwāṇī lagānā*, "to recite the Pandava story," or *pāṇḍavoṃ ko nacānā*, "to cause the Pandavas to dance"; and metonymically in terms of major episodes, namely, *kolyūṃ kauthīk*, or "the pine tree spectacle" (see chapter 4); *gaiṇḍā*, or "the rhinoceros" (see chapter 3); *sarāddh*, or "the funeral rite" (see chapters 3 and 4). Related traditions of recitation (though without performance) include the *pāṇḍav jāgar* of Kumaon (Leavitt 1988, 1991), the *paṇḍuāṇ* of western Garhwal (Zoller 1997), and the *paṇvīṇ* of Himachal Pradesh (Kaushal 1997). Note that there is also a central Indian tradition called *paṇḍvāṇī* (Flueckiger 1996).

herds and muleteers were outnumbered by truckers, the shops mostly made of concrete, and the banks of the river littered with rubbish.

At the end of three interminable days, I finally departed Ghat along with Kunvar Singh, his eight-year-old son, his mother's brother, and two nephews. But we did not start until midafternoon, which left us insufficient time to trek the twenty-four kilometers to Sutol before dark. Or perhaps my friends did not realize how slowly I walked. Along the trail, we saw peasants leading cows, shepherds using whistles and switches to drive their mixed flocks of sheep and goats, schoolchildren returning home in their faded uniforms with satchels clutched under their arms, women bowed under the weight of huge loads of grass for the livestock and wood for the cooking fires. We paused at the tea stall near a junction in the trail, where men sat smoking *bīḍīs* and drinking tea, while buffaloes wallowed in a pond next to the turbulent river. The proprietor, thinking that I was one of the dozen or so Western trekkers who wander up the valley every year on the way to Rupkund, offered me a plate of cold beans at a mercenary price. Chuckling to myself, I reached into my pack and drew out the most typical of Indian lunches: still-warm *parāṭhās* wrapped in newsprint, with a dollop of pickled chilis to waken the weary traveler, all prepared by a friend in Ghat. The proprietor, appropriately humbled, did not charge me for my tea.

We continued through the charming village of Gulari, with its rambling hedge of wild roses, and rested at the tiny store in Sitel across from the Forest Department bungalow, where one of Kunvar Singh's relations eked out a living selling tea, sugar, soap, matches, tobacco, and other necessities. Then came the toughest section of the trail, a steep climb up to Gaumvari Pass, where we crouched in the cold, windy dark, drenched with sweat, while Kunvar Singh lit a lamp to signal a friend to bring us some moonshine for refreshment. We quickly passed the bottle around and, invigorated by the sharp, clear liquid, walked the final five kilometers to Sutol in what seemed like no time at all.

As it turned out, I need not have been frustrated by our delayed start, because when we arrived in Sutol the performance had not yet begun.[2] But within minutes of our arrival, the village children ignited a haystack to provide light and began a tug-of-war. The two sides were designated "Pandavas" and "Kauravas," so the outcome of the contest was hardly in doubt. Inevitably, the Kauravas were dragged down the main path into the flagstone dancing square in the middle of the village—a tiny, bright patch of warmth in the icy blanket of a Himalayan winter.

The drummers played the "summoning" rhythm as more and more villagers entered from every direction and settled themselves on the cold, flat stones of the dancing square. In a far corner was a niche in the wall, with flags on either side. It was the shrine of the village god Danu, the *bhūmyāḷ*, or "earth protector" (plate 1). A small, wiry man named Shiva Singh stood

2. According to my notes, the performance began on the seventh solar day of the month of *kārttik*.

Plate 1. The Pandavas' altar in Jakh village. Note the calendar art and wooden weapons. Photo by William S. Sax.

and approached the shrine; the drums fell silent. Shiva Singh worshiped the god with light and sound, circling the niche with oil lamps and uttering his powerful mantras Then he turned to the crowd and, assuming a stance that would become very familiar to me over the following months and years, cupped his right hand behind his ear, bent forward a bit at the waist, and began a peculiar singsong chant while pacing back and forth across the square.

> O five Pandavas, for nine days and nights
> the rhythm of the season will sound through these hills.
> We have summoned our neighbors, and the faraway city dwellers.
> O singers and listeners, we have summoned the five gods
> to this gleaming stone square.
> I bow to the netherworld, the world, and the heavens,
> to this night's moon, to the world of art.
> The gods will dance in the square like peacocks.
> They will dance their weapons in the square until dawn,
> when they will be absorbed by the rays of the sun.[3]

Until this point the drums had merely punctuated the singer's message at the end of each line. But now both drums—a large two-headed *ḍhol* played

3. Unless otherwise noted, all translations are my own.

Plate 2. The large, two-headed ḍhol is played by Gadi Das, while the small damāūṁ is played by his assistant. Bhatgwali Village. Photo by William S. Sax.

with a single stick and a small tympani-like *damāūṃ* played with two sticks (plate 2)—rolled out a complicated rhythm that grew louder and louder as the drummer Dharam Das, his brilliant white teeth flashing in the light of the fire, exultantly summoned the gods. Two boys began blowing seven-foot-long brass trumpets; the noise became overpowering as members of the audience looked expectantly about them. Suddenly a scream pierced the night air, and a man bounded into the center of the square and began dancing wildly, grotesquely, like a puppet manipulated by an inexperienced child. Some people next to me whispered that it was Kali, the fierce, blood-drinking goddess of destruction, who was using the body of her medium[4] to enjoy a dance during her fleeting embodiment (plate 3).

Meanwhile, Kali seized one of the flags next to the village god's shrine and began parading back and forth across the square, reeling as if drunken. He—or rather "she," since she is addressed in the female gender while possessing her medium—replaced the flag and again did a frenzied dance in the center of the square, arms and legs akimbo, head snapping back and forth. I wondered that the medium's neck did not break. Finally she was given a flaming wick, and while still dancing, she held it to her face, grinning madly, licking her lips as though in anticipation of a special treat. She raised it above her head, looked up, and popped it into her mouth! Soon

4. Hindi *pasvā*, "animal"; Garhwali *ḍuṅgaḍī*, "little horsie," reflecting the common north Indian belief that gods "mount" their oracles like horsemen.

Plate 3. Dancers possessed by the goddesses Kali and Nanda Devi in Sutol. Photo by William S. Sax.

she was joined by Danu, and then by Nanda Devi, goddess of the Himalayas (again possessing a man), who held her hands above her head in a gesture of benediction as she danced.[5]

The men playing the main parts began to dance in a circle around the three deities. They mimed the actions of the central characters of the story: Arjuna shooting his bow, Krishna throwing his discus or blessing the Pandavas (plate 4), Bhima wielding his club. After that, the man playing the part of Arjuna—Padam Singh, whom I later came to know as a great loremaster—stepped forward, a brazier of burning incense in his left hand, a handful of grain in his right. He approached the fire burning in one corner of the dancing square and waved the brazier in front of it, offering *ārati*—a ritual in which guests are welcomed by waving burning lamps before them—first to the fire and then to the three other directions. Next he began spinning rapidly in a circle, the brazier dramatically shooting off sparks and smoke. He placed the brazier on the ground and spun about again while throwing handfuls of grain into the air. Each time after hurling the grain with his right hand, he pounded his left fist (in which he clenched the remaining grain) into his open right palm, thus "closing" the direction and keeping beneficial energies inside the village, as well as inauspicious beings out.

One by one, the five Pandava brothers embraced the three deities. After each embrace, the Pandava would exchange rice auguries with the god or

5. See Sax 1991a for a full-length study of the goddess Nanda Devi.

Plate 4. Krishna blesses Bhima and Arjuna as they dance. Sutol Village. Photo by William S. Sax.

goddess, hurling handfuls of rice at the other's raised, open palm, which he or she would then catch and count. This would continue until an auspicious number (either one grain or an even number of them) was caught. After many such auguries, Padam Singh turned to address the drummer:

Good fortune to you, Kali Das.
May you live thousands of years, may you live for aeons.
Your guru made you a good pandit, you are an exemplary disciple.
Ages have passed, but you have not forgotten your devotion.
There are other books for other sciences,
but there is no book for what you play:
it is there in your heart.

He commanded the drummer to summon Kunti, the mother of the Pandavas, which he did by drumming her distinctive rhythm while reciting her "summoning chant" (*birad*, from Skt. *vṛddhi*, or "growth"):

O greatest of gods! In king Santanu's line
in Citra and Vicitra's line, in Hansurai's line,
in Kunjarai's line, hey five Pandavas:
I will forget, but you mustn't forget!
In Mahabharata's line, in Kurukshetra's line,
in king Gudha's line, in old Pandu's line,

in king Dharma's line, in king Indra's line,
O greatest of gods! I will call the Pandavas today
and send them away tomorrow to Victory Palace in the plain.[6]
The burning wood hisses! My heart jumps!
I will send a pair of honeybees to take an invitation.

o parameśvar devatā! to rājā santan ke pāṭā
citra-vicitra ke pāṭā, haṃsurāī ke pāṭā
kuñjarāī ke pāṭā, to he pāñc pāṅḍavo
maiṃ bhauḷā jaulā, tum bhulā na jaiyā!
mahābhārat ke pāṭā, kurūkṣetra ke pāṭā
gūḍhā rāj ke pāṭā, būḍhā pāṇḍū ke pāṭā
dharmarāj ke pāṭā, rājā indra ke pāṭā
parameśvar devatā! to nyūtī bulaulā
bhauḷī paiṭyūlā syalī jaintī bārau.
maiṃ pahoḍī parājā, hīḍā bhāḍulī
moharī rebārā bhauṃryā jauḷyā bhejulā.

In king Santanu's line, O greatest of gods!
The truthful mother got her boon children,
the five Pandavas. The truthful Kunti,
How she served the Ganges for twelve years!
How she served the god Indra for twelve years!
How she served the lord Dharma for twelve years!
How she served the god Brahma for twelve years!

to rājā santan ke pāṭā, paramesvar devatā!
satyevantī mātā, to bart ge putra ju chayā
ye pāñc pāṇḍav, satyakuntāmātā ne
bārah varas kain gaṅgā jī kī sevā!
bārah varas kain indar kī sevā!
bārah varas kain dharamarāj kī sevā!
bārah varas kain barmājī kī sevā!

She served old Pandu. Serving and serving,
her hair turned white like the khasa grass.
She was bent in three places like a lock from Banaras,
and her petticoat was torn to the knee.

to būḍhā pāṇḍū kī sevā. sevā karte karte
muṇḍalī phūlaigī khāṃsā beṭūlī.
tigūḍī nyūḍī banārasā tāl
ghāgarā phāṭī kvaṇyūṃ māthā.

6. *Śailī jayantī bāra* ("the palace of Victory in the plain") is the local name for what the Sanskrit versions of the epic call "Indraprastha," the Pandavas' capital. In north India, this is widely believed to have been located at or near the present site of Delhi

She served the gods with a necklace-shaped brazier.
She served the gods with a golden pitcher.
O greatest of gods! She took laughing barley and speaking leaves[7]
and entered the assembly of gods, true mother Kunti.

devatoṃ kī sevā par hār kī dhūpyāṇī.
sovan kā gaḍuvā paramesar devatā.
haiṃsaṇ juṇyāḷo bulānī pātī
devatoṃ kī sabhā par cal gaī satī kuntī mātā.

As Dharam Das sang this summoning chant, a very old woman danced into the square, possessed by Kunti. While dancing she blessed the Pandavas by extending her hands upward in front of her, palms down, while each of the five dancing Pandavas in turn touched her feet. Padam Singh now commanded the drummer to summon the Pandavas' common wife, Draupadi, who is considered to be an incarnation of Kali (see chapter 5). She danced into the square and up to the fire burning in the corner, which she circumambulated, thereby honoring the sacrificial flame from which she took birth. She danced with each of the Pandavas in turn, but when she began her dance with Arjuna, the rhythm suddenly changed, and so did her movements. Now she crossed and recrossed her arms above her head, the sign of war and destruction, while Arjuna danced opposite her, ducking and weaving, attempting to evade her destructive power.[8]

More characters were summoned: Krishna, the divine ally of the Pandavas, and his sister Subhadra, one of Arjuna's wives; Hanuman the monkey god, companion of Rama in India's other great epic, the *Rāmāyaṇa*; the notorious mythical busybody and sage Narada; Nagarjuna, son of Arjuna and king of Manipur, along with his sister Nagarjuni and his mother, Vasudanta, the serpent princess, Arjuna's paramour; Kaliya, the ironsmith from across the seven oceans, who forged the Pandavas' weapons, and his wife, Loharini; Nari Ucchanga, the demoness-lover of Bhima; Tilbilla and Tilbilli, a brother and sister from Tibet; Prince Uttara and his sister Uttarā, whom they called "the daughter-in law" (*bvārī*); beautiful Basanti the flower girl, with her captivating smile, with whom I was soon to became infatuated.[9] Once this "army" of the Pandavas had been summoned, they danced together in a circle while the drumming built to a powerful crescendo. Then, suddenly, it was finished, and the audi-

7. "Laughing barley" (*haiṃsaṇ juṇyāḷ*) and "speaking leaves" (*bulānī pātī*) are two proverbially powerful substances in Garhwali oral literature. Informants in Chamoli are unable to gloss these terms, but according to Claus-Peter Zoller (personal communication), they are still used in religious rituals in Bangan, to the west of the Tons River basin, especially in the worship of the god Mahasu.

8. Biardeau (1989) thinks that this particuar movement also signifies sacrifice.

9. In Sanskrit versions of the epic, Nagarjuna is known as Babhruvahana, and Vasudanta is known as Citrangada (see chapter 4), while Nari Ucchanga is known as Hidimba. Many of the other characters, such as Tilbilla, Tilbilli, and Kaliya Lohar, are unknown in Sanskrit versions of the epic.

ence settled down and listened to Padam Singh's account of the creation of the world, before going home to catch two or three hours' sleep before dawn.[10]

A pattern developed over the next nine days. At about two o'clock in the afternoon, the drums would sound, and people would slowly assemble at the central dancing square. The bard Shiva Singh would begin the performance as he did the first day, by worshiping the village god. Then he would approach the wooden stage erected by the villagers, across which was drawn a curtain somewhat incongruously depicting Rama, Sita, and Hanuman. As the drums and bugles and chanting rose to a crescendo, the curtain would rise, and Shiva Singh would hurl a fistful of barley seeds at the five Pandava brothers, standing shoulder to shoulder behind it. They would tremble and shake, indicating that they were now possessed by the Pandavas, then the drums' rhythm would change, and they would leap off the stage and on to the stone courtyard to begin their group dance. Then one by one, members of the Pandavas' army would be introduced. On this "opening night" they all made an appearance, thus creating a "twelve-garland court" (*bārah-hār sabhā*), but it was several days until they were all gathered together again.

Hanuman was played by my host, Kunvar Singh. He was the best alpine guide in the region, with an inexhaustible knowledge of local flora and fauna. He was also a shy man, and I hardly expected him to dance such an important role. But on the first night, after the bard had sung Hanuman's praises and the drummer began to play his distinctive rhythm while calling out his *birad*, Kunvar Singh, who was sitting next to me, started trembling. His body shook a bit, then stopped; trembled, then stopped again. As the tempo of the *birad* increased, so, too, did Kunvar's physical reaction, until finally he was quite literally pulled from the bench where we were sitting and spun around the courtyard like a top. Then, as Hanuman, he danced the famous battle with his half brother Bhima.[11] Kunvar danced the part of Hanuman every day, and when the Pandavas donned costumes, he wore a Hanuman mask, purchased along with the stage curtain from a shop in Delhi

10. This was a very long story, chanted in several different meters by Padam Singh, describing the incestuous union between the birds Pankhi and Pankhina, the creation of the world from a primordial egg that was the result of that union; the creation of Brahma and Vishnu; the birth of the demons Kainth and Madhukainth and their conflict with Vishnu; the birth of Kali, who slays the demons; the creation of the world from their bodies; the churning of the milky ocean; the creation of Kaliya the ironsmith and his stabilization of the world; the creation of human beings, and the sending of a mouse across the sea to obtain grain for them to eat.

11. Bhima and Hanuman are half brothers, sons of Vayu, the god of the wind. The story goes that Bhima was wandering in the Himalayas, boastful and proud of his strength, so Hanuman decided to teach him a lesson. The events of the *Rāmāyaṇa* had taken place in Tretayuga, the previous world-age, and so Hanuman was ancient and white-haired by now. He lay down alongside the trail Bhima was following, leaving his tail lying across it. In India it is quite impolite to step over anyone's outstretched legs (and presumably over a tail as well), so when Bhima saw the old, white-haired monkey lying there, he told him to move

that supplies properties for *rām līlā*, the well-known north Indian dramatization of *Rāmāyaṇa*.[12]

Daytime performances were limited to dancing and were finished by about six o'clock, when villagers would return to their homes, prepare the evening meal, and perhaps enjoy a few hours' rest. Sometime around midnight, the drums would beckon once more, and people would shuffle groggily down the cobbled paths and assemble in the chilly square. The afternoon dance sequence would be repeated, and often the local elementary and junior high school students would perform a skit. Padam Singh would recount the story to that point and give a brief synopsis of what would be enacted that night. Then, from about two o'clock until dawn, they would enact the *līlās* proper: vignettes from the *Mahābhārata* story, important episodes enacted upon the rough stage.

We watched as the Pandavas and their rivals the Kauravas competed with each other at school. The Kauravas were depicted as country bumpkins who could not write or even address their teacher properly, calling him *gorū-jī* (honored cow) rather than *gurū-jī* (honored teacher). We saw how the wicked Kauravas attempted to assassinate the Pandavas by burning them in the palace made of lac, the mother and her five sons huddling under a sari while another actor raced around them with a torch. The drummers' song describing the Pandavas' exile was especially moving. Mother Kunti and her five sons danced sadly, slowly, while the Das sang his lament. Basanti the flower girl cried out, "May you live forever, O people of my village, who made this, our reunion!" Kunti was weeping as she danced, and so were many other characters not involved in the scene, who sat and watched from the side. Amid this outpouring of emotion, the Das sang:[13]

Here is fire, my mother, much fire,
and smoke in the Pandavas' faces.
Among the five is the warrior, Arjuna.
Among the five is the woman, Draupadi.
Among the five is the champion, Bhima.
Among the five is the pandit, Sahadeva.
Among the five is the prince, Nakula.

yakh āg huṇī bhotī mātā bai
takh pāñcāṃ rājā dhūpasarā bai.

---

his tail, and Hanuman told Bhima to move it himself. But when Bhima tried, he found himself unable to do so. One thing led to another, and eventually they fought. To represent this confrontation, Hanuman lies on his back in the middle of the square. Once Bhima comes along, they stand up and "face off," glaring at each other as they circle the square. Then they "fight" by spinning their hands in a circle, much as one winds a skein of wool. The fight ends with their mutual recognition and embrace.

12. For more on *rām līlā*, see Awasthi 1979; Hein 1959, 1972; Lutgendorf 1991; Sax 1990a; Schechner 1983; and Schechner and Hess 1977.

13. Every line was sung twice by the drummer, as well as by his chorus (i.e., it was sung four times), except for the line in boldface, which was sung only once, presumably for effect.

takh pāñcāṃ yodhā arijunā bai.
takh pāñcāṃ durepate bai.
takh pāñcāṃ yodhā bhīm baḍ bai.
takh pāñcāṃ sahadeva paṇḍito bai.
takh pāñcāṃ nakula kuṃvar bai.

In their home in the Victory palace in the plain,
their doorframe was carved with crocodiles and fish.[14]
They had spinning pinnacles and a gleaming stone courtyard.
Fog, dissolve so I can look around. In Victory palace, how the drums are beating!
The Pandavas shed bitter tears, how those gods shed tears of blood.
The Pandavas shed tears, and heavy was their load!
The gods of Victory palace; O God, how these drums melt my heart![15]

pāṇḍapom śailī jaintī bārā bai
bāndhyālī magaramacchī kholī bai.
bāndhyālā phiraṇ kalaśo bāndhyālī phaṭāngiṇī cauk be.
phāṭā kuherī cāū pherī. jaintī bārā kan bājyo bājaṇī bai!
pāṇḍapo netarā chvauḍyailo bai, devatāoṃ raṇgo kaiso būndo bai.
pāṇḍapoṃ netarā coḍyailo bai, pāṇḍapoṃ o bhārī sāmalo!

Those gods were in Victory palace, and how their drums were beating!
The Pandavas left Victory palace and moved along the steep paths.
They moved along the paths until they reached a sandy bank,
and there they ate rice made of sand. They reached a deep and shady wood,
they reached a hula-grass clearing, they reached the forested region.
They reached a clearing of tall hula-grass in the deep dark forest.

devatāoṃ śailī jaintī bārā bai devatāoṃ kan bājo bājaṇ bai!
jaintī bārā chvauḍyailo payāṇo bai, pāṇḍapoṃ bāṭā laige paiṇḍā bai.
tab calegā ulāḍī o bai, devatāo bāloḍī bagaḍ bai
pakaigī bālo go bhātā bai pāṇḍapoṃ raṇ-baṇ jaṅgal bai.
ve gayā hulāḍī pātal bai, ve gāyo vaṇakhaṇḍī pātal bai.
ve gāyo vaṇakhaṇḍī negā bai, devatāo hulāḍī pātal bai.

In the evenings, local children would sometimes worship Krishna by waving a lamp before him as he sat in a makeshift "temple" bedecked with plastic flowers. Then, accompanied by a harmonium, they would sing songs in Hindi and Garhwali, after which the dancers would often present humorous skits. One showed a doctor torturing patients with patent medicine that

14. Regarded by Garhwalis as typical plains motifs.
15. This translation of the boldfaced text was spontaneously offered by my research assistant, Dabar Singh Ravat, while translating the text from Garhwali into Hindi.

made them more ill. Another dramatized a scene from the Pandavas' exile: when the five brothers reach the court of King Virat incognito and apply for work, they are given job interviews by his secretary. "What work can you do?" the secretary asks Arjuna. "Well," replies the latter, "I can teach singing and dancing." "Singing and dancing," replies the secretary. "Hmmm. Things are pretty tough these days. Tell you what—don't call us, we'll call you." Seeing the divine brothers thus treated like ordinary hillbillies, the audience responded with howls of laughter.

As the days went on, I began to participate more in the performance, sometimes taking part in the collective dances, but more often pacing up and down in the square next to Padam Singh, cassette recorder in hand. And, indeed, he was not averse to using my presence to underscore some of his didactic points. One night, for example, when he thought the audience was not being sufficiently attentive, he sang:

Just keep quiet, will you? Your home-land's chatter is being recorded:
you'll be disgraced! Just think a bit on your homeland's shame:
all this chatter will be sent abroad.
O Lord, all your nonsense will be heard there!

zarā hallā kam kari dyao! tumāro is mulk ko hallā yakh rīkārḍ huṇ cha maityo!
badanāmī hvaī jālī hvalī! apnā mulk ko badnām kā vāstā zarā soci kari dyau
tumāro ya sārā hallā-gullā videśoṃ jālo maityo,
to dhani nāraiṇ, to hamārī haiṃsī hamārī kholī hvalī vakh!

I was also the butt of a few jokes told by the local comedian, a man playing the part of Narada the sage. During one of his routines he said, "I've harvested many grains; they've all ripened. The sahib, too, has ripened in our *līlā*. Sahib, look over here. Give me your glasses! [He puts them on.] Now I can't see! Who knows what sort of animal he is? There's no telling his caste."[16]

On the first few days, the dancers looked like simple farmers in tattered workaday clothes. Their dancing was sluggish, few spectators from elsewhere attended the performances, and even their fellow villagers were barely interested. But as the days went by, the artistry of the performance grew along with the size of the audience. We watched as the dancers skillfully evoked Bhima's battles with various demons, the Pandavas' fateful dice game, the tragic death of Abhimanyu in the Kauravas' "Circular Array" (see Chapter 4). On the third day, dancers began to wear costumes. On the fifth day, they took out their weapons. By the eighth day, the entire army of the Pandavas had been summoned, the dancing was superlative (plate 5), and hundreds of spectators were coming from nearby villages for each night's drama.

16. I hasten to add that the Sutol villagers did not usually call me "sahib" (*sāhab*); it was used by the joker for effect.

Reciting the whole *Mahābhārata* story from start to finish is impossible because of its great length, and Padam Singh had to use his own discretion in selecting which stories to tell. It was evident from his choice of episodes, as well as from the language he used to "frame" each night's performance, that he based his selection on the edifying qualities of the episodes. For example, in recounting how difficult it was for the Pandavas to regain their kingdom, he invoked the Hindu theory of reincarnation, stressing how difficult it is to obtain the most precious of births—a human one—and how such a birth should not be squandered. On another occasion, his "song" went like this:

> When someone does a pilgrimage, O brothers,
> to Badarinath or Kedarnath,[17] what is there?
> The temple the Pandavas built that day.
> But now is not the faith of yore:
> Thieves do pilgrimage to Badari-Kedar,
> That is why God is hidden away.
> These days, God hides in idols of stone
> because there is only one religious soul in a hundred.
> No one trusts anyone anymore.

After four or five days, everyone in the village had become absorbed in the performance. Most people slept only two or three hours a day, but they danced all night. On the fourth day, I went to interview Padam Singh, who told me he had been awake for thirty-one hours and asleep for one. This was typical of the performers, who considered going without sleep to be a meritorious activity, a kind of asceticism that added to the power of the drama. Kunvar Singh told me that he stayed awake all night for devotional reasons—that it was a kind of *tapasyā*, a method for generating spiritual power. He also said (using the English word) that it was an *order* from the village. People were slightly disoriented from lack of sleep: it seemed as though the drama had become the "real" world, while workaday life was merely a stage drama. I, too, found myself being drawn farther and farther into the performance. Often it was Basanti the flower girl who shyly took my hand and united me with the circle of dancers. Kunvar Singh and his wife heard me singing a Garhwali song, and every day they begged me to sing at that night's performance. "Hundreds of people from all the neighboring villages have come for the play," they said. "Please sing your song. No one will laugh; everyone will be amazed that a foreigner knows our language." But the mere thought of performing solo before a few hundred villagers, in a strange place so far from home, gave me a severe case of stage fright, and I steadfastly refused. Then, one night when the largest crowd I had yet seen was gathered in the square, Padam Singh introduced, in his chanting style, several notables who were present: the headman of the neigh-

17. Famous Hindu temples located nearby; see chapter 2.

Plate 5. The five Pandava brothers dancing. Sutol Village. Photo by William S. Sax.

boring village, a visiting official, a local boy who had obtained prestigious government employment, "and from the University of America, a student who has crossed the seven seas to see our Pandavas dance, and who will now honor us with a song!" I was trapped: no exit. My heart was pounding furiously in my chest. But as I began to sing, the panic subsided, and I discovered that my stage fright was more in the thinking than in the doing. Now my friendship with the performers was sealed. I was invited to share a meal of boiled rice—a great honor for a foreigner—and on the penultimate night of the performance they made me a king. I was dressed on someone's old military greatcoat and made to play the part of King Virat, giving away his daughter in marriage to Abhimanyu, the son of Arjuna.

The most impressive performance came on the eighth day. It was a special day in many respects and was referred to by a special name: *paṇvāṇī*.[18] It began in the morning when the dancers assembled in a field outside the village and began applying colorful face paint to each other (plate 6). Important ritual objects such as the dancers' weapons—along with my camera and tape recorder—were worshiped and daubed with sacred paint. Dancers had to abide by very strict rules that day: no food, no tea, no tobacco, no urina-

18. See chapter 2 for an extended discussion of one segment of this performance. *Paṇvāṇī* means something like "Pandava recitation" and is related to terms for other forms of *Mahābhārata* narration in the region (see note 1).

Plate 6. Kunvar Singh dressed as Mother Kunti, with face painted, for the special paṅwḍī ī *day in Sutol Village. Photo by William S. Sax.*

tion after they had put on their costumes. Because of the strict purity required, women were not allowed to dance.[19] After donning their costumes and makeup, the Pandavas, preceded by the drummer, processed into the central square, where each dancer's feet were washed as he entered. Then the drummer began to direct them in a distinctive manner, orchestrating what amounted to a complete version of the *Mahābhārata* story up to the great war (see chapter 2).

That night, several dozen villagers trekked over the hills from the village of Wan. Although there is extensive intermarriage between the two villages, they are nevertheless great rivals.[20] One expression of this rivalry is the fact that, whereas Sutol produces a *pāṇḍav līlā* every second or third year, Wan produces a *rām līlā*.[21] Several of the youths from Wan entertained the Sutol villagers with a scene from their *rām līlā*, the battle between Bali and Sugriva.[22] After a forty-minute delay that seemed calculated to irritate

19. Villagers said that women were excluded because of the danger of menstrual pollution. Obviously, this is also a method for retaining male dominance (see Sax 1991a).

20. See Sax 1991a, chap. 4.

21. See note 12. In both cases, the drama is seen by many as an enterpreneurial opportunity. In Sutol, for example, there were six stalls selling tea, snacks, and trinkets, even though the village has only seventy-eight households.

22. I have not seen the *rām līlā* in Wan, but I do know that throughout Garhwal, *rām līlās* are associated with Hindu nationalist politics and often are used by social reformers as vehicles for the introduction of forms of Hinduism that are considered more "respectable" than traditional Garhwali customs. For example, in Jakhol village in western Garhwal, where

their hosts, they performed their second number: a rather lewd dance by a young man dressed as a woman. Then, from about four o'clock in the morning until dawn, the Sutol villagers dramatized the great war, in which the deaths of heroes such as Abhimanyu and Duryodhana were represented by dashing squashes to the ground.

On the next day, all the gods were summoned into the dancing square, from whence they proceeded to the river below the village. Everyone bathed to wash away the sins they had incurred in the great war, including Kali's oracle Than Singh, who bathed Kali's "sign" (*niśān*), a small trident believed to contain the *śakti*, or energy, of the goddess. Then they performed the *śrāddha*, or ancestor worship, of King Pandu, the father of the Pandavas (see chapter 3). In this worship, Nakula was the *yajamāna*, or chief worshiper, on behalf of the villagers, while Than Singh represented the local gods.

The villagers processed back to the village carrying a large cedar pole, freshly cut and peeled for the occasion. Padam Singh performed a long recitation, and the goddess Kali was summoned. She possessed Than Singh as he grasped the pole, then she danced out into the square and poured holy substances—milk mixed with cow's urine—over the heads of the other gods, who had by now also possessed their mediums. Hanuman was summoned, and he performed the barley augury with all the dancing gods. One could see that all the auguries were immediately successful: some of the dancers wore confident expressions, others did not even bother to count the grains but smilingly put them in their pockets. The drama had been very successful, and the air was charged with a feeling of religious elation. Hanuman exchanged seeds with the Pandavas, then climbed on to the roof against which the pole had been laid. He waved some incense before the pole, tied a red and white cloth near its top, then helped the others to stand it upright. The village men held the pole upright while Hanuman performed an extraordinarily energetic dance to the wild beat of the drums. After exchanging barley seeds with Kali, he climbed to the top of the pole, followed by Kali, who gave him a smoking incense brazier with which he saluted the summit. He lowered the brazier to Kali, then took grains and fruit—the *prasād* (sacred leftovers) of the ritual—from his bag and threw them down to the crowd below.[23]

---

the main temple of "Duryodhana" is located (see chapter 7), reformers staged a *rām līlā* during the spring festival in 1991, and this was done explicitly to provide a vegetarian and liquor-free alternative to the traditional celebrations associated with the deity.

23. The villagers in Sutol did not offer any interpretation of this *līlā*; however, it might be related to the following story, told by Bacan Singh Shastri: "Once upon a time, a sky-voice came to Dharmaraj Yudhisthira. 'Hey Yudhisthira, bring a pillar and a hero from Lanka and place them in the *mahāviś yagya* [great poison sacrifice] that the Kauravas are performing, and it will be unsuccessful.' So Yudhisthira sent Bhima, who was proud of his strength. And on the way, Bhima encountered Hanuman, whose tail was lying across the path. And he asked Hanuman to move his tail, but Hanuman, who had taken the form of a very ancient, white-haired monkey, said that he was too old and weak to move it, and that Bhima should. (Note the similarities to the famous story recounted in note 11.) Bhima tried and

A pit had been dug for the pole in the northeast corner of the square. Accompanied by Kali (who once again was acting as representative of the local gods), the Brahman priest placed ashes and *prasād* from an earlier fire ritual in the pit, along with sacred paint, incense, rice grains, flowers, a five-paisa coin, and a burning lamp. Fifteen or twenty men lifted and carried the pole over to the pit, into which they began to lower it. I was at the very bottom of the knot of men; I felt the lofty pole swaying above me and saw the lamp, coin, and flowers crushed as the pole was dropped on top of them. At that moment I was swept up in the current of the ritual; I felt a kind of blissful communion with the ecstatic, swaying brotherhood, with the villagers who had taken me into their hearts, eaten rice with me, made me a king and a dancer. My friends became even more delirious: it seemed that everyone was possessed, that divine blessings were flowing through the crowd like water coursing down a Himalayan river. Finally, the assembled men made a tiny circle with their right hands, each grasping the next one's thumb. The village god Danu shouted out, "I'm going to my place now; blessings upon you" and then collapsed onto the circle of hands. The day's performance was over.

On the next day the villagers performed the horse sacrifice (*aśvamedha yajña*),[24] which they also called the royal installation (*rāj tilak*). Some of the villagers told me that this was done to atone for the Pandavas' sin of killing their friends, teachers, and relatives in the great war.[25] In the per-

---

tried; he pulled so hard that his feet dug two trenches in the ground. 'Maharaj,' he said, 'you must be one of the great gods Brahma, Vishnu, or Mahesh. Why are you tricking me?' So they both went to Lanka, and Kumbhakarna's wife asked them who they were and why they'd come. Bhima replied, 'I am Bhima from Hastinapura, and I've come to get the pillar and a hero.' Kumbhakaran's wife said, 'First you have your food, eat your boiled rice, then take it.' Before eating, they went to bathe. Now there were two tanks in Lanka: one was fit for bathing, but the other was made from Kumbhakarna's skull. Kumbhakarna's wife poured water into it every day, so that it would always be full. Bhima went to bathe in it. And he entered the water and sank like a stone. Hanuman said, 'Hey Bhima, what kind of warrior are you, drowning in the skull of him who was vanquished by Shri Rama?' So Hanuman brought the pillar from Lanka and planted it in the Kauravas' sacrifice."

24. In classical times, the royal sponsor of the sacrifice would release a horse to roam over the land, and if it wandered into the domain of another king, that king had either to submit and offer tribute or give battle. The horse traveled north, east, south, and west, then returned to the imperial capital, where its sacrifice consummated a series of rituals establishing the sponsoring king's sovereignty. Its "wandering" was therefore hardly spontaneous; in fact, the horse was usually followed by a large army, and the sacrifice was normally performed only after effective military control had already been achieved by the royal sponsor. For more on the *aśvamedha*, see Agastya 1928; Caland 1932; Dumont 1927; Gonda 1969, 110–15; Puhvel 1955; and Ramachandran 1951.

25. Heesterman notes that the heroes of both *Rāmāyaṇa* and *Mahābhārata* performed the *aśvamedha* on their triumphant return, and that in the *Mahābhārata* this was also done as expiation for bloodshed (1985, 124). Gonda notes that both the *rājasūya* and the *aśvamedha* sacrifices "were considered saṃskāras, consecrations or rather sacraments, purifying a person from sin and evil contracted in the preceding period of his life and fortifying him at an important moment of his existence in order to be fit to enter upon the next stage" (1969, 100, citing MBh 12,65, 2 and Nilakantha's commentary).

formance in Sutol, Yudhisthira sent his four brothers to the four directions, to defeat the kings of the quarters and bring treasure for the ceremony. Arjuna and Yudhisthira rode in from the fields outside the village on "horses" fashioned from sticks and cloth, and capped with carved wooden horses' heads, looking for all the world like grown men on delicately carved hobby-horses. A barrier had been erected to protect the horses from the crowd, which had swelled to several hundred. If the horses were broken, it was said, the village would have bad luck for a year. That night, Indra's elephant appeared in the square. It had been made secretly in the jungle out of bamboo frames and woolen blankets, with large winnowing pans for ears. The men inside it danced wildly for twenty minutes or so, making it look as though the elephant itself was capering in the square before it was worshiped and then carried off by the five Pandavas. Next came two "Tibetans,"[26] leading a yak and carrying bottles of moonshine. The Tibetan language is incomprehensible to local villagers, and when the visitors from across the Himalayas were asked where they came from and what their animal was called, all they could say was, "*Chūṃ! Chūṃ!*" The night's performance ended as the sky began to redden above the mountains towering to the east.

On the final day of the drama, the whole village seemed different. It was very quiet. People were listless, subdued. I went about taking photographs as usual, but, untypically, people neither posed nor stood rigidly at attention when they saw my camera aimed at them. Then I realized why they were acting so strangely. They were not bored or disinterested; they were sad! In the early afternoon the drums played for the last time to summon everyone, but only half the usual number of spectators came, and some of the dancers had not even shown up by the time the invocations began. My friend Divan Singh explained: "We're all sad today. Just think how much grief we will suffer to see this square empty. The *līlā* is finished. The gods have taken their separate paths."

Again the dancers danced, but this time they were listless and forlorn. Already some of the women were crying. Shiva Singh paced up and down the stone courtyard with each character, recounting their pasts and summarizing their futures according to the epic: their coming victories and sorrows, their eventual deaths.

Then, one by one, he bade them farewell and sent them away. Now everyone was crying. Kunvar Singh was weeping uncontrollably, his body racked with sorrow. Perhaps two or three of the players were forcing their tears, but the rest were truly grief-stricken. I asked my friends why this was so and received a similar answer from practically everyone: "We haven't performed a *līlā* for years. Just now we're all together, friends and family united. But who knows who will survive, and who will die before the next performance?"

26. Tibetans are called *hūṇiyās* in the local dialect, from *hūṇa deś*, "the land of *Hūṇ*," the local term for Tibet.

Finally the five Pandavas were dismissed, but before leaving the courtyard, they did one last circuit of the square, exchanging auguries with members of the audience and bidding them farewell. As I gazed at the faces of these good people who had taken me into their hearts, shared their traditions with me, and even made me a king, I, too, began to cry. The flower girl tried to say good-bye, but her tears prevented her, and she turned and raced away toward her own home. I embraced the Pandavas one by one, weeping with each of them, then turned and walked alone down the long path back to Ghat. From there it was two days' bus journey to Mussoorie and my family, and shortly after that a train to Delhi and a flight back across those "seven seas" to my own country. I did not know if or when I would return to lovely Sutol. As the bard says:

O merciful Lord!
The bird flies, but the summit remains.
Man dies, but the Pandavas' story remains.
Speech is immortal, the seasons are immortal,
nothing else in this world lasts.
How many have danced in this stone courtyard,
and how many ages have passed!
And those who will survive will meet again,
to dance the Pandav Lila.

he dīn dayāl ab!
paṅkhī uṛ jālī, ḍhayā rai jālā.
manakhī mar jālā, paṇvāṇī rai jālī.
yā to bol amar huṇī, yā to ritu amar huṇī
dharatī gā bīc māṃ ab amar nī hvayā.
ye paṭhāmgiṇī cauk māṃ katī ghoṛā badalyā hvalā
aur katī juge re badal!
jo bhāgī bacyūṃral
ye paṭhāṅgiṇī māṃ pher bheṇṭ hvaiī jālī.

2

The Dance of the Cowherd

Pāṇḍav Līlā *as a Regional Tradition*

On the first day of the new millennium, in the Garhwali town of Gopeshwar, the headquarters of Chamoli District, there was a cultural program incorporating three distinct local performance traditions: the *lāspā* dance of the local Bhotiya community, the procession of a local goddess's palanquin, and the dance of the Pandavas. The impresario of this event was Shashi Bhushan Maithani from the nearby village of Maithana, whose goal, as he put it, was to "celebrate Garhwali culture as well as to inspire the younger generation to preserve it." The program incorporated performances of all three genres in the large open-air bus stand, speeches by local politicians and other notables, processions of dancers and palanquin-bearers from the bus station to the Gopinath temple and back, more speeches and dancing, and recitals of songs and poetry in the local dialect. It concluded with a collective vow (*saṃkalpa*) by the crowd to maintain their cultural traditions.

Several aspects of this event place it firmly within the postmodern ambit of the twenty-first century. First is the fetishization of "culture." Anthropologists have done their work very well, and the concept of culture has spread throughout the world: in Hindi, the usual term is *saṃskṛti*. In the process of its diffusion, the idea of culture has undergone some remarkable changes, including the common tendency, in India as nearly everywhere else, to objectify it as a thing that can be publicly displayed. Performance is the very type of such a cultural token, and in north India the term "cultural program" (*sāṃskṛtik kāryakram*) almost always indicates a public performance or a series of performances. Such cultural performances are displayed to the self (the audience in Gopeshwar consisted almost entirely of Garhwalis), as well as to others (Maithani was planning to take the same performance to the state capital the following week).[1]

1. See Milton Singer's (1955) seminal discussion of cultural performance.

What is perhaps more definitively postmodern is the combination of three genres that in normal circumstances would never be found together. Watching the performance from a safe distance, my friend Kranti the journalist complained about its artificiality, saying that he found the juxtaposition of *lāspā* and Pandava dances particularly disconcerting. Why were these three types of performance chosen as representative of Garhwali culture? The *lāspā* dance was perhaps chosen because the Bhotiya community is one of the most distinctive local "tribes" (the administrative term is *janjātī*) and is especially prominent in the Gopeshwar area.[2] Palanquin processions are much more conspicuous in Garhwal than in the north Indian plains, and it is understandable that local persons should think of them as a distinctive local custom. If Garhwalis traveled to the neighboring Himalayan state of Himachal Pradesh as much as they do to the plains, they would perhaps realize that palanquin prossessions are typical of the entire central Himalayan region, and not just Garhwal (see Sax forthcoming a).[3] That leaves the Pandava dance: Why was it chosen to publicly represent Garhwalis, both to themselves and to others?

In the introduction, I asserted that public rituals are an important site for the construction of identities because in such rituals, communities and persons define and represent themselves, to themselves as well as to others; that we should look to the specifically performative aspects of such rituals to understand this self-definition; and that *pāṇḍav līlā* is an excellent example of the process. But Garhwalis come in many shapes and sizes: young and old, male and female, parent and child, members of different castes. The self of a Garhwali person, like that of people everywhere, is constructed of numerous overlapping parts. In the following chapters, I shall explore the ways in which some of those parts are shaped by the *pāṇḍav līlā* and how they in turn shape it. In this chapter, I discuss the most encompassing level, that of Garhwal as a region and *pāṇḍav līlā* as a regional tradition. I begin by locating Garhwal in relation to the rest of India and show that at representational and historical levels, *pāṇḍav līlā* is an icon of Garhwal. Most Garhwalis live in villages, and so in the second section of the chapter I show how the practical, concrete actions associated with *pāṇḍav līlā* construct and define persons at a more restricted level, as corporeal parts of organically conceived villages. I conclude by returning to the relationship between text and performance, and the question of how dance constructs identities through embodied movement.

The *Pāṇḍav Līlā* of Garhwal

Pāṇḍav līlā is first and foremost a Garhwali tradition. The former Himalayan kingdom of Garhwal is located in the central Himalayas of north India

2. For more on the Bhotiyas of Garhwal and Kumaon, who formerly controlled the trade with Tibet in this region, see Brown 1992; and Srivastava 1979.

3. For more on Garhwali palanquin journeys (*ḍolī kī yātrā*), see Sax 1990b, 1991a.

in India's twenty-seventh state, Uttaranchal, which was inaugurated on November 9, 2000. It consists mostly of deep river gorges winding among extremely rugged mountains, which culminate in the Greater Himalayan range. It is bounded on the north by Tibet; on the east by the former kingdom of Kumaon, which constitutes the bulk of the remaining area of Uttaranchel; on the south by the Tarai, a marshy and densely forested region that, together with the Siwalik mountain range, constitutes a natural border between the hills and the vast Gangetic Plain; and to the west by the Tons River, beyond which lies the state of Himachal Pradesh. In ancient times, Garhwal consisted of a number of independent chieftans who ruled from small fortresses or *gaḍhi*, hence the name Garhwal (*gaḍhwāḷ*), the "land of forts." These small chiefdoms—traditionally numbered at fifty-two—were first consolidated by Ajaypal Pamvar in the thirteenth century. In 1790, invading Gurkhas from Nepal conquered the neighboring kingdom of Kumaon, and fourteen years later they defeated the Pamvar dynasty of Garhwal and killed the reigning king, Pradyuman Shah, in a battle at Dehra Dun. In 1815, the British defeated the Gurkhas and reinstalled Pradyuman Shah's son, Sudarshan Shah, as king of the new state of Tehri Garhwal, which consisted of the western portion of the former kingdom, the British having retained control of the eastern portion (figure 1).[4]

Throughout its long history until the time of the Nepali conquest, Garhwal was little affected by external forces. Because of the natural defenses provided by the Tarai and the Siwalik range to the south, it was spared domination by foreign Muslim rulers who eventually established control over most of north India from the tenth century onward.[5] Guha (1991) claims that the Pawar dynasty enjoyed "nearly 1300 years of continuous rule" and was the oldest in north India, but the evidence does not seem to bear out his assertion. Garhwal has by no means been unaffected by the turbulent history of north India; however, because of its relative isolation it has, rather like Nepal, maintained a number of cultural forms that were lost elsewhere in north India. The *pāṇḍav līlā* is one of these.[6]

Garhwal has particular significance to Hindus because it contains a number of well-known pilgrimage places. For centuries, the pilgrim traffic has been an important source of revenue for local persons and governments and has provided a cultural link with the rest of India. The main pilgrimage places include Haridwar, where the Ganges enters the plains of north India, famous both as a place to perform the ancestral *śrāddha* ritual (see

4. For more on the history of Garhwal, see Atkinson 1974 [1882]; Bahadur 1916; Dabaral 1965–78; Guha 1991; Ratūḍī 1980 [1928]; Rawat 1983; and Sakalani 1987.

5. Compare Schnepel's concept (1995, 1997) of the "jungle kingdom," which resembles Garhwal in certain senses: its peripheral location, the preponderance of "tribal" people, and its relative independence from major overlords.

6. See chapter 3 (especially note 27) for a detailed discussion of one such tradition.

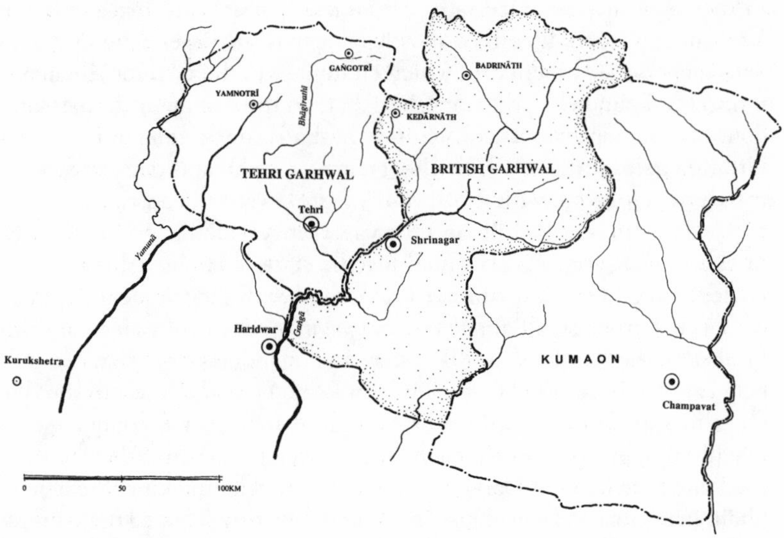

Figure 1. Map of Garhwal and Kumaon. Drawing prepared by Niels Gutschow.

chapter 3) and as the site of the Kumbha Mela, the largest religious gathering in the world (Sax 1987); Jamnotri, the source of the Yamuna River on whose banks far downstream in the plains of north India Krishna was born; Gangotri, the putative source of the Ganges; and Kedarnath, which is one of the twelve *jyotirliṅga*, or "lingas of light," manifestations of the great god Shiva. Most famous of all is Badrinath, one of the four *dhāms*, or "abodes," of divinity, the most geographically encompassing of all Hindu pilgrimage systems, located roughly at the four corners of kite-shaped India.[7] Indeed, the temple of Badrinath is so bound up with Garhwali history and kingship that the ruler of Garhwal was traditionally styled *bolāndā badrī*, "the speaking Badrinath," and Badrinath was the state deity. Badrinath is also closely associated with the *Mahābhārata* story (see later discussion).

The *pāṇḍav līlā* tradition is strictly limited to Garhwal. One would of course not expect to find it in Buddhist Tibet, but it is rather surprising that it is not found in the adjoining areas of Kumaon, Himachal Pradesh, or the north Indian plains. While traveling in Kumaon in 1993, I found that few Kumaonis had even heard of it. Like most regions of India, the areas adjoining Garhwal—Kumaon to the southeast and the Simla Hill States to the northwest—have their own traditions of *Mahābhārata*-related recitation (see, e.g., Kaushal 1997; Leavitt 1988); however, these traditions are quite

7. The other *dhām* are Jagganath in the city of Puri on the eastern coast in Orissa; Rameshvaram in Tamil Nadu near India's southern tip; and Dwarika in the westernmost state of Gujarat.

distinct from (and much less elaborate than) *pāṇḍav līlā*.[8] In all of South Asia the only other performance tradition comparable to *pāṇḍav līlā* in its complexity is the Terukkuttu studied by Hiltebeitel (1988, 1991) and Frasca (1990). As Hiltebeitel puts it, there are "astonishing parallels" between Terukkuttu and *pāṇḍav līlā*, "one from the high mountains of India's far north, the other from the lowlands of the deep south, and with nothing to link them geographically or historically but Hinduism" (1988, 132).

Although *pāṇḍav līlā* is unknown in neighboring regions, it is found throughout Garhwal, especially in the higher-altitude regions where old customs are better preserved. Since participating in my first *pāṇḍav līlā* in Sutol in 1986, I have attended eleven other performances, in Lobha Chandpur in the easternmost part of Garhwal adjoining Kumaon; in Nagpur, the region lying between the Alakananda River flowing down from Badrinath, and the Mandakini River flowing from Kedarnath; and in Singtur in the far west, in the region adjoining Himachal Pradesh. In the western parts of Garhwal, many villages, especially in the Jaunsar region, have squares that are dedicated to the dance of the Pandavas. This close association of *pāṇḍav līlā* with Garhwal and the fact that it appears to be strictly circumscribed by its borders suggest a historical link with the old kingdom. Unfortunately, extensive research has failed to disclose any historical evidence of such a connection.[9]

There is some historical and textual warrant for the close association of the *Mahābhārata* story with the central Himalayas. Badarinath was well known to the redactors of Sanskrit *Mahābhāratas*, and recent research suggests that the kingdom of the Kurus was located along the foot of the Himalayas (Witzel 1995, 1997).

Among the people of Garhwal, there is little doubt that the events of the *Mahābhārata* story occurred here. Throughout India, people identify notable local landmarks with events from the *Mahābhārata* or from India's other great epic, the *Rāmāyaṇa*.[10] This boulder is said to have been placed there by mighty Bhima; that ancient ruin is believed to have been built by the Pandavas; here is where Rama, Sita, and Lakshmana made camp during their forest exile; there is the place where Hanuman's foot left an impression in the rock.[11] A. K. Ramanujan called this phenomenon "localization," and with regard to the *Mahābhārata* story, it is nowhere as extensive as in

8. Nanda writes that the "northernmost limits" of *Mahābhārata*-related recitation "can be found in stray southern portions of Lahaul valley" and that the tradition dwindles in Kumaon (1982, 48). Nautiyal (1971) provides an extensive description of *pāṇḍav līlā* performances and texts from Garhwal.

9. The only shred of evidence I have come across to suggest such a connection is Gaborieau's amplification of Gairola's assertion that "before the end of the eighteenth century, at the time when the local kingdoms were still in existence, the bards would entertain kings and their courtiers in the royal palaces, and encouraged warriors on the battle-field. There is no documentary evidence for such a claim, but a few allusions in the songs themselves make it very likely" (1977, xvi).

10. For an excellent study of the sacred geography of the epics, see Bhardwaj 1973.

11. For examples, see Bandhu 1997; Herath 1997; Mishra 1993.

Garhwal. The Pandavas are thought to have been born in Pandukeshwar, a well-known temple town lying above Joshimath on the Badrinath road. The ruins at Lakhamandal in the Yamuna valley are believed by many to be of the capital of the kingdom of Virat, where the Pandavas spent their exile, while others say that they mark the spot where the Kauravas attempted to assassinate the Pandavas by burning them in a lac palace (Thukral and Thukral 1987, 42). Another story, well known in Garhwal from its occurrence in a local primary school Hindi reader, tells how once when the Pandavas were roaming through the mountains, Draupadi saw a beautiful flower floating downstream and asked someone to bring her more flowers like it. Bhima followed the stream to its source, where he found a high alpine meadow full of flowers, which is now famous as the "Valley of Flowers."[12] The local village of Bhyumdar, it is said, means "Bhima's cave" (from *bhyūṃ* [Bhima] + *uḍyār* [cave]). The magnificent Svargarohini peaks in the far west of Garhwal are said to mark the spot where the Pandavas climbed toward heaven at the end of their lives, as described in Sanskrit versions of *Mahābhārata*. Near Nandikund at the source of the Madhyamaheshvara River in Chamoli District are a series of naturally terraced fields (*pāṇḍav syerā*) that are believed to have been made by the Pandavas. A similar set of fields with a similar name is found near the Sahastra Tal, seven high-altitude ponds on the border of Uttarkashi and Tehri Districts. Below these lakes, on the way to the remote village of Gangi, are three more lakes named for Bhima, Arjuna, and Draupadi. Another local tradition (said to derive from the *Skanda Purāṇa*) attributes the origin of the pilgrimage system of the Five Kedars to the time of the *Mahābhārata* war. According to the story, the only way the Pandavas could atone for the sins they had incurred was to obtain a vision of Shiva. They went to the holy city of Varanasi, Shiva's dwelling place, but he refused to give them a vision and instead fled into the Himalayas. The Pandavas followed him to Kedarnath, where he disguised himself as a buffalo, hiding among a herd that was grazing there. Mighty Bhima straddled the valley and drove the buffaloes out, knowing that Shiva would not demean himself by passing under Bhima's legs. When only one buffalo was left, Bhima reached for him, but he dove into the ground, leaving only his hindquarters, which are now worshiped at the temple. Subsequently, Shiva manifested various parts of his body at the remaining four Kedars: his midsection at Madhyamaheshvara, his hands at Tunganath, his face at Rudranath, and his matted locks at Kalpanath (figure 2). When I asked the priests at Kedarnath temple about this tradition, they connected it with Nepal's national shrine of Pashupatinath, where they say Shiva's head became manifest.

12. A parallel story, in which Draupadi sends Bhima to get her a flower and he meets Hanuman, is also found in the Pune edition of *Mahābhārata*. This is conventionally known as the critical edition, but I refer to it as "the Pune edition" to emphasize that it is but one of many versions of the epic.

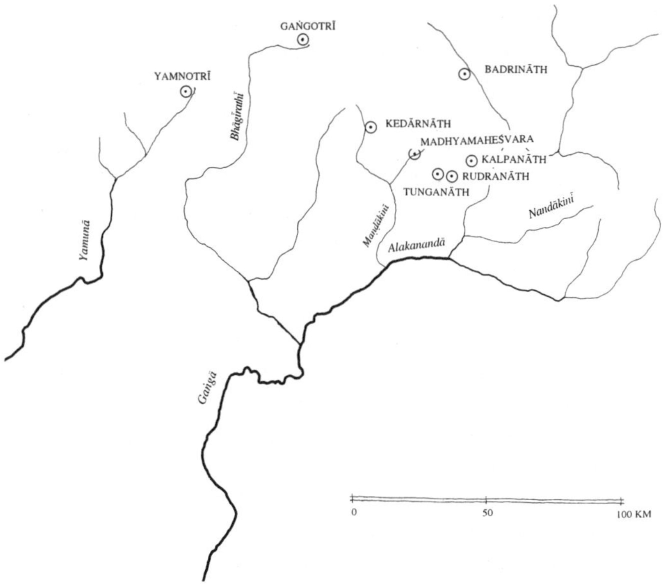

Figure 2. Sacred places of Garhwal. Drawing prepared by Niels Gutschow.

When I asked Padam Singh from Sutol why *pāṇḍav līlā* was so popular in Garhwal but unknown in Kumaon and Himachal Pradesh, he invoked the holiness of the landscape, asserting, "The gods emerged here first of all: in Badrinath, Kedarnath, and other places. The gods have hidden here [*guptavās lenā*] during Kaliyug. If you go to the west, you will find little devotion [*devabhakti*]. The gods have come to Garhwal, as numerous as the stones."

But it is not just through the landscape that Garhwalis link themselves to the *Mahābhārata* story. It informs local mythology, folklore, proverbial wisdom, and popular history, in many other ways as well. For example, my assistant Dabar Singh Rawat explained that south Indian cross-cousin marriage originated with the marriage of Arjuna to the sister of his classificatory "brother," Krishna. According to another story, the cow killed by Vidyadhar the Brahman (see chapter 3), was reborn as a *śamī* tree (locally regarded as a pine) on Gandhamadana mountain. An "American king" was performing asceticism there and acquired the tree as a boon from Shiva, and that is why the pine tree originated in America.[13] Yet another tale tells of how the Pandavas, having survived the Kauravas' attempt to assassinate them in the lac palace, went to bathe in a river. But the demon Angar Pran blocked their way, and they had to kill him before they could proceed. Garlic came from his ankle, and because of its origin in the corpse of a demon, it

13. Reference to the "American king" was probably added for my benefit.

is still regarded as impure. Such stories, which are legion, illustrate the truth of Chandola's claim that throughout Garhwal the "most extensive body of folklore is that based on the *Mahābhārata* tales" (1977, 18).

One particularly striking example of the way in which *Mahābhārata* stories and themes are incorporated into local traditions is provided by the cult of the deity Jakh, also known as Jakspati or Vazir. His main temple is located in the village of Gwar, a few kilometers from Gopeshwar, the headquarters of Chamoli District. Perhaps the most striking aspects of this village god's cult are his periodic ritual processions (*dyorā*), which occur every few decades. In 1997, for the first time in thirty-six years, he emerged from his village (i.e., his image was taken out on a palanquin) and processed for six months throughout his territory, keeping to the true right bank of the Alakananda River[14] as far as Badrinath, from whence he returned to Gwar. Jakh is identified with Babarik, a character who is unknown in the Pune edition of *Mahābhārata* but well attested in folk traditions from Garhwal to Tamil Nadu, where he is known as Aravan (Hiltebeitel 1988, 1995b). When Jakh travels on his periodic ritual processions, he is accompanied by eighteen masked dancers, including Karna, Duryodhana's famous ally from the *Mahābhārata*.[15]

In making *Mahābhārata* their own, Garhwalis represent it in rustic and homespun ways. A fascinating example is the story of the five Phandata brothers from Singtur *paṭṭī*[16] near the confluence of the Rupin and Supin Rivers in western Garhwal. According to the musician Bhuli Das of Dyora village, the Phandatas used to graze their sheep and goats in an alpine meadow called Manir. But every year before they took their animals there, the Bhungarata clan from nearby Panchgaim demanded that the Phandatas sacrifice their best animals to the Bhungaratas' god Rathchalya. This went on for twelve years, until old Maisu Phandata had five sons who were so fierce that people were scared even to talk to them. Empowered by their goddess Nakuti, the Phandata brothers not only took their flocks to Manir without sacrificing to Rathchalya but also cut down the god's sacred tree and lit their campfire from it. Rathchalya's followers learned that this outrage had been perpetrated not by the score of men who used to come to Manir but by a mere five brothers. They bided their time, and a few days later they surrounded the Phandata brothers' camp under cover of darkness. Just as they were about to pounce on the Phandatas and rustle their sheep, the goddess came over the youngest brother, who stood up and called out:

14. The god Jakh has an old dispute with the deity residing on the left bank of the Alakananda, also known as Jakh (!); hence he did not cross except in one instance, at Pipalkoti, where sheer cliffs on the right bank make passage impossible.

15. For more on the cult of Jakh, see chapter 4.

16. *Paṭṭīs* are traditional territorial units, analogous to the *parganahs* of north India. The *paṭṭīs* of Garhwal have been reorganized many times, and often take their names from nearby forts (Traill 1828: 178).

When the goat is killed, the guests gather
Wait, you hunchbacked hillbilly pigs:
Let my elder brother Bidhi finish his pipe![17]

The Bhungaratas were so startled that they missed the most auspicious moment to begin their attack, and when they fell upon the herders and their flock, the god Pokkhu helped the Phandatas to leap high into the air and escape. At the urging of the youngest brother, the Phandatas fashioned knives out of sharp bamboo and attacked the Bhungaratas, who were routed. The Phandatas recovered their sheep but discovered that the best ram, the one that belonged to the eldest brother, Bidhi, had been killed in the fray, sacrificed as it were to the god Rathchalya. In revenge, they captured and killed a low caste man from Panchgaim.

This story of five brothers who prevail against a numerically superior foe has striking parallels with the *Mahābhārata* story, parallels that are underscored by the fact that the god Rathchalya is more commonly known as Duryodhana! (see chapters 6 and 7; also Sax 1999). But whenever I mentioned this parallel to local people, suggesting that the story was a kind of "mini-*Mahābhārata*," they were surprised. They could see the logic of my idea, but it had never occurred to them, which suggests just how thoroughly the *Mahābhārata* story has been "localized" in Garhwal.

Pāṇḍav Līlā as a Village Ritual

Pāṇḍav līlā is a thoroughly amateur tradition: there are no printed scripts or paid performers of any sort. Like most public rituals in Garhwal, performances are sponsored and organized by villages, which are thought of as biological and moral entities, constituted by the persons who dwell in them, even as they constitute those persons. Such a conception of the village is already implied by the fact that the core of most villages consists of an exogamous patrilineal clan, and that this clan often takes its name not from an ancestor but from the village itself: in theory, all Nautiyals "originally" hail from Nauti, Dimaris from Dimar, and so on. Instead of the eponymous ancestors so familiar in the anthropological literature, one instead finds in Garhwal eponymous villages!

To be sure, one need not necessarily reside in the village to be a part of it. Like Indians elsewhere, most Garhwalis think of their ancestors' villages as their own, even when they have not resided there for generations. Furthermore, although a "village daughter" typically lives elsewhere (because of the residential rule of patrivirilocality, according to which a new bride takes up residence in her husband's father's home), and is therefore a legal

17. *mārīn jab bhākurī, uttārī ghālitī bheya*
thāmathāmī paḍyā ṭūṭyā sungaḍā
bidhī dādā tamākū khāṇ deya

resident of her husband's village according to both customary and civil law, she does not therefore cease to be a member of her natal village, and her presence is required on important ritual occasions. Clearly, the village is much more than a mere physical location, a collection of houses and associated lands where people dwell. It is instead a complex biomoral entity made up of place, soil, persons, and history.[18]

Ritual is the chief means by which villages, in a rather Durkheimian fashion, collectively constitute and reconstitute themselves as biomoral units. In *pāṇḍav līlā*, everyone has specific responsibilities in preparing for a performance: gathering firewood and foodstuffs, fashioning weapons and other stage props, making costumes, clearing performance areas, and so on. Normally in Chamoli District, every high-caste household is required to contribute cash, rice, and flour to a common store used to feed dancers, guests, and others. This collective store is called a *melāk*, a word that derives from the root *mil*, meaning to "mix" or "join." Villagers join together and mix their contributions, and thus the blessings of the Pandavas are shared by all. As part of the *pāṇḍav līlā* in Nauti village in 1990, for example, the Pandavas went in procession to every high-caste household, where they were worshiped and gave blessings in return.[19] Because there were so many houses, the village had to be divided into three parts, and the exchange of blessings for worship took three days. By the end of the performance, every household in the village had been blessed, including those of the lowest castes, who had not contributed to the common store and were not visited by the Pandavas but instead received blessed food through higher-caste intermediaries. I was particularly surprised when I saw "Hanuman" steal fruit—just like a monkey—from trees belonging to several different houses, then redistribute it to his entourage. Normally, the trees' owners would have loudly objected to such cheekiness, but in this collective performance the fruit was in a sense "owned" by everyone, and they remained silent.

In the neighboring village of Bhatgwali, a much longer *pāṇḍav līlā* concluded when a goat representing the rhinoceros (see chapter 3) was sacrificed, cooked, and collectively eaten. Just prior to this feast, one woman from each house brought a cloth-covered platter containing foodstuffs[20] that were mixed together, blessed, and then redistributed to the villagers: a shared meal with which the communal performance culminated.[21] Heads of households were expected to provide clothes and sweetmeats (*kalyeū*) to their outmarried daughters before sending them back to their marital homes.

18. For an extensive discussion of these matters, see Sax 1990b; 1991a, chap. 2; also Daniel 1984.

19. The exchange of blessings for worship has been said to be a central paradigm of popular Hinduism (Wadley 1975).

20. Each platter (*thālī*) contained fried sweetbread (*roṇṭ*), clarified butter (*ghī*), milk, sweet semolina pudding (*halvā*), and flowers.

21. In Gugali village in 1993, each household sent a woman bearing a platter containing barley and mustard seeds that would later be used in the fire sacrifice that closed the performance.

When I asked villagers why they went to so much trouble and expense to stage this performance, I was told, among other things, that *pāṇḍav līlā* "completes the circle of relatives."

The staging of a *pāṇḍav līlā* is thus a communal affair, and the benefits that are believed to flow from a successful performance—health and well-being—are also communal, accruing to the village as a whole. By working collectively, mixing and sharing food, and especially through their rituals, villages constitute themselves as biomoral entities, and this is typical not just of *pāṇḍav līlā* in particular but of public ritual generally in Garhwal (Sax 1991a, 202–8).[22] Ritual is thus an important site for the construction of identities: in ritual, communities (in this case, villages) define and represent themselves and their constituent parts, both to themselves and to others. In this way, villages are created and re-created in ritual.

Garhwalis say that regular performances of *pāṇḍav līlā* ensure the health, well-being, and prosperity of villages and their residents, fields, and livestock. This is exemplified by the following blessing, given by "Arjuna" to the head of a household that had just publicly feasted the Pandavas following an afternoon performance:

May your storehouse be full!
May your buffaloes in their corral be healthy!
May your children be happy and healthy!
May your own Jayanti Palace[23] be splendid!

During periodic outbreaks of hoof-and-mouth disease, it is not unusual for village men to gather at a shrine of the Pandavas (particularly if the shrine is dedicated to Arjuna) and promise to perform a *pāṇḍav līlā* if they escape the disease. Performances I attended in Nauti and Bhatgwali in 1990–91 resulted precisely from such vows. In less extreme circumstances, people still believe that regular performance of *pāṇḍav līlā* confers definite (if vague) benefits to the village community. At a minimum, the Pandavas should be "danced" at least once every generation. Conversely, failure to perform *pāṇḍav līlā* may result in ontological diseases of the collective body. These are called *doṣ* (Skt. *doṣa*), an important term with a range of meanings, including "fault," "blemish," and "sanction" (see Sax 1991a, 92). A *doṣ* is believed to be not so much the result of a divine being's ill will as an automatic result of people's failure to complete their religious duties. Thus the verb is almost always used in a passive rather than an active sense: "The *doṣ* adhered" [to us] [*doṣ lag gayā*] rather than "The god gave us a *doṣ*" [*doṣ lagāyā*]. Although the negative sanction resulting from a failure to perform *pāṇḍav*

22. This is also the case elsewhere in South Asia (e.g., Seneviratne 1978). Of particular interest is the fact that in Hinduism, one of the few occasions on which fractious "caste society" is united is in the context of the annual temple ritual (Fuller 1992; Srinivas 1969 [1955]).

23. See n. 6 chapter 1.

līlā—like the positive one resulting from regular performance—is more or less mechanical, nevertheless villagers consider it imprudent to discuss it openly. In Taintura village in 1991, I watched as householders took the Pandavas on their shoulders from the dancing square to a private house nearby, where they were publicly feasted. I asked the four male adults if they were not doing this to gain some desired object (*manautī karnā*), but they resisted my suggestion, insisting that they received no particular reward but only a kind of generalized blessing from the Pandavas, whom they regarded as gods (*dev*). Later I asked a somewhat larger group of men why they had "danced" the Pandavas that year.

A: [The Pandavas] are also gods. A *doṣ* affects the entire village. We only do it every five or six years, every ten or twelve years, when we have the opportunity.
Q: Does the *doṣ* really fall?
A: Definitely. Some trouble in the fields, or the children get sick, whatever. Then we do the *pāṇḍav līlā*, and everyone is made well again.
Q: Was there some trouble this year?
A: No, no. We are doing it from happiness [*khuśī se*]. [In the background a man can be heard whispering: What can we say? The tape is going. There would be trouble.]

In order for blessings to be generated, the performance must be insulated from contamination by inauspiciousness and impurity. Dancers are required to maintain strict purity for the duration of the *pāṇḍav līlā* by remaining celibate, following a vegetarian diet, avoiding intoxicants, limiting their sleep, and so on. One village had a strong tradition that *pāṇḍav līlā* should last for eighteen days,[24] but in the middle of its performance, an elder died and the performance was halted, only to be resumed after twelve days of mourning.

Because *pāṇḍav līlā* is a village ritual, permission to perform it must first be sought from village deities, who are also responsible for distributing the sacred and powerful weapons with which the characters dance. The cooperation of village deities is not guaranteed; sometimes they refuse to distribute weapons to a particular person because of a perceived moral failing or ritual error.[25] In Sutol, the goddess Kali suddenly possessed her oracle Than Singh in the middle of an afternoon performance and shouted out:

24. The number eighteen is of particular symbolic importance. Sanskrit versions of *Mahābhārata* have eighteen "books" (*parva*), and a classical Indian army had eighteen divisions (*akṣauṇī*).

25. Such weapons are associated with blood sacrifice, which is forbidden by Sutol's village god Dyosingh. That is why they are not prominent in the Sutol *līlā* described in this and the preceding chapters. See chapter 3 and chapter 4 for an extended discussion of the weapons.

> There's no sugar for the tea, the rules are not being followed! Pollution has fallen in your courtyard! Don't blame me, and don't blame the high gods! . . . There's no order in this Pandavas' exercise! The god of this land is watching your ritual! I cannot burn the stomach-water of the transgressor![26] Promise, promise me—and I will swear to you. I won't accept the blame myself. . . . I am not a [blood-] sucking goddess; demand a boon from your old established [village] gods, too! Dance your dance! Do your play! Perform your drama![27]

Kali's accusations were borne out the next day when it was discovered that the wife of the man who was dancing the part of Krishna had given birth; thus he was in a state of pollution and unfit to dance. But some people still insisted that Kali's accusations actually referred to the onset of menstruation in one of the female dancers.

Ghosts, demons, and other disruptive spiritual beings must be pacified, often by offering them raw vegetables and uncooked grains both before the *līlā* begins and at the beginning and end of every performance. The *bed-bāṇ* ritual performed by Padam Singh at the beginning and end of performances in Sutol (see above) is typical of such rituals. In the Chandpur region, they "bind" the four "passes" (*caukhāḷ*) or "gates" to the village before the performance begins, thus preventing the entry of negative beings and forces. In this ritual, a bamboo workbasket is torn into four pieces, each of which is filled with equal parts of squash, yellow pumpkin, a mixture of seven grains, green and yellow powder, and an uncooked mixture of rice and lentils. Four men then take these basket shreds (*caṅgatīra*) to the village periphery and fix them to the ground at the four cardinal points with cut lengths of bamboo and split nails fashioned from iron plow heads. These offerings placate any malevolent beings who might be tempted to disrupt the *līlā* and also bar their entry into the village.

Although *pāṇḍav līlā*s are performed throughout Garhwal, there is little regularity in their duration, the season in which they are performed, or the episodes with which they culminate. They may last anywhere from half a day to nine days. A minor, half-day performance is usually incorporated into some major event such as an annual festival in honor of a village deity, and in Chandpur it is often referred to not as *pāṇḍav līlā* but as *kaḍhāī*, or "the pot" (see later discussion). Once villagers have collectively decided to produce a *pāṇḍav līlā*, they consult a Brahman astrologer, who must take into

26. In other words, "You must punish him/her yourselves."

27. *Cāī meṃ cīnī nahīṃ hai, koī nīti sīdhī nahīṃ hai, chuāchut paṛī tumārī akhaḍī* [*sic*] *meṃ. Māī par doṣ mat rakhnā. Aur maiṃ pāṇḍavoṃ ko bacan diyā* . . . (*unclear*) . . . *pañcanām devatoṃ par koī purānā doṣ mat rakhnā. Is pāṇḍavoṃ kī akhaḍī meṃ koī śāsan nahīṃ hai. Bhūmī kā mālik tumāra kārya dekh rahā hai. Ham ko bacan de do ki peṭ kā pānī maiṃ kisī kā nahīm jalā saktī hūṃ. Mujhe bacan de do, bacan de do, maiṃ sab ko dharam detā hūṃ. Māī apne par koī doṣ nahīṃ rakhegī. . . . Māī koī cūsnewālī devī nahīṃ hai. Tum apne purāne sthit devatāoṃ se bhī bacan māngo! Nacāo! Khilāo! Apne khel-khud karo!* Note that when speaking through their human oracles, gods very often use Hindi, which is more prestigious than the local dialect.

account the astrological signs of Arjuna, the village, and its guardian deity and bring them all into line with each other before determining an auspicious date to begin the performance.[28] *Pāṇḍav līlās* occur at different times of the year in different regions, each of which tends to have its own performative specialty. Thus in the far west of Garhwal, in the basins of the upper Jumna and Tons Rivers, a typical performance lasts two to three days and is called a *sarāddh* (from Sanskrit *śrāddha*, a type of ancestral ritual; see chapters 3 and 5). These performances occur in the months of *māgh* (January–February), *śrāvaṇ* (July–August), and *mārgaśīrṣ* (November–December). In the Mandakini River basin in Chamoli District, performances last up to six weeks and culminate in the *cakravyūha*, or "Circular Array," which dramatizes the encirclement and death of Arjuna's son Abhimanyu during the great battle (see chapter 4). Here, performances occur in the months of *kārttik* (October–November) and *mārgaśīrṣ*(November–December), but in the neighboring Alakananda and Pindar River basins, *pāṇḍav līlās* take place in the month of *pauṣ* (December–January). Full-length performances in the latter area include the *śamī* tree episode in which a large pine tree is ritually felled, dragged to the village square, and joyfully erected as a symbol of the Pandavas' ultimate victory (see chapter 4); and the "rhinoceros" (*gaiṇḍā*) episode involving the killing by Arjuna of a rhinoceros belonging to his son Nagarjuna (known as Babhruvahana in Sanskrit versions of the epic), followed by a battle between father and son (see chapter 3). In the latter instances, the designated *śamī* tree or the pond where the rhinoceros grazes may be five or six kilometers distant, making an effective performance area of dozens of square kilometers.[29] Even the musical instruments used in *pāṇḍav līlā* vary from region to region. In the southeast of Garhwal, musicians typically use the *ḍhol*, a two-headed drum played with one stick and one hand, and the *damāūṃ*, a single-headed drum played with two sticks (plate 2); in the northwest a large "battle-horn" (*raṇa siṃha*) is sometimes used, and the *damāūṃ* is replaced by a gong (*bhaiṇā*). Despite these significant variations in time and duration of performance, most villagers in Garhwal are probably within walking distance of a *pāṇḍav līlā* in any given year.

Among upper-caste males, there is considerable variation regarding who may or may not dance the major characters. In the most remote villages, women participate fully in the performance, but they are discouraged or prohibited from doing so in villages that have been strongly affected by the culture of the north Indian plains (usually, those closest to the road). The outstanding exception is Kunti, the mother of the Pandavas. Even in those villages that have nearly eliminated public dancing by women, the part of Kunti must be played by a senior Rajput woman. (Usually, certain ritually important dances and actions of Draupadi must also be performed by a

28. The first letter of a person's name indicates his or her astrological sign. This principle is applied to determine horoscopes for villages and deities.

29. Compare Richard Schechner's remarks (1983, 1993) on *rām līlā* and environmental theater.

woman.) The chief male parts are usually danced by Rajput men, and sometimes by Brahman men as well. Despite such variation, there is a tendency for male and female parts to be hereditary. Thus, the part of Arjuna tends to pass from father to son and in such cases the part of Arjuna's wife Draupadi may go to the wives of father and/or son. On the other hand, female parts may devolve independently from female to female, sometimes passed on in a powerful amulet or other piece of jewelry (see chapter 5). Thus a woman who dances the part of Draupadi may pass on an amulet containing Draupadi's "energy" (*śakti*) to one of her daughters-in-law, who will subsequently dance the part. In all cases, high-caste persons of the appropriate gender are normally welcome to dance any part they wish, so that, for example, the main Bhima dancer may be accompanied during group dances by several other "Bhimas." In those villages where the principle of hereditary transmission is well established, the sons of men dancing the lead parts have opportunities to practice with their fathers during performances. In other villages, older men are appointed to teach the youths how to dance, and still elsewhere, youths informally learn to dance. In Taintura, for example, every day about an hour before the evening performance, the village children would assemble in the village square, and the drummer Bhanu Ram would play a number of rhythms so that they could practice their steps.

Pāṇḍav līlās incorporate at least five main features. The first of these is drumming. Garhwali folk drumming is a sophisticated art and is indispensable in virtually all public rituals (Chandola 1977). The musicians' esoteric knowledge, magically powerful spells, and especially their drumming induce possession and provide the highly charged ambience of a performance. Although the musician (*dās*) caste has a low rank, individual musicians are often highly respected for their learning and artistry. Taintura villagers told me that their 1990 *pāṇḍav līlā* was performed for the benefit of Bhanu Ram, the local Das, in order to obtain his blessing; and during a *pāṇḍav līlā* in the village of Dargan in Singtur in 1994, I was struck by how Bhuli Das, an eminent local musician, was consistently addressed by his patrons as *gurūjī*, a highly respectful epithet normally reserved for Brahmans (see chapter 5).

Drumming is always accompanied by dancing; hence, *pāṇḍav līlā* is often referred to as *pāṇḍav nṛtya*, the "dance" of the Pandavas. Each character dances with a specific weapon. Yudhisthira dances with a staff; Bhima with a club; Arjuna and his son Nagarjuna with bows and arrows; Mother Kunti with a strongbox; Nakula and the female characters Draupadi and Vasudanta with scythes; Sahadeva with a student's slate; and the Mohars, companions of the Pandavas, with bamboo baskets filled with flowers used to make garlands. These dances are often associated with characteristic actions: gluttonous Bhima gobbles huge amounts of food while dancing; Kaliya Lohar, the low-caste ironsmith who forged the Pandavas' weapons, circumambulates the fire, and so on. Moreover, what I have called "possession" is conventionally understood as a kind of dance. Village gods and goddesses, along with the Pandavas, are said to enjoy "dancing" in the bodies of human beings (cf. Berreman 1964), and another common expression for staging a *pāṇḍav līlā* is "causing the Pandavas to dance [*pāṇḍavoṃ ko nacānā*]."

Along with drumming and dancing, *pāṇḍav līlās* include discrete *līlās*, vignettes from the *Mahābhārata* story. These dramatize a range of episodes, but they tend to focus on martial themes such as the battle between Arjuna and his son Nagarjuna or the slaying of the rhinoceros (see chapter 3). Harmless childhood confrontations between the Pandavas and the Kauravas are a favorite theme in the Alakananda basin, where people decline to perform major battle scenes because, as they say, these generate too much fervor (*joś*).

A fourth characteristic of *pāṇḍav līlā* is competitive bardic recitation of the *Mahābhārata* story. This did not occur in Sutol, where recitation was dominated by Padam Singh, but in nearby Chandpur such competition is common. Recitation is performed in a distinctive style, with the reciter cupping one or both hands behind the ears, pacing back and forth across the flagstone square, and chanting the relevant narrative in the local dialect. Sometimes the performing bard is politely and formally challenged by another to recall an obscure detail from the *Mahābhārata* story. If he is able to do so, he continues his recitation; if not, the challenger takes over. Village sponsors encourage well-known local bards to attend their *līlās*, and modest cash prizes are sometimes awarded to superlative performers. But such recitation seems to be something of a dying art: though it has many exponents in the Alakananda and Pindar basins, it is remembered only by very old men in the Mandakini basin, where newer forms of recitation (from handwritten scripts held by the performers) are more prestigious. I have not heard any such recitation in the Tons basin.

A fifth characteristic of *pāṇḍav līlā* is the feasting and hospitality by which it is framed. A successful performance attracts hundreds of relatives and neighboring villagers. Because Garhwali villages tend to be dominated by single castes, performances are in effect caste gatherings, where marriages and other kinds of alliance are negotiated, and matters of common political and social interest are discussed and acted upon. Hundreds of guests must be fed and housed, at considerable expense to the sponsoring village. In Chandpur, all *pāṇḍav līlās* involve a kind of subperformance, a ritual within a ritual, known as "the pot" (*kaḍhāī*), in which the Pandavas are given festive foods by some or all of the families in a village.[30]

The Dance of the Cowherd

It should be clear by now that for Garhwalis, *Mahabharata* is much more than just a book. This seems to be obvious enough, but academic special-

30. People in Chandpur District connect this custom to Bhima's slaying of the demon Baka. The feast is said to be a thanksgiving festival instituted by a grateful king.

ists in Indian culture must periodically be reminded of it.[31] The problem is clearly stated by Goldman, who notes that modern scholarship

> has turned the great and fundamentally oral ancient epics of India into *books*. If we "establish" the text . . . then we have a book we can put on our shelf, hold in our hand, and sit quietly and read, scratching our head in wonder at the bizarre kinds of books the ancient Indians produced and read. The volumes may look gigantic on our office shelves but in fact they were delivered and consumed orally in discrete performance units over a period of time as is indicated in the Ramayana. My suspicion is that when one conceived of a text like the Mahābhārata as a whole, if ever one did, it was not so much as a book but as a whole body of literature from which specific characters, incidents, or scenes could be adduced from memory to illuminate questions in social life, etc. (1986, 19–20)

In this chapter I have tried to show how Goldman's "suspicion" is confirmed by *pāṇḍav līlā*. Nevertheless, many Indologists persist in thinking that there is a single *Mahābhārata*, of which the regional versions like *pāṇḍav līlā* are deviations.[32] But the *Mahābhārata* is no monolith. Though it is deservedly known as India's "great epic," it has also been translated into many languages of many nations, traveling throughout Asia as far as Vietnam and Indonesia.[33] In certain places it was as thoroughly indigenized and "localized" as in Garhwal; for example, in Indonesia, where it was "an integral element in the concept of the State, . . . the Indonesian kings considered themselves to be incarnations" of the Pandavas (Chandra 1990, 221). Even today, the most intimate of the several names of a Javanese man—even

31. Richman (1991) introduces her excellent volume on the *Rāmāyaṇa* tradition by noting five assumptions shared by the contributors: that all incidents are worthy of attention, that there is no "urtext" for the *Rāmāyaṇa*, that tellers of the story other than Valmiki are worthy of our attention, that there are important genres in addition to the literary, and that different versions of the story may be in conflict with each other. Why has a book based on similar assumptions not been written or edited for the *Mahābhārata*, which is even more obviously oral and "multiple" than is the *Rāmāyaṇa*?

32. One example is Hiltebeitel, who continues to insist that traditional performances of the *Mahābhārata* story, such as the Terukkuttu that he has so thoroughly studied, are ultimately derived from a textual source, despite his earlier (and to my mind more sensible) assertion that "[i]t is thus not a case of two separate worlds—classical and modern, Vedic and Tantric or Śākta, Āryan or Sanskritic and Dravidian, Great Tradition and Little Tradition—but of two parts of a continuum, one that has always involved interplay, selection, and change" (Hiltebeitel 1982, 78). Cf. de Bruin 1988, who, like me, opposes the idea that textual versions are more pure, and oral versions somehow inferior or degraded.

33. Cf. Rassers's reflections on Indonesian dramatizations of *Mahābhārata* stories. These are vitiated by his assumption that there is a single *Mahābhārata* to which the Javanese episodes either correspond or fail to correspond. In this light, "the Javanese drama . . . consists largely of an accumulation of misunderstandings, and is a product of the most unsystematic confusion" (1959, 111). See also Desai's (1970) discussion of the spread of the *Rāmāyaṇa* story throughout Asia.

though he is most likely a Muslim—is that of one of the Pandavas: Yudhisthira, Bhima, Arjuna, Nakula, or Sahadeva. We must also remember that *Mahābhārata* originated as an oral epic, "an open, fluid text transmitted orally by rhapsodists. Recent studies . . . have clearly shown the importance of regarding the *Mahābhārata* as an oral epic" (Kunjunni Raja 1990, 89; see also Fitzgerald 1991, 154, citing the comments of both O'Flaherty 1978 and de Jong 1975 on Grintser 1974). So there are many good reasons for thinking of *Mahābhārata* not as a book but as a *tradition* of which written texts are but a single (albeit a very important) element. As Fitzgerald puts it, "In its largest sense, 'the *Mahhābhārata*' is a wide and varied tradition which has existed in ancient and 'medieval' India in several forms (oral, written, dramatic, danced, in puppet performances) in many languages and in numerous versions, and it is entirely uncharted as such a super-textual tradition" (1991, 153).

The critical edition of *Mahābhārata*—which I lightheartedly refer to throughout this book as "the Pune edition"—was "established" on the basis of several regional recensions that differed so greatly among themselves as to create unprecedented problems for the editors.[34] In fact the editor of the critical edition, V. S. Sukthankar himself, wrote that "[t]he essential fact in Mahābhārata textual criticism is that the Mahābhārata is not and never was a fixed rigid text, but is fluctuating epic tradition. . . . To put it in other words, the Mahābhārata is the whole of the epic tradition: the entire Critical Apparatus" (1933, cii).

In short, *Mahābhārata* is not just a book. It is also a political model, a bedtime story, a form of dance, a dramatic spectacle, a geographic template, and a charter for personal identity. It is a "super-textual tradition" (Fitzgerald 1991, 153), an "institution" (Gitomer 1992, 231). In Garhwal, far from being understood as a book, *Mahābhārata* is a kind of ancestral history that is remembered by the wise and periodically enacted in *pāṇḍav līlā*. Although printed versions are available in most villages, they are rarely consulted, even when there is disagreement over the accuracy of some bard's version. The decisive factor in settling such disagreements is never a printed text but rather the collective memory of the senior men present, especially those who recite.

Obvously it would be a mistake to regard our bound and printed copies of *Mahābhārata* as the thing itself, and equally misguided to regard *pāṇḍav līlā* as the performance of a written text. How, then, to characterize it, how to describe the way in which it "constructs" or "embodies" identity? For the Western scholar who lives in a world of books, human social and cultural life is a text, and *paṇḍav līlā* might be seen by such a scholar as a kind of textual charter, a representation of a set of "beliefs," including beliefs about the self. But such a view would be fundamentally misguided, for *pāṇḍav līlā* is neither a text nor a theology, neither a set of systematic beliefs to be

34. See Fitzgerald 1980, 59; O'Flaherty 1978, 22ff.; Proudfoot 1987.

deconstructed nor a set of propositions to be logically evaluated. It is a performance, a dance, which can easily be observed, and even participated in, by informants and anthropologists alike. If we attempt to reduce *pāṇḍav līlā* to a text, or to a set of beliefs that should (or even can) be analyzed as a text, we neglect all the numerous extratextual elements that make it a living tradition.

Part of the problem stems from thinking of "belief" exclusively as a state of mind, from failing to recognize that it is also a state of the body. In typical academic fashion, experience is reduced to text, text is analyzed in propositions (true or false?), and the distance between disembodied intellectual subject (the scholar) and embodied acting object (the native) is maintained. But, as Bourdieu reminds us, "Practical belief is not a 'state of mind,' still less a kind of arbitrary adherence to a set of instituted dogmas and doctrines ('beliefs'), but rather a state of the body." Moreover, the body "believes in what it plays at: it weeps if it mimes grief. It does not represent what it performs, it does not memorize the past, it enacts the past, bringing it back to life" (1990, 68, 73). Performance theorists know that Bourdieu's assertion is grounded in the human organism. To smile is to physiologically dispose the body to feel happiness; to frown is not simply to mime the feeling of sadness but actively to elicit it.[35]

Garhwalis associate *Mahābhārata* not only with their region but also with their own bodies. Garhwali Kshatriyas—those belonging to the "class" (*varṇa*) of warriors—say that they are descended from the Pandavas. To honor the Pandavas is thus a kind of ancestor worship, and *pāṇḍav līlā* is often referred to colloquially as a *sarāddh* (Skt. *śrāddha*), the obligatory ritual of ancestor worship.[36] It is remarkable that, despite variations in *pāṇḍav līlā*, this definition of it as a kind of *śraddha* is virtually universal in Garhwal. Much of the action of a performance is directly related to this idea. For example, in most *pāṇḍav līlā* performances, the Pandavas process from house to house, where they dispense blessings and in return are worshiped and feasted by the household and are given various items such as grain, jaggery, fruits, and sometimes hashish and liquor. This collection is conceived of as a gathering of the materials required for the *śrāddha* of the Pandavas' deceased father, King Pandu. Moreover, every *pāṇḍav līlā* involves a *śrāddha* ritual of some sort, performed by a priest for Nakula, who is believed to be the only biological son of Pandu. In Chandpur, the complete *śrāddha* ceremony is performed, authentic in every respect. In these ways the *pāṇḍav līlā* is directly tied to Garhwalis' deepest identities as descendants of the Pandavas.

The patterned movements of public rituals and ceremonies of all kinds help to shape the identity of Garhwalis; this is perhaps clearest in *pāṇḍav*

35. See Schechner's (1990) discussion of a "universal language of emotions" that is linked to the autonomic nervous system.

36. See Pande 1969 for a detailed study of Hindu life-cycle rituals (*saṃskāras*), including *śrāddha*.

līlā, which relates the *Mahābhārata* story to the most mundane details of peasant life. For example, many of the dances mimic typical rural activities. In Sutol, one of the most common dance steps was "pounding grain," an activity that can be observed every evening in any Garhwali village, when girls and women husk grain by placing it in a hollow that has been carved in one of the flagstones in front of the house, then pounding it with a large wooden pestle. In Bhatgwali village, one of the group dances (called *paiñjī*) began after the dancers had gone in procession to an irrigated field, where they danced the following series of actions: cleaning the field of its debris, opening the irrigation canal, plowing the field, pushing down the sprouted paddy shoots, transplanting paddy, harvesting it, loading it on the back, and returning to the house.

Other skits are more humourous and/or lewd and are referred to by the common north Indian term *śauṅg* or *svāṅg*. These often center on oxen, which are essential for agricultural work but often are rather troublesome. In Taintura village, the bard Gautam Singh became a kind of "director" one night for a *svaṅg* lasting several hours, in which elements of self-parody were ubiquitous. It began when a man came to the market to sell a pair of oxen. Gautam Singh teased the seller, telling him that he must be a real country bumpkin because his hat and clothes did not fit properly. He asked the price, and the seller replied that he would yoke the oxen together and demonstrate how well they plowed; then they would discuss the price. They continued to haggle, while the audience laughed at the antics of two village youths, who were required to crawl about in the dancing square on their hands and knees, sometimes rearing up and snorting, at other times stubbornly refusing to budge. Gautam Singh then took them through an entire season of preparing the ground and planting, transplanting, and harvesting rice.

In Sutol, the musician Dharam Das also directed *svāṅgs* that represented the annual agricultural cycle, month by month. His most impressive *svāṅg* lasted for most of the sacred *paṇwālī* day (see chapter 1) and included a number of rustic activities. After leaving Hastinapura and building their new city of Jayanti, the Pandavas go to Nagiloka (the serpent realm) to buy a cow. Accompanying himself on the drum, Dharam Das chanted:

Now the Pandavas
They went to Nagiloka
and they brought from there a cow
And in Hastinapur was the cowherd of the Kauravas.
And here was the cow of the Pandavas.
Now, O kings, here is what happened one day:

(sings:)
"Today I must herd the cows and buffaloes in the forest.
Today I must herd the cow calves and buffalo calves in the forest."
Then along came the Kauravas' shepherds—
in which forest will the cows graze today?

[Two cowherds dance. One represents the hundred Kauravas, and the other represents Nakula.]

Today they will graze on Sandy Bank:
the hundred shepherds assembled.

(chants:)
So, hey, great kings!
From Hastinapur the Kauravas' herdsmen came.
And there at Sandy Bank was the Pandavas' cow.
All were there.

[Dharam Das directs the four Pandavas to stand to one side; he tells Nakula to say, "Hey, brother, what game should we play today?"]

(sings:)
They began to make boiled rice out of sand
They began to make fried snacks out of sand.

(chants:)
Hey, great kings,
They made boiled rice from sand!
They made fried snacks from sand!
They made tasty treats from cow manure!
They made sugar from stones!
All the hundred herdsmen ate it,
and Nakul ate it too.

(sings:)
The cow from Jayanti Palace went back to Jayanti Palace,
and the Kauravas' cow went back to Hastinapura.

(chants:)
I'll tell you in five years:
everyone ate their food.
The next day came.
The Kauravas' herds came from Hastinapura.
The Pandavas' herds came from Jayanti Palace.

(sings):
"I must graze the cows and buffaloes in this forest.
I must graze the cow calves and buffalo calves in this forest."
To which forest will the shepherd go today?
Today he will go to Giratoli Field.

(chants:)
So, hey, great kings!
They all came,
all the cows from both sides:
the hundred shepherds of the Kauravas,
and Nakul came too.

[Dharam Das directs the Kaurava to ask Nakula:]

"Today what game shall we play, little one? Today we will play *gilli*."[37]

[Dharm Das directs them to dig a hollow and fetch a stick]

(speaks:)
Now the Kauravas say to Nakul: "You make a hollow for the stick, and we'll put *you* in it. There's a hundred of us, but only one of you!"

(chants:)
So, hey, great kings:
on that day,
in Giratoli field,
they played *gilli*.

[They play *gillī* to the beat of the drums.]

(speaks:)
Now the Kauravas say, "There's a hundred of us versus only one boy! Why is he beating us time and again?"

(sings:)
The cow from Jayanti went back to Jayanti,
and the Kauravas' cow went back to Hastinapura.

(chants:)
Hey, great kings! O great gods!

37. A very common game, "*gillī* and *daṇḍā*" is played thus: first a small hole is dug in the ground, perhaps four inches deep. Then a *gillī* twig is placed across the top. It should be about nine inches long, with projections at either end such that it can be struck and caused to fly. The first player plants his stick (the *daṇḍā*) in the hole beneath the *gillī* and, with a rapid upward motion, launches the *gillī* as far as he can. If the second player catches the *gillī*, the first player is out. Otherwise, the first player places his stick across the hole, and the second player tries to hit it with the *gillī*. If the *gillī* strikes the stick, the first player is out. If it does not, the first player flips the *gillī* into the air with his stick and tries to keep it aloft by striking it as many times as possible before he finally knocks it as far as he can. He has three chances to do this. The final score is calculated in terms of the number of times he manages to strike the *gillī* while it is in the air.

The next day came
"You go now!" said Mother Kunti.

[Dharam Das directs the dancer: "Mother Kunti, you go, too."]

Mother Kunti says, "Hey son Bhimsen,
you go in Nakula's place today.
He is getting weak going with the cows.
Today I will wash him and comb the lice from his hair.
Today you go with the cows and buffaloes."
Hey, great kings! O great gods!
Today Bhimsen will go with the cows!
Mother Kunti gave Bhima Nakula's herding stick.

(sings:)
"Today I must graze the cow and buffalo calves in the forest.
Today I must graze the cows and buffaloes in the forest."

[The dancer does so.]

In which forest will today's shepherd take his herds?
Today's shepherd will graze his herds in Giratoli forest.

(speaks:)
O great kings! The hundred shepherds all collected in Giratoli forest. And then the Kaurava shepherds said:

(sings:)
"A shepherd has come from some village or other.
Which mother's son has come here today, my brother?"
The Kauravas' herdsman is staring.

(speaks)
Today's shepherd is big brother Bhima!
One shepherd says, "Hello, big brother!"

[Dharam Das directs the dancer: "Say it! Say "Hello, big brother!"]
One shepherd says, "Hello, big brother!"

[Now Dharam Das directs the shepherd to say to Bhima:]
"Big brother, you sit here. I will take the cows out to graze today."

The Kauravas' shepherd has guessed that Bhima has come to avenge the slight to his younger brother Nakula. Bhima points with his shepherd's staff and asks, "Why have you made this pit? Have you been playing *gillī*?" The Kaurava shepherd says, "No, no, I don't play *gillī*. I herd cows." Bhima replies, "Yes, you have—you've been playing *gillī*," and the Kaurava answers, "No, we didn't. We didn't play." Bhima says, "Then how did this pit come about?" and they answer, "It's from the cows' hooves." The Kaurava shepherd begs Bhima to forgive him, saying, "Bhimsen, we won't play with you anymore. And we won't play with Nakula. Our noses have been rubbed in the dirt today."

(chants:)
Hey, great kings! O great gods!
The Pandavas rubbed the Kauravas' noses in the dirt seven times.

(sings:)
Then Jayanti Palace's shepherd came home,
and the Kauravas' shepherd went back to Hastinapura.

(chants:)
Hey, great kings! O great gods!
The Kauravas said to Nakula,
"You went and told some lies about us!
And we got our noses rubbed in the dirt seven times!"
The Kauravas say, "Today we won't play *gillī*, we'll have an ox-fight instead."

[The drummer recruits two youths to play the part of oxen. "Yes," he says, "these two will do nicely." One ox represents the Kauravas and another, the Pandavas.]

(sings:)
"Both oxen were bellowing" [the youths bellow; lots of laughter].
"Both oxen dug trenches with their hooves."

[Dharam Das directs: "You go to this side, you go to that!"]
"Both oxen were bellowing!"

(chants:)
The earth from the underworld was thrown to the sky.
A cloud of dust arose.
Both oxen were bellowing.
Both oxen locked horns.

[The two oxen fight as the drums play frantically. After some time, Dharam Das continues his performance in prose. First he directs a youth playing the part of the Kauravas to say, "The Kauravas' ox's horn has come off!" Then he tells the Kaurava to hit the Pandavas' ox on the forehead with it.]

Now his head is naked!
So the two oxen came and fought.
They caused the dust to fly:
so much dust that it clogged up their yokes!

To the reader, these skits may seem crude and artless, and indeed they were not very sophisticated. But they do embody peasant experiences and concerns, and they were immensely popular with audiences, who laughed and clapped with delight, especially at the antics of the young men who took the part of oxen. In these skits, the heroes of *Mahābhārata* were portrayed not as great kings and princes but as simple folk with lice in their hair, as ancestors with whom the villagers felt an experiential and physical bond.

This identification by Garhwalis of themselves with the Pandavas is perhaps nowhere clearer than in the dance of Nakula the cowherd. His other brothers were born of gods and had miraculous powers, but according to the Garhwali version of *Mahābhārata*, Nakula was the sole biological son of Pandu, the human son of a human father. If the Rajputs of Garhwal are descended from the Pandavas, then it is Nakula who provides the genealogical link. Nakula's dance is among the most popular dances of *pāṇḍav līlā* and is performed nearly everywhere in Garhwal. In the Chandpur region, it may be performed as many as ten or fifteen times a night, as pairs of local men come to display their skills to the assembled crowd. Thus the dance goes on for hour after hour, and villagers never seem to tire of it. In the dance, Nakula bathes and dries himself, exhibiting the kind of concern for personal cleanliness that is appropriate for a Rajput nobleman. He takes his carrying stick in hand, then strides along the Himalayan paths to the grassy meadows, lying verdant under a sunny sky. He cuts great swaths of grass with his sharp hand scythe, binds them tightly to his carrying stick, hoists them on to his back, and carries them home. After reaching his farm, he feeds the grass to his cows, then milks them. He pours the milk into a barrel and churns great mounds of butter from it. And when all the butter is churned, he places it on his domestic altar, offering it to the gods who have been so generous with their blessings, their love, and their bounty.

These dance steps are neither heroic nor miraculous. They are the rustic actions of a simple Himalayan farmer. But the grace with which the dancers mime them, the enthusiasm with which they come forward to perform, and the evident pleasure taken by both dancers and spectators in witnessing this dance over and over must be seen to be appreciated. This pleasure and skill, this embodied performance, clearly show that in the dance of the cowherd, as in the other dances and skits of *pāṇḍav līlā*, the peasants of Garhwal dance their own selves, and that these selves are merged with the heroes of *Mahābhārata*.

3

Hunting the Rhinoceros

Pāṇḍav Līlā *as a Man's Sport*

It is not, however, the contents of the myth that keep analysis Freudian. It is the method. —Hillman 1991, [1987], 130

In this chapter, I will explore the way in which Garhwali men represent themselves in *pāṇḍav līlā*, to themselves and to others, as fathers and sons. This is an especially significant issue because for Garhwalis the most compelling of the many episodes dramatized in *pāṇḍav līlā* is the battle between Arjuna and his son Nagarjuna. For reasons that will become clear in due course, this episode is known as "the Rhinoceros" (Hindi *gaiṇḍā*).

A parallel episode is found in the Pune edition of *Mahābhārata*,[1] where Arjuna's son is called Babhruvahana. That version has been subjected to a Freudian analysis by Robert Goldman (1978), and part of my purpose in this chapter is to provide an alternative to Goldman's interpretation, but to do so I must first set the stage by describing the mythology and performance of the Rhinoceros in some detail. After doing so, I will summarize Goldman's analysis of the corresponding episode in the Pune edition of the epic, then offer my own interpretation by taking into account Garhwali patterns of child rearing and Hindu theories of personhood, family, and caste. I conclude that the episode derives its extraordinary dramatic power from the ambivalent and highly charged relationship between father and son, which is represented, and in a sense "resolved," by means of public, embodied performance.

In chapter 2, I discussed the ways in which *pāṇḍav līlā* varies in time and duration of performances, chief episodes dramatized, musicians' instruments, and other features. In later chapters, I will discuss another variation that amounts to a kind of inversion: a valley where the Kauravas rather than the Pandavas are the chief focus of worship. Given such regional variation, it is remarkable that one episode is consistently dramatized throughout

1. See n. 12 chap. 2.

Garhwal.[2] That episode is known as "the Rhinoceros," and the following is the Rhinoceros Tale:[3]

The Rhinoceros Tale (as told by Bacan Singh)[4]

King Agnidhar's son Utkal was sick, so he sent for Atmadeva, his Brahman priest. Atmadeva pleaded that he was too old to come, and as he had sent his eldest son, Dharmishtya, to Kashi to study Sanskrit, he directed his younger son, Vidyadhara, to go the king's palace, instructing him to accept any gift from the king except for red garments. However, it was fated that only by accepting such a gift would the king's son get relief. The king tempted Vidyadhara with a golden scythe and a golden staff, and the Brahman youth accepted them along with the red cloth.[5]

But God did not approve of this. He took the form of a cow along the path, and when Vidyadhara approached, he threw rocks at her, but she did not give way. So he struck her with the golden scythe and killed her, and the cow cursed him, saying, "Go, Brahman. You were born in a Brahman family, but you killed me. Go! You will now take birth in a demon's home."[6]

Many years later, Vidyadhara took birth in the home of a demon named Keshi. And Keshi named him Surya. One day, Keshi and his wife went to the jungle to eat meat and drink liquor. They stayed there overnight, while their son was home alone, crying with hunger. At that moment, Atri Muni and Anasuya Devi were flying through heaven in their aerial cars. Anasuya said to her husband, "A child is crying from hunger." She landed her aerial car and fed

2. The village of Sutol, whose *līlā* is described in chapter 2, is one of the very few villages where the Rhinoceros is not performed.

3. Most of what follows is based on research on the left bank of the Alakananda River and in the Pindar River basin, where the Rhinoceros *līlā* is most highly elaborated (see map 2). For convenience' sake, I will refer to this area as Chamoli. The Rhinoceros also predominates in Nandakini District and perhaps in the Painkhanda region. It should, however, be noted that parts of Chamoli District located on the right bank of the Alakananda specialize in the *cakravyūha*, or "Circular Array," the encirclement and death of Arjuna's son Abhimanyu during the great battle (see chapter 4). I suspect that these regional variations correlate with the ancient division of Garhwal into petty chiefdoms, each with its own fort, or *gaḍhi*, hence the name Garhwal (*gaḍhwāḷ*), "land of forts."

4. Bacan Singh "Shastri-ji" is a loremaster from Toli village, Malla Chandpur, Chamoli District. The version translated here was told in Hindi.

5. Obviously the king requires Vidyadhar to accept some of his "negatives" in the red cloth, and he bribes him into doing so with the golden scythe and staff. The passing on of such negatives in the form of prestations to Brahmans is common in north India; see Raheja 1988b.

6. In a separate telling, Bacan Singh said that Vidyadhara thought that his father had gone senile: "He takes bags of rice and salt, and wants to leave this golden scythe behind." So Vidyadhara took the scythe, along with a yellow cloth (not a red one), and the cow he killed with it was actually dharma, personified as an ox (*dharmarūp bail*).

him a spoonful of nectar. The next day, the parents of Surya the demon came home. They said, "Eat, son." He said, "I'm not hungry." They asked why, and he said, "You two went to the jungle and stayed there for two days. In the meantime, a man and woman came from the sky and fed me something, and my hunger and thirst have been satisifed." So his mother and father sent him to search for the couple who had helped him.

Surya scrambled and climbed and crawled to Atri and Anasuya's ashram in the mountains. Atri said to Anasuya, "Devi, I told you that day not to feed him, now see what trouble has come. I will change his name." He taught him some mantras and gave him some good clothes and named him Devasura. When Devasura learned the mantras, he remembered his previous life: how he had been born in a Brahman's home, had taken the gifts of gold, killed a cow, and been cursed to be reborn as a demon.

He told all of this to Atri Muni, who said, "Go, son, you are guilty of bovicide. There are 360 rivers in India: go bathe in all of them, then return to me." Devasura did so, returned to Atri Muni, and asked him to liberate him from his demonic body. Atri told him to search out a pilgrimage place with a great boulder on the banks of the Ganges, where he would be liberated. So Devasura searched and he searched and he searched and he searched, and finally he found the great boulder named Gomati at Gaya. Then he summoned all the gods, and they dug a large, deep pit and placed him in the bottom, and rolled a big stone over the top of it, and performed a sacrifice on top of the stone. When only Devasura's bones were left, they joined them together to make an effigy.

Then Vishnu said to his charioteer Dvaruka, "Go, and grab whatever you first see in the bazaar and bring it here." The first thing Dvaruka saw in the bazaar was a cake of jaggery, so he took it and brought it back. They mixed it with honey to make flesh. By the power of their mantras, they established breath in it. Then they put the ash from the sacrifice[7] between his eyes, and it grew and grew until it formed a horn. Since he was born in Gaya in the month of Bhadrapad, he was called Gayasura, the demon [*asur*] from Gaya. And because of the horn he was called "rhinoceros." He was the Rhinoceros Demon of Gaya [*gayāsur gaiṇḍā*].[8]

7. Hindi *yajña-tilak*, black ashes from burned barley and sesamum.

8. According to popular religious literature available in Gaya, Gayasura was a demon who performed asceticism until he received the boon that anyone who touched his body would go to heaven. Soon the netherworld (*yamaloka*) began to be depopulated as all its residents went to heaven, so the gods went to Vishnu, who directed Brahma to do a sacrifice (*yajña*) on the body of Gayasura. Afterward, Gayasura tried to rise up but was prevented from doing so by the gods. Yama placed a stone on top of him to keep him down, and Gayasura promised that he would not get up anymore if Vishnu and the other gods would continue to dwell on top of him (Pandeya n.d.; Prasad n.d.).

When the gods saw him, they were afraid. They didn't know what to do with him, so they said, "Let's give him to Indra, king of the gods." Indra made a copper pavilion for him and put him inside. He was too ornery and dangerous to be let out, so they pushed his fodder into the copper pavilion with a crooked stick, and his drinking water flowed in through an opening at the base of the wall.

Then came *dvāparayug*, the third age of the world. Once upon a time, King Pandu took his bow and went to hunt in a jungle where a rishi and his wife had taken the forms of deer so that they could enjoy sexual relations.[9] Pandu shot the stag, and the rishi's wife resumed her human form and said, "Look what you've done, you've killed my husband!" She cursed him: "Should you ever have sex with your wife, your head will split."

So the Pandavs were not born of Pandu's seed. Mother Kunti recited the mantra of Dharmaraja, and Yudhishthira was born. She recited the mantra of Vayu, and Bhimsen was born. She recited the mantra of the Ashvin Kumars, and Sahadeva was born. Once when King Pandu was observing the eleventh-day [*ekādaśī*] fast, he thought, "I have two wives, but I have never enjoyed them sexually." His heart began to beat for his second wife, Madri, and he forced himself on her, had intercourse with her, and Nakula was conceived.[10]

Now in former times, when a man died, his wife would burn herself to ashes together with him on his funeral pyre and become a *satī*. But the gods said, "Mother Kunti is one of the deities—she can't be a *satī*. And Madri is pregnant. She can't be a *satī*, either." So King Pandu wasn't cremated for ten months, not until Nakula was born.[11] In our Hindu religion, we break the skull of the cremated corpse because the *dhananjaya vāyu*[12] is inside it, and if it is not released, it becomes a ghost, but if the skull is broken, it flies away. So because King Pandu's skull was not broken, he became a ghost.

Now about this time, Narada the rishi was wandering in the forest, and he saw King Pandu on the path. He said, "King Pandu is dead. How is it that he has appeared to me on the path?" So he went to the Pandavas' capital and said to King Yudhishthira, "Your father has not reached heaven. I've seen him on the path. You perform a *nārāyaṇa-*

9. Literally "so that he could give her *ṛtudān*," the householder's obligation to have monthly intercourse with his wife after her period. In Garhwal, this is a polite euphemism for sex.

10. Accordig to the Pune edition of *Mahābhārata*, both Nakula and Sahadeva were conceived by the Ashvina Kumaras, so that Pandu had no biological children at all. See discussion below.

11. In India, human gestation is traditionally reckoned to last ten months.

12. For *dhanaṃjaya vāyu*, Monier-Williams gives "a particular vital air supposed to nourish the body" (1976, 508).

bali,[13] and he will reach heaven." So Yudhishthira asked Narada, "How should I do it? What do I need?" and Narada said, "You need the earth from an elephant's footprints, soil from Malari, barley from Jauras,[14] sesame from Sesame Grove, gold from Tibet, and the hide of a rhinoceros."[15] So the Pandavas held a council and decided that they would do Pandu's *nārāyaṇa-bali śrāddha*. Mother Kunti called her four sons, but Arjuna wasn't there. Why not?

Once upon a time, they would tell stories in the Kauravas' capital of Hastinapur. At that time, Arjuna was just a child: he filled their hookah and so forth. Afterward, Lord Krishna would stand up and ask if anyone would like to go to the gates of death. But everyone refused; none of them wanted to go because they knew that whoever goes to the gates of death does not return.

Mother Kunti asked Arjuna what stories they were telling there, and he said that he didn't understand the stories, but afterward Shri Krishna would arise and ask if anyone was willing to go to the gates of death, and they would all refuse. Mother Kunti said, "Son, one day you agree; tell Shri Krishna that you will go to the gates of death." So one day Arjuna said to Shri Krishna, "Yes, I'll come," and the gods were upset by this.

Now there was a girl named Vasudanta, the daughter of Vasuki the Serpent [*nāga*]. She performed asceticism for Shiva for twelve years, seeking the boon of a husband. If she didn't get that boon, the earth would burn up from the falling of her tears, so Shiva-ji concocted an enchantment. . . . Shri Krishna and Arjuna came to Shiva's realm. Shri Krishna began to play the drum, and Arjuna began to dance the *kāñcanī* dance. Shiva-ji was charmed and said, "Kanchani, tell me what boon you seek." Arjuna said, "First you give your oath." Shiva gave his oath, saying:

13. The *nārāyaṇa-bali* is mentioned in the Hindu ritual manual *Dharmasindhu*. In Garhwal, it is performed for any person whose last rites have not been completed. An effigy made of *ḍūba* or *kuśa* grass is placed on a bier and taken to the cremation ground, while the bearers chant "*Rāma nāma satya hai, satya bolo gatya hai*" (Rama's name is truth; speak truth; this is everyone's destiny). All other, related rites are observed, including tonsure and *kapāla-kriyā*.

14. These places are in Garhwal's neighboring province of Kumaon. They are at high altitude and are associated with the Bhotiyas, trans-Himalayan traders and transhumant pastoralists.

15. It is said that a rhinoceros-hide ring may be substituted for the more conventional *kuśa*-grass ring in *śrāddha*, the obligatory mortuary rite, and that such rings were often employed in Garhwal in times past. In some parts of Kumaon and Garhwal, Brahmans use either a ring made of rhinoceros bone or a small piece of rhinoceros hide during their *śrāddha* performances. Such rings are also mentioned in the *Dharmasindhu*, a Hindu ritual manual (Mihirachandra 1984, 576). The *Mānavadharmaśāstra* (3.272) gives a list of oblations to the ancestors, asserting that those of rhinoceros flesh are the most effective, satisfying the ancestors forever and thus obviating the need for future *śrāddhas*. Although rhinoceroses are not now found in the Tarai region adjoining the central Himalayas, historical evidence shows that they were once common there (Bautze 1983).

I swear once, I swear twice.
May Brahma and Vishnu,
the banyan and pipal trees, bear witness:
if my oath wavers, may I go to hell![16]

"Tell me what you want!" And Arjuna said, "I want Vasudanta for my wife." Then Shiva-ji asked Vasudanta what she wanted, and she said she wanted a husband like Arjuna. So Shiva placed Vasudanta's hand in Arjuna's and said, "This is your wife." And he placed Arjuna's hand in Vasudanta's and said, "This is your husband." Then they returned to Hastinapura along with Shri Krishna.

At Caupanthi Caukhal [lit. "four paths, four passes"], Vasudanta said, "Revered husband, we are husband and wife only because Shiva-ji gave us to each other as a boon. Let us visit my father Vasuki in Nagiloka [Skt. *nāgaloka*], and he will marry us properly. He'll erect a banana tree, make an altar, bind us together with a cloth, and lead us around the fire altar.[17] Then we'll be man and wife." From there, Vasudanta and Arjuna went to Nagiloka, and Shri Krishna went to Dvaraka.

Now mother Kunti said, "Arjuna should bring the rhinoceros skin, but he's not here." He had gone to Nagiloka. She sent a letter to Dvaraka saying "Hey, Krishna, my nephew, Arjuna was with you. Where has he gone?" And Shri Krishna sent an answer, saying, "Father's sister, your son has gone to Nagiloka with Vasudanta."

So Mother Kunti rolled some of the dirt from her body into a ball, breathed life into it, and made two bumblebees. She wrote a letter to Arjuna and placed it beneath their wings. Then she said, "Go, bumblebees, to where my Arjuna is." So the bumblebees went to Nagiloka: "*gauṃ-gauṃ-gauṃ-gauṃ*." Arjuna was sleeping next to his wife on his cloth bed. She was fanning him with a yak-tail whisk.[18] When the bumblebees alighted, she thought they might bite him, so she struck them with her whisk, but then they multiplied a thousandfold. They became a thick cloud that blotted out the sun. Vasudanta thought, "O God, what will I do now?" and fled.

Arjuna's conch shell, named 'Devadatta', was lying on his chest, and it sounded a note from the breath of his nostril. Arjuna awoke and said, "Where have these bumblebees come from?" He struck the

16. *ek bācā, do bācā*
baramā viṣṇu bākī
baḍ pīpal sākhī
bacan ṭalegā to narak paḍegā

17. elements of an orthodox Hindu wedding

18. In the dance-drama, Vasudanta fans the rhinoceros with a whisk. Is some kind of equivalence being established here between the two sacrificial "victims," Arjuna and the rhinoceros?

earth and said, "If they are from my mother, let them become as many as were sent from Hastinapur. If they are from my enemy, let their number remain as it is." The thousands of bees became two, and alighted on Arjuna's lap. He stroked them and found the secret letter. His mother had written, "Son, come quickly. Your father, Pandu, is stuck between heaven and earth. We are performing his mortuary rites—come quickly! If you're eating rice, then come here to wash your hands. If you're getting dressed, then come here to button your shirt."

Arjuna said to his wife, Vasudanta, "My mother has sent these bumblebees—I must go to Hastinapura." Vasudanta said, "The male of the species is very bad. You will forget me and marry again. Give me your token." Now, Arjuna had a special ring that enabled him to travel very quickly, and his ten names were written on it. He left it with her, and therefore it took him twelve years to reach Hastinapura. And the child Nagarjuna was born in Nagiloka and grew to be twelve years old.[19] When Arjuna reached Hastinapura, he touched his mother's feet and asked her what was wrong, and she said, "Narada the rishi told us that your father is stuck between heaven and earth. Now you must do his *nārāyaṇ-bali*. It requires the hide of the rhinoceros demon of Gaya. You go and bring it from Indraloka."

Meanwhile, Nagarjuna had grown to be twelve years old. He laughed and played with the people of the city. The other children teased him, calling him a bastard.[20] He went crying to his mother and told her how the other children teased him. He said, "Mother, who is my father?" and she said, "You have no father." He said, "Then how was I born?" and she replied, "I ate some roots, flowers, and fruits." He said, "Then why don't you eat some more and have another child—why are you telling me such a story?" She said, "Look at this ring. There's a copper plate inside: read it. On it is written that your father is Arjuna, who lives in Hastinapura. And your grandfather is Indra, who lives in Amaravati."[21] So he asked, "Which is farthest, Hastinapura or

19. It is odd, to say the least, that Arjuna gave up his ring and thus took so long to reach Hastinapura. This detail is anachronistic: it facilitates the aging of Nagarjuna, so that he will be an adult when Arjuna confronts him, but what did Arjuna's family do for twelve years while they waited for him? A more satisfying explanation is given by a bard from Agast Muni. He says that Nagarjuna was going to attend the *rājasūya yajña* but lost his way at Caupanthi Caukhal. He went to Indra's city of Amaravati by mistake and danced before Indra, who was pleased and gave him a boon. He asked for the rhinoceros, knowing that Arjuna would come to get it from him. When the *rājasūya yajña* begins, Arjun is sent to obtain the rhinoceros hide. Indra tells Arjuna that Nagarjuna has already taken the rhinoceros, but he does not tell him that Nagarjuna is his son.

20. Gwli. *cor-jār putra*, lit. "son of a thief," a common term for "illegitimate son" in the local dialect.

21. This is similar to the penultimate story in the *Kathāsaritsāgara* (retold by Doniger 1988) of the thief Muladeva, who leaves his pregnant wife with a ring with his name on it, which the son, when taunted about his illegitimacy, uses to find his father.

Amaravati?" His mother answered, "Your grandfather's house is closer; your father's house is very far away."

He said, "I'll go to Amaravati." He went there and did obeisance to his grandfather. Indra was disturbed, saying, "Why does he call me grandfather?"[22] Nagarjuna answered, "I am Arjuna's son." Indra said, "Why are you calling me by this false name? If you are Arjuna's son, then go give some water to the rhinoceros and bring him here. He is fed with a crooked staff and watered by a trough. No one can untie him. If you are Arjuna's son, then bring him here."

Nagarjuna said, "If I am truly Arjuna's son, then the rhinoceros won't kill me. But if I'm a bastard, then he will surely kill me." He went to the rhinoceros and called out, "I am Arjuna's son." The rhinoceros answered him, and then Nagarjuna went in, stroked him, untied him, and led him to water. The rhinoceros drank, and Nagarjuna brought him back and tied him up again. Indra said, "This is surely Arjuna's son. My troubles with the rhinoceros are over." Indra had a new hat and suit of clothes made for Nagarjuna, and gave him sweets and fried grain.[23] "Go," he said. "And take the rhinoceros with you."

Later, Arjuna came to his father Indra's palace in search of the rhinoceros. He did obeisance to Indra, who said, "Who are you?" Arjuna said, "I'm Arjuna, your son."

"Why have you come?"

"I've come to get the rhinoceros."

"Your son has taken him to Nagiloka."

"What son?"

"No, no, he's taken the rhinoceros to Nagiloka."

Arjuna got angry: "What son?"

Arjuna returned to Kunti in Hastinapura and said, "Mother, a thief has stolen our rhinoceros and taken him to Nagiloka." Mother Kunti said, "Go to Nagiloka and bring him back." Arjuna got angry with his mother and said, "You always send me to such difficult places! First you sent me to Indraloka, now to Nagiloka!" He left angrily, without even doing obeisance to his mother. At the place where four paths and passes meet, he saw eight different ways and didn't know which way to go.

He returned and said, "Mother, there are eight paths; which one should I take?" She said, "Son, that's what happens to children who do not respect their parents' word. Go back to that place. My little sister, Mother Earth, lives there—summon her and ask her which way

22. Note how fathers (and grandfathers) consistently fail to recognize their sons (and grandsons) throughout this story. Cf. Ulbricht, who in his discussion of Indonesian shadow puppetry and especially the "Pandwa Cycle" of *lakons* (dramas), notes that "Ardjuna's own encounters with his unknown sons likewise give rise to much confusion and many surprises" (1970, 60).

23. Such prestations are typically made to close kin in Garhwal at the conclusion of a visit.

to go. She has a son named Bhumasura, and his son is named Bhagadatta. He will go with you." So Arjuna returned, called on Mother Earth, and asked her which way to go. She said, "This is my grandson Bhagadatta. He will go with you."

Where the four paths and four passes meet, in one place there is nothing but stairs, stairs, stairs . . . that path goes to heaven. And where there are elephant prints, that path goes to Amaravati, where Indra lives. The bull hoofprints lead to Gandhamadana Mountain, where Shiva lives—Mount Kailash. And where there is cow manure, that road goes to Grassy Wood. And where there are single footprints, that road goes to the Monoped Kingdom. And where there is the sign of a stick that's been dragged, that path goes to Nagiloka, the Serpent Realm. So Arjaun followed the path to Nagiloka.

Now on the day that Shiva-ji gave Vasudanta to Arjuna, he also gave her a quiver full of arrows as a dowry. Arjuna and Vasudanta had left it at a place called Dharmashila.[24] So when Arjuna went to Nagiloka to get the rhinoceros, he stopped at Dharmashila and took out the blood-drinking arrow. When he reached Taluka Pond, he built a hunting blind in a tree.

Now the rhinoceros woke up very thirsty, every morning. Nagarjuna would untie him, send him to Taluka Pond, and say, "Drink your fill, and return." When the rhinoceros drank, he would first offer some water to heaven, then to the underworld, and only then would he drink.[25] Arjuna was sleeping in the blind, and when the rhinoceros cast the water toward heaven, some of the drops fell on Arjuna's chest, and he awoke, thinking, "Where has this rain come from?" He saw the rhinoceros drinking water and shot him. As the rhinoceros died, he bellowed forth, and from the noise of his cry the earth trembled: "*Tha-ra-ra-ra!*" Nagarjuna heard the cry and said, "Oh, mother, someone has killed my rhinoceros." So he went to that place and called out, "Who are you? You thief—you've killed my rhinoceros! If you are a true Kshatriya, then come forth and do battle!"

They were father and son, and they both had the same weapon—the one that Shiva had given to Vasudanta. They shot their arrows, but the arrows did not strike home. They met in midair and then returned. They fought fiercely, but the arrows did not strike home. So Nagarjuna went to Kaliya the ironsmith and had him make the *gurū*-less arrow [*nigur bāṇ*], the arrow that doesn't obey the word of the *gurū*, that kills anyone, that has no discrimination [*vivek*]. He struck Arjuna

24. This detail is repeated in many tellings of the story throughout Garhwal, emphasis being laid on the fact that during his first sojourn in Nagilok, when he conceived Nagajuna, Arjuna had been without weapons. He is armed only when he returns to hunt the rhinoceros.

25. Similar to the morning ritual that orthodox Hindus are supposed to perform: this is a very pious rhinoceros!

with that arrow, and Arjuna fell mortally wounded. Then Nagarjuna took Arjuna's *gāṇḍapī* [Skt. *gāṇḍīva*] bow, went to his mother, and said, "I have brought the weapon of him who killed my rhinoceros."

She gasped, "Son, you've killed your father. This is his bow!" Then Mother Kunti came there, and so did Shri Krishna. They revived Arjuna with the "laughing barley" and the "speaking leaves."[26] Then Nagarjuna fell at his feet and said, "Oh, father, I didn't know you were my father." Nagarjuna lifted Arjuna on to his shoulders and carried him about, dancing and playing. He said, "Please forgive me for my errors." Then Arjuna took the rhinoceros hide, and Nagarjuna came with him to perform Pandu's last rites.[27]

The Rhinoceros Ritual

By itself, this episode might seem rather obscure and unimportant.[28] However, the Rhinoceros Tale is not only a myth but also a public ritual performance that lies at the very heart of *pāṇḍav līlā*. In Chamoli District, where the episode achieves its greatest elaboration, the Rhinoceros metonymically designates an entire performance. People do not normally speak of going to see a *pāṇḍav līlā* but rather of "going to see the Rhinoc-

26. See chapter 1, note 7.

27. According to an extensive oral version of *Mahābhārata* collected by D. R. Purohit, the rhinoceros lived in the Thick Woods (*gājulī van*), not in Manipura or Nagiloka. The pond where he grazed along with 239 other rhinoceroses (*bārah bīsī gaiṇḍā*) was called Nandani Pond (*nāndanī baḍār*). When Arjuna shot it from his blind, the other rhinoceroses stampeded over to where Nagarjuna was sitting, and he noticed that the white rhinoceros, his favorite, was not among them. So he killed Arjuna with a bow made of *kuṇjā* and an arrow made of *tāchḍiyā*. Then he went to the home of his mother, whose name was Subarnika. There a garland had withered, and the milk had turned to blood. His mother informed him that he had just killed his father. She went and danced before Indra, who was pleased and asked who she was. She replied that she was the wife of Arjuna, that the five Pandavas were her brothers-in-law, and so forth. He offered her a boon, whatever she wished, and she asked him to revive Arjuna.

28. The rhinoceros episode is known in Rajasthan, where, as in Garhwal, it is associated with the *śrāddha* (see later discussion). On the twelfth or thirteenth day after death, certain communities hold a nightlong ritual called *rātī-jug* (all-night wake), where they tell one or two out of a repertoire of twenty-eight stories. One of these stories involves the rhinoceros and is called *sāvakaraṇ* (Hindi *syāmakaraṇ*) *ghoṛā*, that is, the "golden" (*aśvamedha*) horse (a variant of the Rhinoceros Tale in Garhwal also involves the *syāmakaraṇ ghoṛā*) (Komal Kothari, personal communication). This ritual is performed mostly in eastern Rajasthan by Muslim Jogis and is probably the source of the "folk *Mahābhārata*" collected by J. D. Smith in which Arjuna slays a rhinoceros in order to make a shield from its hide so as to deliver Pandu from Nagaloka, and is slain in the attempt by Nagiya, his son by a Naga princess (Smith n.d.). Similarly, in the oral *Mahābhārata* of the Bhils of *tahsil* Dāṃtā in Gujarat, Arjuna goes twice to the underworld (*pātāl lok*). First he goes to obtain gold for the *yajña* of his father's *śrāddha*, then he goes again to make a shield of rhinoceros skin in order to obtain success in war (Patel 1997, 48–55, 91, 92, 104–5). Clearly the Rhinoceros tradition is widespread in north India.

eros." The story is competitively recited by local bards several times during every performance, and its culmination in Arjuna's slaying of the rhinoceros and subsequent battle with his son is represented via both dance and drama. In half-day performances,[29] a rhinoceros is made by inserting four small bamboo "legs" into a pumpkin, which is decorated with leaf "ears," soot "eyes," and often a black moustache.[30]

The performance culminates when Arjuna slays the rhinoceros and is in turn slain by Nagarjuna, then magically revived and reconciled with him. Full-blown, nine-day *pāṇḍav līlā*s include a number of elaborate enactments, including the uprooting and erection of the *śamī* tree (see chapter 4), the slaying of various demons, and blessing-visits to individual households by the Pandavas and their entourage. But here, too, the culminating episode is the slaying of the rhinoceros, enacted over and over again, with the rhinoceros successively represented by a bit of fried bread, a pumpkin (decorated as described earlier), and finally a goat that is sacrificed on the spot. Such elaborate enactments provide scope for visual and dramatic elaboration: sometimes the pumpkin is intricately painted, and often it is fanned by a female character, usually Nagarjuna's sister, Nagarjuni, but sometimes his mother, Vasudanta (see note 18). The audience members are of course aware of the impending violence of the sacrifice, and their dramatic anticipation is often heightened by the use of comedy in the buildup to it. The joker in this case is Bhagadatt, the grandson of Mother Earth, who knows the way to Nagilok. Now Datt is a typical Brahman name in Garhwal, and *bhag* (Skt. *bhaga*) means vagina, so this character's very name—a Brahman called "vagina-born"—is considered humorous. Moreover, Bhagadatt's cowardly vacillation contrasts with the calm determination of the Pandavas. He is frightened of going to Nagilok, so he must be flattered, cajoled, and finally bribed with a pair of golden earrings in order to act as guide. As the drummers' tempo increases, the three dancers approach ever closer to the goat, while Bhagadatt tries to bolt in fear. But he cannot even flee successfully, because he is overcome with greed for the proferred bribe, or loses his way, or becomes entangled in his own turban, or (in a bit of "jokering" that is common in local folk dramas, and must have been derived from Western slapstick via the Hindi cinema) receives the proverbial pie in the face. In the end, he turns away as Arjuna shoots the fatal arrow.

This is followed by the "Arjun-Nagarjun dance" [plate 7], which in Chandpur is performed more than any other single item in *pāṇḍav līlā*.[31]

29. In Malla Chandpur, these shorter *līlā*s are called *pāṇḍav roṇṭ* or *roṇṭ khājā*, terms that refer to the deep-fried bread (*roṇṭ*) and the dry-fried grain (*khājā*) that are offered to dancers and guests during performances (see chapter 2).

30. Few, if any, of these mountain dwellers have ever seen a rhinoceros, so the effigy is a bit odd.

31. Other dances are more prominent elsewhere. For example, the dance of Arjuna with his son Babarik (see chapter 4) is more prominent in Nagpur *paṭṭī*, across the Alakananda River from Chandpur, and the *cakravyūha līlā* (see chapter 4) is also more prominent there than the rhinoceros *līlā*.

Plate 7. Arjuna-Nagarjuna dance in Bhatgwali village. Photo by William S. Sax.

Virtually every surrounding village sends its best pair of dancers, and many men from the host village are also eager to display their terpsichorean talents, so that perhaps twenty pairs of dancers perform in a single night. The dance can be divided into two parts. In the first part, the two male dancers slowly circle each other, then mime the actions of bathing, drying, weaving, and then donning the so-called sacred thread; meditating, grinding sandalwood, applying the resulting paste to "the gods of the four directions" and then their own foreheads; and finally admiring themselves in a mirror. In the second half of the dance, Guru Dronacarya, who taught the Pandavas the science of war, stands up. In one hand he holds a bow and in the other an arrow, to which a set of harness bells have been tied, so that they jingle loudly as he shakes them. The dancers embrace Dronacarya and take their weapons from him, holding them horizontally over their heads and slowly spinning around while shaking them furiously. Dronacarya resumes his seat, and the two dancers enact a long battle, stalking and finally confronting each other. Expert dancers embellish their performances by alluding to various episodes in Arjuna's life: certain steps represent his shooting an arrow through a fish's eye while looking at its reflection in a pot of oil, stringing the bow with his own tendon when no bowstring was available, and so on. The actual moment of Arjuna's death is ambiguously represented: as the drums reach their climax, the two dancers merely "hop" once or twice, and this is quickly followed by an embrace that, as informants are quick to point out, signifies reconciliation.

The slaying of the father by the son is often enacted in extended dramatic form on the culminating day of a *pāṇḍav līlā*, when the crowd's reaction can be overhwelming, as many people are spontaneously possessed by malevolent demons. Once I saw pandemonium break loose as members of the audience—mostly women and children, but some men, too—swoon, cry out, and exhibit other signs of demonic possession immediately following the "death" of Arjuna. During the moments of collective vulnerability before Arjuna is revived, malevolent beings hovering on the edge of the dancing square are thought to seize the opportunity to possess members of the audience. Normally a pumpkin is smashed and its pieces thrown in the four directions to appease these spirits, while members of the audience attempt to revive those who have swooned by uttering special mantras, sprinkling them with *pancāmṛta*,[32] or hurling the ritually potent *satanāj*, a mixture of seven grains, at their faces.

In summary, both the Rhinoceros Tale and its ritual enactment are of central importance in *pāṇḍav līlā*. They are among the few elements that are found throughout Garhwal; the story is widely known and recited throughout the region; in Chamoli District it is the metonymic designation of, and the culminating episode in, a full-scale performance; the Arjuna-Nagarjuna dance is the most frequently performed of the major dances;[33] and dramatic representations of the episode can have powerful and startling effects on the audience, as well as on uninvited guests like the malevolent spirits watching the performance from the shadows. Why is this episode so important?

I believe that the answer to this question has to do with the typically ambivalent relationship between fathers and sons in north India, and also with the ways in which the Rhinoceros Tale encodes certain masculine values that are of surpassing importance to Garhwalis. But before explaining why this is so, I must first discuss the Sanskrit version of this story and Goldman's interpretation of it.

A Freudian Interpretation

The Rhinoceros Tale is strikingly similar to the battle between Arjuna and his son Babhruvahana in the Pune edition of *Mahābhārata*. This story

32. The five products of the cow: milk, buttermilk, butter, curd, and urine. Sometimes a mixture of urine and camphor is used instead. Containers holding one or another of these mixtures are always near at hand to counteract malevolent influences or inadvertent pollution.

33. The only dance to rival the complexity of the Arjuna/Nagarjuna battle dance is Nakula's, the dance of the cowherd (see chapter 2). Other forms include the *cop*, or circular dance, a popular dance form performed on many occasions; the "dancing" of Mother Kunti's *sat* (see chapter 5); and other brief representations of such events as the dice game.

is found in the *Āśvamedhikaparvan*, or "Book of the Horse Sacrifice," which takes its name from the ancient Indian sacrifice that is its central event.[34] In classical times, the sponsor of the sacrifice would release a horse to roam over the land; if it wandered into the domain of another king, that king had to either submit and offer tribute or give battle. The horse moved in a "sunwise" pattern—north, east, south, west—then returned to the imperial capital, where its sacrifice consummated a series of rituals establishing the sponsoring king's sovereignty. Its "wandering" was therefore hardly spontaneous; in fact, the horse was followed by a large army, and moreover the sacrifice seems normally to have been performed only after effective military control had already been achieved by the royal sponsor.[35]

In the "Book of the Horse Sacrifice," Yudhishthira is distraught after the great war, and Vidura counsels him to perform several sacrifices, including the *aśvamedha*, to expiate his sins.[36] This requires immense wealth, which Yudhishthira obtains by recovering the gold left over from a previous sacrifice of King Marutta in the Himalayas (XIV.1–71).[37] Once the horse sacrifice begins, the five brothers assume various responsibilities: Arjuna protects the horse, Bhima and Nakula protect the kingdom, while Sahadeva looks after invited guests in the capital. Arjuna goes to the north and the east, fighting a number of battles and defeating various rivals, notably the Trigartas, the Saindhavas, and Arjuna Vajradatta, son of Bhagadatta, king of Pragjyotisha, who seizes the horse and takes it to his capital but is defeated by Arjuna after a three-day battle. The fathers of most or all of these adversaries had already been slain by Arjuna in the great battle at Kurukshetra, and in the battles recounted in the *Āśvamedhikaparvan* he is consistently chivalrous, sparing his opponents whenever possible, as instructed by Yudhishthira (XIV.66–77).

The crucial episode occurs at XIV.78–81, when the horse wanders into the kingdom of Manipur, ruled by Babhruvahana, son of Arjuna by the princess Citrangada. At first Babhruvahana does not wish to fight his father and goes instead to welcome him but Arjuna is enraged and, as Goldman puts it, reviles him "as an unmanly coward and betrayer of the knightly tradition" (1978, 330).

The Serpent Princess Ulupi, who is one of Arjuna's wives and thus one of Babhruvahana's classificatory "mothers," appears and urges Babhruvahana to fight Arjuna, telling him that this is the only way he will appease his father. So Babhruvahana fights, and Arjuna is indeed gratified, especially

34. Ramanujan reports that a popular Kannada *yakṣagāna* play is also based on it (1983, 235).

35. For more on the *aśvamedha*, see Agastya 1928; Caland 1932; Dumont 1927; Gonda 1969, 110–15; and Puhvel 1955.

36. See chap. 1 n. 25. For more on the expiatory functions of both the *aśvamedha* and the *rājasūya* sacrifices, see Keith 1925, 343ff.; and Oldenberg 1988.

37. Residents of the upper Tons basin claim that Marutta's sacrifice occurred in their region, which will be the only part of the earth to survive an imminent nuclear holocaust.

when his son shoots him through the collarbone! The battle rages until Babhruvahana kills his father, then himself succumbs to his wounds and falls unconscious. At this point, Babhruvahana's real mother, Citrangada, comes to the battlefield. She berates Ulupi for inciting the fight and threatens suicide unless Ulupi revives Arjuna. Babhruvahana revives and, overwhelmed with guilt at his parricidal act, he, too, proposes to fast to death. Ulupi remembers a gem that revives the dead, and thus thought of, it appears. She informs Babhruvahana that he has not really killed his father, who is in fact invincible and has only come to test his son's strength in battle. The gem is employed to revive Arjuna, who embraces his son and then asks Ulupi the reason for his "death." Ulupi explains that she arranged it to help Arjuna expiate his sin of killing his own "grandfather" Bhishma unfairly, as a result of which he would have gone to hell. The only expiation for this sin was death at the hands of his own son. The entire company is delighted by Ulupi's resourcefulness, Arjuna invites Babhruvahana to the horse sacrifice, Babhruvahana accepts, and the reconciliation is complete.

Robert Goldman has referred to this story as "the only unambiguous example of parricide that I can find in the Sanskrit epic literature" (1978, 329)[38] and has interpreted it in oedipal terms. As Goldman sees it, the narrative employs various techniques—notably Ulupi's multiple explanations of the events—to "strip the story . . . of its central content," the slaying of the father by the son. Nevertheless, "the parricide and the horror that it engenders are hardly concealed" (332); moreover, Ulupi's "final and most fundamental" explanation, invoking as it does Arjuna's own slaying of Bhishma, confirms the centrality of parricide to the story. Goldman goes on to interpret the episode as an example of disguised oedipal aggression, with the mother's role in the oedipal triangle played by Shikhandin when Arjuna slays Bhishma, and by Ulupi/Citrangada when Babhruvahana slays Arjuna. For Goldman, these episodes are "positive oedipal material . . . at the very heart of the epic story itself . . . with the son in each case overcoming his filial deference and dread to conquer the father. . . . Understood correctly, the stories of Bhīṣma, Arjuna and Babhruvāhana provide dramatic evidence of the viability of the positive oedipal stance in ancient Indian literature" (337).

Confronted with the material from Garhwal, Goldman would no doubt conclude that the Rhinoceros Tale and its ritual enactment confirm his hypothesis. The battle between father and son is central to *pāṇḍav līlā*, and the dramatic representation of parricide induces extreme psychological dismay and spiritual vulnerability in the audience. This might well be regarded as confirmation of the existence of a positive oedipal stance, in which the act of parricide represents a real, underlying hostility toward the father that, because it is normally repressed, causes distress when it is overtly represented.

38. In a Telugu women's telling of the *Rāmāyaṇa*, however, Rama's sons Lava and Kusha kill and then revive their father (Narayana Rao 1991).

Consideration of this issue takes us into the heart of debates over whether there is or is not an Oedipus complex in India, and if there is, what form it takes. The literature surrounding this issue is by now fairly extensive.[39] Like many debates relating to the psychoanalytic paradigm, this one is associated with the characteristic difficulty that the very things that cast most doubt upon psychoanalytic interpretations—explicit rejection of them by informants, inconsistent or plainly contradictory elements in the material being interpreted—are regarded by Freudians as evidence of "distortion, displacement, projection and various forms of substitution" (Goldman 1978, 362), or of repression, secondary elaboration, and so forth, even though the concept of repression is unsupported by any controlled laboratory evidence.[40] The more strenuously the Freudian interpretation is denied, the more confident the Freudian feels, leading to an impasse between defenders of the approach and its critics.

One way forward is illustrated by recent attempts, like those of Obeyesekere (1990) and Kurtz (1992), to modify psychoanalytic theory so as to take account of culturally variant socialization patterns and family relationships,[41] a project that was even hinted at by Freud himself for whom the classical oedipal triangle was not the only formation but merely the culturally operative one, the one that "we are accustomed to regard . . . as the more normal."[42] It seems only reasonable to suppose that as patterns of socialization and family structure vary, so will the contents of infantile fantasy.

I am sympathetic to such attempts and hope that this chapter will contribute to them in a small way. But in the main, my analysis is ethnographic, not psychoanalytic. My central question is, Why is the Arjuna-Nagarjuna episode so central to *pāṇḍav līlā*? I rely upon empirical entities such as public ritual performances, ideas about masculinity and father-son relationships, child-rearing patterns, and the complex institutions of family and caste—what a psychoanalytically oriented analyst might call "surface features"—to explain why the battle between father and son is central to *pāṇḍav līlā*, and why its dramatic representation evokes such a powerful response from

39. See Goldman 1978 and references therein; also Kondos 1986; Kurtz 1992; Obeyesekere 1990; Ramanujan 1983; Shulman 1993; and Spiro 1982.

40. See Holmes 1990, 96, cited in Crews 1994, 54.

41. Kurtz, however, finds that Obeyesekere's psychoanalytic approach, like that of others, inevitably tends to "pathologize non-Western cultures" (Kurtz 1992, 227–31) by finding them deficient with respect to its central (and eminently modern, Euro-American) goal of "individuation." As for Obeyesekere's model, I am skeptical as to whether, by the time he has extended the oedipal triangle to a "circle of oedipal relationships" (p. 98) and "subsidiary models" (p. 106), we are not left with the rather tame observation that mythology is associated with problematic family relationships.

42. Obeyesekere 1990, 85, quoting Freud 1923, 31–32. I find it difficult to reconcile this statement with Obeyesekere's assertion that Freud held "that the Oedipus complex is based entirely on the erotic nature of the son's tie with the mother and the sexual jealousy he has for the father, all of this reinforced, if not caused, by the witnessing of the primal scene" (1990, 71).

the audience. If I can propose an explanation that makes sense to local participants as well as to outside observers, then why invoke the hidden messages and secret codes of psychoanalysis?

A Local Interpretation

Filial piety is a core value in Garhwal, and in Indian civilization generally. As Goldman notes, Indian epic literature represents the ideal son as utterly subordinate to his father (1978, 337ff.). Ethnographers, too, find that in life as well as in literature, filial piety is a fundamental social value, inculcated in boys from an early age. A male must obey and respect not only his father but also his elder brothers and his father's brothers, all of whom partake to some degree in the father's authority. In north India the father's elder brother is entitled to much greater deference than the father's younger brother, thus reiterating the age-based structure of authority. Among the world's cultures, this association of strong paternal authority with intense filial piety is hardly unusual, and in most of north India these features were traditionally underpinned (as they still are throughout Garhwal) by their association with agnatic descent, primogeniture, patrivirilocality, intracaste hypergamy, and indigenous theories of the agnatic lineage (Gwli. *svaurāṃ*; Skt. *vaṃśa*) as a collective body, the authority and agency of which is concentrated in the senior adult male. Such features are broadly typical of north Indian Hindu families, for example, the Bengali *parivāra*, in which the father is both "generous and kind, at the same time he has to be harsh in the treatment of his sons; he is a disciplinarian, a figure of authority" (Fruzetti and Ostor 1982, 39; see also Inden and Nicholas 1977, 6–7). Taken together, these values, customs, theories, and institutions are the political and institutional foundation of male dominance among north Indian Hindus, and I have argued elsewhere (Sax 1990b, 1991a) that they persist in part because they serve the collective interests of males.

The Rhinoceros Tale is an explicitly and self-consciously moral tale about the value of filial piety: those displaying it are exemplary, while those who violate it are at best tragic, at worst demonic. The story begins with Vidyadhara disobeying his father's explicit command, as a result of which he is transformed into a demon. Appropriately enough, the demon renounces his own hard-drinking parents before finding a truly nurturing mother and father who acquaint him with his "real" identity. The main episode focuses on Arjuna's abandonment of his wife, Vasudanta, in order to attend his father's *śrāddha*, and his properly filial search for the rhinoceros hide that will enable him to release his father's spirit. The story culminates with a tragic and unwitting parricide, the perversity of which is indicated by the fact that it can only be accomplished using a weapon that explicitly resists the principle of filial piety, the "*gurū*-less arrow (*nigur bāṇ*), the arrow that doesn't obey the word of the *gurū*, that kills anyone, that has no discrimination." This is quickly followed by a reconciliation between father and son. In every instance, the story valorizes filial piety and stigmatizes its violation: it is nothing less than a moral tale about the value and importance of respect for one's father.

This interpretation is confirmed by public, ritual performance. I refer not only to the battle between father and son and their subsequent reconciliation, which I have already shown to be central to *pāṇḍav līlā*, but also and equally significantly to Pandu's mortuary ritual (*śrāddha*), which follows the Rhinoceros episode. In Chandpur this is neither a pseudo-rite nor a dramatic representation of a ritual, but rather an actual *śrāddha*, conducted by a qualified Brahman priest and, so far as the villagers are concerned, authentic in every respect.[43] In Lobha Chandpur, the Pandava brothers wander from house to house gathering materials required for Pandu's obsequies, as they do also in the far west, where *pāṇḍav līlā* is metonymically referred to as "the *sarāddh*." In many parts of Chandpur, a sacrificial goat is cooked and distributed among the agnatically related core of the village, further confirming the episode's fundamental concern with continuity between fathers and sons. Now in the Pune edition of *Mahābhārata*, Pandu has no biological sons. But in Garhwal, Nakula is believed to be the biological son of Pandu (by Madri); hence he performs the *śrāddha* along with the village priest. Once again, the tremendous local stress on father-son continuity goes far toward explaining this "local variation" in the *Mahābhārata* story: Pandu required a biological son in order to complete his mortuary rites. This also explains the fact that in Garhwal, the Arjuna-Nagarjuna episode is consistently linked to the *rājasūya* sacrifice, whereas in the Pune edition of *Mahābhārata* the Babhruvahana episode takes place in the *Āśvamedhika parvan*. In fact, the most extensive oral version of *Mahābhārata* to be recorded in Garhwal to date contains little on the horse sacrifice.[44] Once again, the importance of father-son relations explains the "discrepancy": Pandu's *śrāddha* must be performed before the royal installation can take place. Both the Rhinoceros of eastern Garhwal and the *sarāddh* of western Garhwal culminate with Pandu's obsequies, which are in an important sense the raison d'être of the entire event. The rituals and dances, the feasts and ceremonies, and the Rhinoceros Tale itself are all clearly and explicitly about the moral and religious importance of fulfilling one's filial obligations.

Why is the father-son relationship so important in *pāṇḍav līlā*? An unreconstructed Freudian would no doubt answer that the battle between Arjuna and Nagarjuna is a working out in a specific cultural context of universal oedipal male fantasies of aggression against the father, fantasies

43. In other regions, attenuated versions of the *śrāddha* are performed.

44. D. R. Purohit, personal communication. See, however, note 55, where the bard Gautam associates the battle between Arjuna and Nagarjuna with the horse sacrifice. We may be faced here with a widespread north Indian oral tradition of the hunting of a rhinoceros, which is sometimes associated with the *rājasūya yajña*, and elsewhere with the *aśvamedha yajña*. However, my fundamental point remains valid: that the crucial issue here is the relationship between father and son.

that are forbidden and thus repressed. This was argued by Spratt (1966), whom Goldman cites approvingly, and also by Goldman, who "follows the classic Freudian argument that there is everywhere a positive Oedipus complex and that the Hindu is but a transformation of it" (Obeyesekere 1990, 82). In fact, Obeyesekere agrees that Indian Hindus have an Oedipus complex, and he modifies the Freudian paradigm only to the extent of asserting that this complex is characteristically "passive" rather than "active" as in the case of the Sinhalas. He suggests a number of reasons for this, including the Hindus' pronounced "familial sacramentalism" (attenuated or absent in Buddhism); their predilection for joint families (Obeyesekere claims that nuclear families are more common in Buddhist societies); the differences in their respective kinship systems; and the fact that the Sinhala father is typically less distant than the Hindu father (1990, 160–61). These observations are generally accurate for Garhwal; so how do we account for the centrality of the Rhinoceros Tale, which enacts what the psychoanalytically oriented analyst would have to call an *active* Oedipus complex, thus providing a compelling counterexample to Obeyesekere's hypothesis?

Let us take a closer look at social and familial patterns, and especially at relationships between fathers and sons. In north India, such relationships tend to be rather difficult. As has often been noted, north Indian fathers are normally rather formal and authoritarian toward their children and particularly their sons.[45] Within the joint family, fathers should not express overt, public affection toward their own children; these feelings are reserved for nieces and nephews. Anthropologists usually explain this in functional terms: the joint family must protect itself from the threat to its solidarity that would be posed by the development of strong affective links in any of its potential "nuclear" families, and so it discourages the formation of such links (cf. Dern 1995, 42–47, 85–89).

In Garhwal, as in the rest of north India, relations between fathers and sons are characterized by distance and formality; the loving and nurturing father is an anomaly. Inden and Nicholas contrast the "easy," egalitarian love between siblings and between spouses in Bengal with the "hard," hierarchical love between parents and children (1977, 25–29); and Parish notes that among the Newars of Nepal, respect rather than affection is the norm governing relationships between fathers and sons (1994, 134). Does the father's emotional distance give rise to feelings of ambivalence in the son? Are Garhwali sons frustrated because they receive so little affection from their fathers? I cannot say for sure; however, the idea is strongly supported by the Indian psychotherapist B. K. Ramanujam (1986), who shows among other things that the absence or premature death of a strong father figure can have serious psychological repercussions for Hindu males, who display a vital need for a positive and nurturing father. Renuka Singh points out

45. "The Punjabi daughter's early experience of her father . . . is indeed very different from that of the Punjabi son; the mutual adoration and idealization characteristic of the former relationship is missing in the latter" (Kakar 1982, 140).

that Indian men often adopt surrogate "fathers" in later life (personal communication), and Sudhir Kakar writes of a characteristic "oedipal alliance" that has to do not with attraction toward the mother and hostility toward the father but rather with the "deeply buried and unfulfilled need of many male patients for the firm support, guidance and emotional availability of the father" (1980, 47). It is of course precisely this sort of relationship that is often absent in north Indian families, and certainly in the Rhinoceros Tale, where Nagarjuna's father gives no love to the serpent prince. As a result, Nagarjuna aims to establish an enduring filial relationship. He is teased by his playmates as a bastard and embarks on a journey to discover his real fathers, Arjuna and Indra. But, as Prakash Desai suggests (personal communication), there are no loving fathers in this story (and precious few in the Sanskrit *Mahābhārata*): Indra denies his grandfatherhood, challenging the young prince to prove it by taming the rhinoceros. Nagarjuna swears that if he is a bastard, he will die, but if he is truly Arjuna's son, he will tame the beast, and tame it he does, by calling out, "I am Arjun's son." He transforms the fierce and warlike rhinoceros (with its prominent, erect horn) into a soft and cuddly pet.

But Nagarjuna 's domestication of this beast is short-lived because soon thereafter Arjuna kills it, exemplifying once again the absence of paternal love. Thus provoked, Nagarjuna kills his father, but this is immediately followed by the latter's revival and reconciliation with his son. The distant, hostile Arjuna is finally and permanently transformed into a loving, supportive father, and the dance of Arjuna and Nagarjuna culminates in their loving embrace. The Freudian would say that this final embrace serves only to disguise the fundamental hostility of the myth, but I would argue on the contrary that it is precisely the point of the story, which is about the recovery and replenishment of a stable and loving relationship between father and son.[46] Can we not see in this final embrace a dramatic representation of just such a relationship? Do we really need the full-blown oedipal triangle to account for the power of this story? Is it not sufficient to interpret it in terms of a model that takes account of the characteristically north Indian tension between, on the one hand, a family structure that encourages paternal distance, and, on the other hand, the son's desire—and perhaps the father's as well—for mutual affection and friendship?

Actually, I believe that the answer to this question is no. Such an explanation, while perhaps accurate, is nevertheless insufficient because it fails to take into account certain martial elements that are inseparable from both the tale and its ritual enactment.[47] These elements, and especially the episodes

46. As Inden and Nicholas put it, among Bengalis in their personal and family relationships "the maintenance of order (dharma) centers concretely around the problem of sustaining the proper balance of difficult and easy relationships" (1977, 22).

47. Oedipal interpretations of the parricidal Rhinoceros episode are also undermined by the fact that the filicidal slaying of Abhimanyu by his uncles the Kauravas is of considerable importance in *pāṇḍav līlā* narrative and dramatization (see chapter 4).

that are chosen for dramatic elaboration, will be discussed at length in the next chapter. For the moment, I will concentrate on just one such element—the weapons, and especially the iron arrowheads (Hindi *bāṇ*)—which are without doubt the most sacred and powerful objects in a *pāṇḍav līlā* performance. They are fashioned in the dancing square by ironsmiths specially summoned for the purpose, and they are regarded as extremely powerful and dangerous. Women, children, and lower-caste men (other than the ironworker) are not allowed to touch them (plates 1, 8).

Normally, either Guru Dronacharya or Nagarjuna's mother, Vasudanta, distributes arrows to the dancers before each night's performance, and I have seen them refuse to give them to someone who is drunk or ritually impure (because of a recent birth or death, for example). If a high-caste man takes the arrows in his polluting left hand or, worse yet, accidentally drops them, the penalties can be severe (usually a sacrificial goat or its cash equivalent). Not only is it disrespectful to drop them, but they are believed to be full of energy (*śakti*), which, like electricity, can be discharged into the earth if they come into contact with it. In effect, they embody the military power—the *kṣatra*—of the local Kshatriyas.

Each of the major characters dances with a particular weapon: Yudhisthira with a staff, Bhima (and sometimes his son Babrik) with a club, Arjuna and his sons Nagarjuna and Abhimanyu with bows and arrows, Nakula with a herder's stick or a grass-cutting scythe, Sahadeva, "the pandit," with a student's slate,[48] Draupadi and the other female characters with womens' grass-cutting scythes, Krishna with a discus, and the Mohars (companions of the Pandavas) with bamboo baskets filled with flowers used to make garlands. In some villages, the Pandavas' mother Kunti dances with a strongbox or its key,[49] but usually she needs no weapon other than her own truth, or *sat*. In addition to these weapons, there is also a second set that is removed from some safe and secret place—usually under the eaves of a house—and kept on the altar until the completion of a performance, when it is disposed of in some pure location (often a spring or other water source) along with other ritually powerful objects. In Taintura in 1990, for example, the deity Diba possessed his oracle on the first day of the performance[50] and distributed new weapons to the various performers. The old weapons were removed from a small, locked armory, the key to which was in the care of the woman playing the part of Nagarjuna's mother, Vasudanta, and placed on the altar, where they remained for the duration of the performance. A priest, who had inherited this duty from his father, was required to stay by the altar twenty-four hours a day, even in the pouring rain, and

48. Tamil tradition also considers Sahadeva "a great astrologer" (Hiltebeitel 1988, 321).

49. Traditional Garhwali keys are made of iron and often are more than a foot in length, making rather effective weapons!

50. Actually, it was the first day of the second half of a performance that had been interrupted by the death of a respected local man.

Plate 8. Wooden weapons being ritually bathed in Jabari Village. Photo by William S. Sax.

to properly dispose of the older set of weapons after the conclusion of the performance. In most villages, *pāṇḍav līlā* happens only once in a generation, so that this older set of weapons will have been used as many as twenty or thirty years earlier, by the previous set of dancers. Because roles in *pāṇḍav līlā* tend to be passed from father to son, this means that the old weapons, taken out from under the eaves and present on the altar for the duration of a performance, represent the previous generation, now mostly deceased. The ancestors are thus virtually present on the central altar, in the weapons with which they once danced.

These themes are all illustrated by a fairly typical sequence that occurred in the village of Gugali in Nagpur *paṭṭī* in 1991. The local ironworker came to the dancing square at 9:30 A.M. to forge the new set of weapons, assisted by his son on the bellows. The village deity Kshetrapal possessed his medium, who led a procession to the god's shrine below the village. This was a crude structure, consisting merely of a few large pieces of slate standing in a kind of A-frame, on the hillside below a huge pipal tree. The procession was led by drummers from the musician caste, followed by horns, Kshetrapal's oracle, and other participants. No females whatsoever participated. The medium worshiped Kshetrapal's sign (*niśān*), consisting of two copper and two silver images hanging from a trident, and then brought it up to the dancing square. Almost immediately another procession formed, again consisting solely of males. It passed by the Shiva temple and proceeded to a wild cherry tree on a hill above the village.[51] Incense was lit, the tree was cut down, and leaves and grass were placed on the stump to cover the "wound"; this was done "out of respect." The tree was cut into lengths, which were brought back to the dancing square, where they were fashioned into clubs for Bhima and his son Babarik [figure 3]. One young man explained the significance of the weapons: "If an arrowhead falls to the ground, even by accident, then the whole affair may be ruined. We are afraid, because great misfortune [*hānīkār*] may befall us. Because we are doing this after twenty-four years, we must be especially careful. Most of us don't know exactly how it's done, and we must rely on the old men to show us the way. Then when we are old, we in turn will show the way."

Now the old weapons were brought to the dancing square, covered with white cloth. Most of them had nearly rotted away; one especially large and fierce-looking weapon was taken out and given to the ironsmith to reforge—this was Draupadi's dagger. A man turned to me and said:

> This is the real thing. We have to join our hands before them in respect. Nowadays, intelligent people say it's all a fake [*ḍhakoslā*], but our older people say that at one time, these weapons would return to the hands of their owners. Someone would be going for a [ritual] bath,

51. The wild cherry (*payyāṃ*) tree flowers in winter and is used extensively in local rituals.

> and all of a sudden the arrowhead would disappear from their grasp, only to reappear later just as suddenly. So when we see such things with our own eyes, we are compelled to join our hands before them. This is why we go to so much trouble and expense to do a *pāṇḍav līlā*.

After the weapons were prepared, they were rinsed in water, then bathed with a mixture of turmeric and oil to make them strong and lustrous. The Brahman priest performed a purifying ritual on both the weapons and Kshetrapal's four "signs," using turmeric, water, sesame seeds, barley, milk, vermilion powder, flowers, *ḍūba* grass, and sugar. For the rest of the performance, the old weapons remained on the altar, while the new weapons were used in the Pandavas' dance. I did not stay for the closing rituals in Gugali, but at the conclusion of a *pāṇḍav līlā* I attended in Kaphalori in 1990, villagers took the older set of weapons along with the *śamī* tree (see chapter 4) in procession to a small spring at some distance from the village, where they could be left undisturbed. This was described as a "funeral procession" because the tree went headfirst, "the way a corpse is taken to the cremation ground." The oldest set of weapons was thus truly "dead," while the new set of weapons, which had been handled by the dancers in the just-concluded performance, were hidden under the eaves of a local house.

By means of such practices, the interrelated patrilines of the village are substantialized in the weapons, which are explicitly linked to the principle of agnatic descent. The martial energy of the deceased fathers is recycled through these weapons to their adult sons who dance the main roles. Meanwhile, members of a third generation—the young men who will constitute the next generation of dancers—look on, as understudies of their fathers, and are not allowed to grasp the powerful weapons. My interpretation of the myth is unambiguously confirmed by public ritual: it is all about solidarity and continuity between fathers and sons.[52] It is a way of resisting death by ensuring the continued life of the patriline.[53]

It is also about the honor of the Kshatriyas, which is intimately related to such martial virtues as bravery and an eagerness to fight. In Bacan Singh's oral version, Nagarjuna first challenges the killer of the rhinoceros: "You thief—you've killed my rhinoceros! If you are a true Kshatriya, then come forth to do battle!" In the Pune edition, the challenge is issued by the father

52. Parish notes that among the Newars, "a father experiences his son as part of the self and that, like the Tamils discussed by Trawick, "the father longs for continuity, but the son longs for independence" (1990, 158)—that is, until the father dies, when the son, who has now taken his father's place, seeks continuity rather than independence. Similarly, Ramanujam has noted that the individual within Hindu culture "strives to maintain his place within the family and the community by following the traditions allowing for continuity from generation to generation" (1986, 82).

53. Sudhir Kakar writes of a "mythological motif, depicted in some old temple relics, in which a boy holds fast to his father's penis to escape Yama, the god of death and the harbinger [*sic*] of that ultimate narcissistic injury—the extinction of the self" (1980, 52; cf. Kakar 1979).

rather than the son. But whether it is the father or the son who issues the challenge, the central point has to do with Kshatriya bravery—or its lack. This was made clear in the performance of Shiva Singh, a bard from Sutol:

> When the child Nagarjun heard the rhinoceros was slain, he was furious. He grabbed his *gāṇḍapī* bow [paradigmatically associated with Arjun], saying, "I am of Kshatriya lineage. I must kill in war, or be killed. Today I shall kill him who shot our rhinoceros, or else myself be killed."
>
> His mother, Vasudanta, made one request: that he bring her a token of whomever he killed. He went and saw the slain rhinoceros; he circled the pond where the rhinoceros bathed,[54] but saw no one. Then he shouted:
>
> If your mother was married, then come and fight;
> if she was unmarried, then stay and hide![55]
>
> So Arjuna came forth, and they began to fight with arrows. Nagarjuna shot his father and took his ring and brought it to his mother, Vasudanta. When she saw that it was Arjuna's, she said, "Son, today you've killed your own relative: you've killed your father." Nagarjuna replied, "But mother, he killed our rhinoceros."

Far away in Gith *paṭṭī*, at the headwaters of the Yamuna River, almost identical words are sung by the local bards during the enactment of the Rhinoceros *līlā*:

O my champion, who has killed my rhinoceros,
which kingdom are you from, which *thāt*[56] are you from?
Tell me how many ancestors you have.
And why did you hide?
If you are the [legitimate] son of your mother and father,
then come forth and stand![57]

And in Taintura village, in December 1990, the bard Gautam Singh recited this version:

54. Here the bard referred to the pond as the "four *dhāms*," that is, the four sacred places of Garhwal: Yamunotri, Gangotri, Kedarnath, and Badrinath (or perhaps India's four *dhāms*: Badrinath, Puri, Rameshvaram, and Dwarika).

55. *rānī ko holo to raṇ paḍlo*
kumārī go holo chipī jālo.

56. In western Garhwal and the adjoining areas of Himachal Pradesh, each village is associated with a *thāt*, a ritual platform connected to a particular deity, where sacrifices are performed to ensure village prosperity.

57. *he merā mālā yab tuj kai rāj ko chan kai thāt ko chan?*
jena merā gaiṇḍo dhāṛū denī sun re mālā
āpaṛ sāṃkhyā gotar lagāyī dīn, kai rāj ko chan kai thāt ko chan?
aur coro kyūṃ marī tūjo?
āpaṛī mātā-pitā ko jāī hvalo tūjo
hab mero yab khaṛo jālo hoī

Krishna sent the warrior to Nagilok to shoot the rhinoceros.
There live nine million Nagas.
There lives the girl Nagarjuni
and her brother Babhruvahana, who is Nagarjuna
the son of Vasanta, who was the warrior Arjuna's woman
for twelve years, and now lives in Nagilok, in Manipur.

There you married Vasanta,
and two children were born.
But you abandoned them,
and they were left fatherless.

And you came to the mortal world,
and their mother did not tell them that they were of a Rajput lineage.
And when the day of the tragedy came,
the warrior loosed the horse
with a copper plate on its forehead,
and the horse wandered
through the earth's nine regions,
but no one could capture it.

Finally Arjuna reached Manipura,
and the warrior Babhruvahana saw the copper plate
and said, "This is my father's horse."
So he took the horse and led it to his father.

When he took the horse back, there was an earthquake,
and the warrior Arjuna went searching for his horse,
and the son Babhruvahana took lamps and incense and went to his father.
Arjuna said, "You bastard! From whence have you come?"
He was furious and asked if his son was truly a Kshatriya.

Babhruvahana said, "I am not a bastard: I will fight with you!"
Then they had a battle; they fought a *Mahābhārata* there.
Babhruvahana knew more of the science of weapons than Arjuna.
Arjuna fell to the ground, then mother Vasanta went there.
She told her son that he had killed his father.
Then mother went to the warrior Hanumant.
She sent him to Sumeru mountain for the life-giving herb, for the pot of ambrosia.
Then mother sprinkled the ambrosia on Arjuna and revived him.
He was revived, and then he returned to Jayanti palace.
Tomorrow you will see this all in detail.
Joining my hands, I serve you in this way.[58]

58. Note that the bard should have recited "Hastinapur" rather than "Jayanti," and that he has incorporated elements of the *Rāmāyaṇa* into his recitation.

The duty of a Kshatriya king or warrior is to fight bravely, against his own relatives, against his father himself if need be.[59] Is this not implicit in the *Mahābhārata* and explicit in the *Bhagavad Gītā* at its core? Textual and dramatic representations of fratricide or parricide are terrible not because they enact suppressed wishes but because they violate the values of filial piety and fraternal solidarity that are so deeply embedded in Indian culture. The tension between filial piety and the dharma of the warrior king is precisely what provides the dramatic interest of the *Mahābhārata*, which is after all about a devastating fratricidal war. This is clear enough in the Pune edition, where Arjuna furiously upbraids his son for betraying the warrior's code. Here is Goldman's translation of Arjuna's speech when confronted with a son who is unwilling to fight:

> Then the wise Phalguṇa (Arjuna), his mind fixed on what is proper, recalling what is proper for a warrior, did not approve and, angered, he said to him, "This conduct is not appropriate for you. You are beyond the limits of what is proper for a warrior. My son, why have you not attacked me who have crossed the border of your kingdom guarding Yudhiṣṭhira's sacrificial horse? Damn you! You fool. You know the rules for warriors yet you greet me peacefully when I have come to fight! Living here you accomplish none of the goals of a man greeting me gently, like a woman, when I have come to fight. Idiot! Lowest of men! If I had come to you unarmed only then would this conduct have been proper."[60]

The martial virtues dramatized in *pāṇḍav līlā* are consciously encouraged not just in males generally but more particularly in Kshatriya males. These men's honor depends not just on their willingness to fight but also on the legitimacy of their birth. This was implied all along in the myth, where Nagarjuna was plagued by uncertainty about the identity of his father Arjuna, who actually called Nagarjuna's legitimacy into question when the two finally met. The filial relationship is not just an abstract principle of social organization; it is a fundamental basis for a man's personal identity. It is not only socially necessary but also psychologically foundational. The bastard is the lowest of men, on the same plane as the despised untouchable, while a real man, a true Kshatriya, must be publicly and legitimately affiliated to his father. Questions about legitimate filiation are also questions about female virtue. Many South Asian customs and institutions are concerned primarily with protecting female virtue to ensure the integrity of the patriline and the caste (Liddle and Joshi 1986; Yalman 1967). As the Garhwalis say, "Only Krishna knows the Gita, and only the mother knows the father[!]"[61]

59. Cf. MBh 12.55. This point is also developed in Ghoshal 1966, chap. 12.
60. MBh 14.78.3–7, as translated by Goldman 1978, 330.
61. *Kṛṣṇa jāne gītā, mātā jāne pitā.*

These points become even clearer in my translation of a recorded, competitive exchange between two bards representing Nagarjuna and Arjuna. This exchange immediately followed the climactic slaying of the rhinoceros, represented by a sacrificial goat.[62] The dialogue took the form of a riddle wherein each speaker challenged the other (and implicitly the audience) to guess his identity. Note the importance here of being recognized as a Kshatriya of legitimate birth.

N: Listen, O listen, my warrior: you are not your father's son. You stayed with another father for twelve months;[63] I think you are a low-caste bastard! You are not the only son of your mother. Those weaklings Nakul and Sahadev have a different mother. Your mother bore three sons, and another bastard in her father's house.

A: Listen a while, O warrior, listen: we were not naturally conceived. We are the boon-children of dharma, not lechers like you. I had gone to the forest; I was wandering there for twelve years, but your mother didn't leave me alone for a minute. A princely man is never beaten; one of Kshatriya blood cannot be defeated; [but] you fled to Nagilok and hid, out of fear of me.

N: Listen, O man, listen: we'll see about your "Kshatriya blood"! You little bastard! Your mother gave birth to Karna in her natal home, and from shame she set him adrift in the river; then she married Pandu. She lived like an unmarried whore! Hai Ram! She never even slept with your father!

A: Listen, O listen, princely man! Why are you saying such things? Our father married our mother and brought her from King Surasen, who is also called King Kuntibhoj.[64] My mother prayed to the sage Durvasa, who gave her a special mantra; that's how we were born. The half of which you've spoken—Nakul and Sahadev—that half was the boon requested by Madri; and the other half were the boon-children of our elder mother [Kunti]. Hai Ram! Who serves the gods receives such boons, but your mother rubbed Shiva's linga![65]

N: Listen, warrior, listen! Today I will show you who's a princely man! I'll tear off your head and throw it all the way to Jayanti, and leave your bloody trunk here! Today you will see a true

62. This event was attended by one of the largest crowds I have ever seen at a public ritual in Garhwal, certainly the largest crowd for a *pāṇḍav līlā*.

63. The reference is to Arjuna's stay with Indra.

64. In the Pune edition, Kunti is the biological daughter of King Shura and was adopted by Kuntibhoja.

65. *mādev go liṅg malyo*. This is an ambiguous, insulting double entendre. It refers not only to sexual play but also to the fact that Nagarjuna's mother, Vasudanta, had earlier received a boon from Shiva. It also calls to mind the Garhwali custom of rubbing ghee on the *śivaliṅga* at Kedarnath in order to obtain sons.

Kshatriya! Beat the drum and blast the horns![66] Now see if I lie or not!

A: My mother is in far Jayanti, and I'm in Nagiloka. If you cut off my head, it will go to my mother's lap! Listen, my warrior: such is a princely man, such is a true Kshatriya. I will return to the mortal world for a year; you stay that year in Nagiloka.

N: You are a Kshatriya, a true Kshatriya.[67] You won't be able to reach your mother's lap until my mother comes with her gourd full of ambrosia, bearing the reviving herb, to restore the breath of your life, and you touch your head to my feet—and then you'll take me with you.

A: Listen, O listen, my warrior: your name is Babhruvahana! I must go to the mortal world. I recognize you as my own, and give you reign over Nagiloka. O princely man, I must go, but you stay here in Nagiloka. I will go to the mortal world.

N: Listen, listen, O princely man! A true Kshatriya will now be seen. Your death is in my hands; I am your son Babhruvahana; I am even more expert in the science of arms than you.

Why is the battle between Arjuna and Nagarjuna so important in *pāṇḍav līlā*? I have tried to show that this question is best answered not by invoking an unmodified Freudian paradigm according to which the battle expresses a universal but repressed hostility toward the father but rather by looking closely at local family and social structure, at child-rearing patterns, and at Indian theories of person and caste. Ritual, oral recitation, and Sanskrit text all place the continuity between father and son and the Kshatriya's concern for honor at the heart of this episode. The battle between Arjuna and Nagarjuna can thus be seen as a didactic episode stressing the ambivalent tension between the principle of filial piety and the principle of Kshatriya valor, and thus consistent with the enduring themes of the *Mahābhārata* story.

66. Literally "let the thirty-six rhythms and the twelve instruments be played!"

67. *khāsā kṣatriya*. This intriguing phrase is a double entendre: it could mean either a Kshatriya who is a *khaśa* (the so-called tribe from whom most local Kshatriyas are descended, a well-known but often-denied fact—see chapter 2); or a "special" (*khās*) Kshatriya. Garhwali Rajputs sometimes say that the word *khaśa* actually means *khās* (special).

4

A Theater of Hegemony

Pāṇḍav Līlā *as a Rajput Tradition*

> *Pāṇḍav līlā* is part of the dharma of the Kshatriyas. Krishna taught the eighteen chapters of the *Bhagavad Gītā* to Arjuna: that no one kills anyone else; that one dies only when one's time comes; that the earth from which we are made must die, but the soul [*prāṇ*] that speaks and flies away is immortal, and only changes bodies as one changes clothes; that everyone must die one day. Krishna taught all of this to Arjuna in the eighteen chapters of the *Bhagavad Gītā*, and Bhishma also taught it to him in the teachings concerning kingship [*rājanīti*], and it inspires our Garhwali youths with enthusiasm. Why shouldn't it? It's true. One must either fight or die. But one only dies when one's time [*āyu*] is finished. And if you win, so much the better. This is why Garhwali soldiers do so well in the military.
> —Padam Singh Negi

In this chapter I analyze the ways in which *pāṇḍav līlā* constructs peoples' identities as members of the warrior class (*kṣatriya varṇa*). In Garhwal, the various castes that make up this class are collectively known as Rajputs. They are politically and economically dominant, and like dominant castes elsewhere in India, they fulfill the "royal function" in several important respects. In what follows, I will show that *pāṇḍav līlā* does not simply "express" the dominance of the Rajputs but actively reproduces it through the medium of embodied performance. This is because in performances of *pāṇḍav līlā*, entire communities not only represent a set of virtues that are paradigmatically associated with warriors and kings but also dramatically embody and valorize a village polity in which Rajputs are dominant. Once again, *pāṇḍav līlā* has strong affinities with its classical antecedents; as Pollock (citing Oldenberg) points out, the Sanskrit epic literature was originally "composed by more or less professional poets for the politically dominant group, the kshatriyas" (1986, 15; cf. chapter 2).

But this drama is not so straightforward as it perhaps seems. The classes of Hindu society, like the persons who constitute them, have many strands, not all of which are in harmony with the others. Close attention to the Rajputs' language and practices reveals that they consider themselves to be like Brahmans in certain important respects, and I will show in detail later that this similarity is an important (though submerged) theme of *pāṇḍav līlā*. But despite the Rajputs' unspoken desires and explicit fantasies, their dramatic and ritual performances of Brahmanhood are embodied in performances that unambiguously give highest rank to actual Brahmans. In other words, despite the Rajputs' best efforts, their economic dominance cannot buy them Brahmanical status, nor can their political dominance compel it. This chapter thus leads directly to a discussion of the relationship between Brahman and Kshatriya, a relationship that has been called "the central conundrum of Indian social ideology (Trautmann 1981)." No doubt this conundrum is central to the study of Hindu society, but it also reverberates well beyond the cloistered world of South Asian studies, being a particular form of a central problem of modern social theory: the relationship between values and power. In the wider intellectual world, the problem is often discussed under the twinned rubrics of dominance and hegemony, and I will conclude by framing it in those terms. But first I must show how Garhwali Rajputs construct themselves as Kshatriyas in the context of *pāṇḍav līlā*.

Pāṇḍav Līlā as a Rajput Tradition

Chapter 3 described the many ways in which *pāṇḍav līlā* is a regional tradition, associated with the unique history and landscape of Garhwal. It is found exclusively within the boundaries of that "little kingdom," events from the story are widely associated with regional landmarks, and *Mahābhārata* themes and stories are incorporated into regional folklore and traditions to an extent that is unusual even for India. But perhaps the most important link is through local Rajputs, who claim descent from the Pandavas themselves. As described in chapter 3, Rajputs explicitly regard *pāṇḍav līlā* as a form of ancestor worship, and performances incorporate the major Hindu ritual associated with the cult of ancestors. So although *pāṇḍav līlā* is clearly a Garhwali tradition, it also is a tradition that is associated more closely with Rajputs than with any other class. In this respect, it resembles the *Lorik-Candā* epic discussed by Flueckiger (1989). Both a caste (the Ahirs of eastern Uttar Pradesh) and a region (Chattisgarh, which is not in eastern Uttar Pradesh but rather in central India) regard the epic as their own. The crucial point is that in both cases, ideas of "ownership" have primarily to do with self-perception. Flueckiger suggests that the Ahirs' claim correlates with their greater strength and solidarity in eastern Uttar Pradesh, coupled with a history of well-organized activism (the Yadav movement). The Raut caste of Chattisgarh, by contrast, perceive themselves as weak and lacking central authority. Nevertheless, they, too, find sufficient resources in the epic to "claim" it for themselves.[1] In my view, this all goes to

1. Flueckiger shows that notions of masculinity and femininity in the different variants are also related to caste. For example, the Ahir versions contain stronger statements of males as "protectors," and so forth, while stressing the martial and downplaying the romantic elements.

show that the "meaning" of this or any other epic is not purely or even primarily determined by the text. Meaning, significance, and especially the power to reproduce social groupings are a function not of text but of context—that is, of culture and history—and so it is to culture and history that we must turn to understand how *pāṇḍav līlā* reproduces the warrior class, and is in turn reproduced by it.

Throughout the central and western Himalayas, from Nepal to Himachal Pradesh, members of the Kshatriya class of warriors are called Pahari Rajputs or "Rajputs of the mountains" (from Hindi *pahāḍ*, or "mountain[s]"). This is problematic because different people have different opinions about who is and who is not a "true" Rajput.[2] The word *rājput* literally means "son" (*putra*) of a "king" (*rājā*) and is normally applied to a range of north Indian castes presumed to originate in Rajasthan, or Rajputana, as it was sometimes known. There seems to have been significant immigration by Rajputs from western India to the central Himalayas in the late medieval period, largely as a result of pressure from invading Muslim armies.[3] It has long been argued that both the Panwar dynasty of Garhwal and the Chand dynasty of Kumaon were founded by such groups, and many prominent local Rajput clans claim descent from the dynastic founders or their courtiers. These high-status Rajputs are usually contrasted with the so-called *khaśa* Rajputs, presumed to be descended from indigenous, "tribal" ancestors. In the 1980s and 1990s, middle-aged Garhwalis could still remember a time when the appellation *khaśa* was unproblematic and even used self-descriptively, but it has since come to be a term of abuse, and in most parts of Garhwal, nearly all Kshatriyas now prefer the name Rajput.[4] At the same time, they typically insist that one or another neighboring group is *khaśa*, even as they object to the term being applied to themselves. Although, after ten years of searching, I have failed to turn up any historical evidence of *pāṇḍav līlā* in the precolonial period, nevertheless it seems reasonable to assume that the tradition arose in a social context where the distinction between *khaśa* and aristocratic Rajput was considerably more salient than it is today. It might therefore be argued that *pāṇḍav līlā* serves to hide or deny the *khaśa* ancestry of the majority of local Rajputs by asserting a royal ancestry in its place. The previous chapter described how the tradition places great emphasis on legitimacy of birth. When this is linked to myths of descent from the semidivine Pandavas, one can see how, in place of a widely known but rarely acknowledged subaltern status, the ritual drama asserts a royal descent of the highest order. I have been told more than once by local Rajputs of indisputable aristocratic descent that *pāṇḍav līlā* is "be-

2. See, e.g., Atkinson 1974 [1882]; Berreman 1972 [1963]; M. C. Joshi 1990; M. P. Joshi 1990.

3. This is, however, a controversial point. For example, in an important essay, M. C. Joshi (1990) has argued that the extent and significance of this migration were "overstressed" by Atkinson and others.

4. Not in Rawain, however, where the higher-ranked Rajputs are called *khas* and the lower-ranked Rajputs, *khūnd*.

neath" them, that it is a custom of the *khaśas*. Elsewhere, though, Rajputs of equally prestigious rank unselfconsciously participated in *pāṇḍav līlā* performances, even as I recorded them on my video camera. Was *pāṇḍav līlā* more closely associated in a bygone era with *khaśa* Rajputs, so that aristocratic Rajputs did not participate? Has the gradual erosion of the distinction between *khaśa* and aristocrat resulted in a "democratization" of the performance, so that the higher-ranking Rajputs participate more willingly now than in previous generations? In the absence of historical evidence, we can only speculate about the answers to such questions.

What is certain is that these days, representations of "Kshatriyahood" as found in *pāṇḍav līlā* do not distinguish between *khaśa* and aristocrat. It is equally certain that these representations associate "true" Kshatriyas not only with the martial qualities of valor and bravery but also and by extension with kingship, the prerogative of the Kshatriya class. This was suggested by the epithet *pāvaryā* (used in the bardic exchange in the preceding chapter), which I translated as "princely man." The term is conventionally applied to a brave warrior, and I suspect that it derives from the patronymic Panwar (*paṃvār*), from which the royal dynasty of Garhwal takes its name. (If the preceding speculations have merit, the term itself could be seen as an appropriation by the *khaśas* of aristocratic forms of address.) The bravery, aggressiveness, and physical prowess of the Rajput are thought to contrast strongly with the detachment, passivity, and intellectual orientation of the Brahman, and also with the cowardice, subservience, and aesthetic orientation of the lower castes. These stereotypes lie behind the humorous contrasts (described in chapter 3) between the brave Pandavas, anxious to go to Nagiloka to slay the rhinoceros, and their reluctant guide, Bhagadatta. The cultivation of martial virtues extends as well to Rajput women, whose participation in the drama is tied more closely to their caste than to their gender identity (see chapter 5). Along with legitimacy of descent, these martial values are crucially linked to personal honor. To be a true Kshatriya is to be a brave warrior who is publicly and legitimately affiliated to his father.

Thus *pāṇḍav līlā* represents and exemplifies the quintessentially Rajput virtues of legitimate descent and martial valor. But it does not simply reflect such values. Like other ritual performances, it actively reproduces them, in the process of producing Rajput persons. As a ritual, *pāṇḍav līlā* generates certain kinds of extraordinary power, and this power is specifically linked to the Kshatriya class. Nowhere is this clearer than in the weapons that are an essential part of the performance.

In the previous chapter, I showed how the martial power of the Rajputs—the *kṣatra* of these Kshatriyas—is cycled and recycled through the generations, from fathers to sons. However, the weapons are important not only as generational links but also as objectifications (and not mere "representations") of martial power. Using Peirce's terms, one might say that they are iconic indexes of power: indexes because they contain it, and icons because they resemble actual weapons. This is perhaps clearest with respect to Bhima's club. In Taintura, the clubs of Bhima and several members of his "army," along with Nakula's herding stick and Sahadeva's slate, were made from the purest and most auspicious kind of wood, that of the wild cherry tree (*payyāṃ*), widely employed in Garhwal for rituals but never for cooking or other mundane tasks. A branch perhaps half a meter long and five centimeters in diameter was cut, and the bottom three-quarters of it was whittled down to make an easily grasped handle, while the remaining quarter was left untouched, with the bark still on. The top of the resulting "club" was plastered with a mixture of rice, clarified butter, and yogurt (figure 3). Clearly this was neither an ordinary club nor a "prop" for a dramatic representation but rather an auspicious container of divine power.

The power contained in these weapons is believed to be directly transferred to those who dance with them. This is especially the case with the bows and arrows that are given by Guru Dronacarya to Arjuna and Nagarjuna during their dance. Accomplished local dancers often fall into trance when they seize these weapons: they tremble violently, their eyes roll back into their heads, and they appear to be taken over by an outside force. I myself had such an experience when I grasped the weapons for the first time, in Kaphalori in 1990. I had been invited to dance several days earlier in another village but had declined when I realized that the villagers would not allow me to dance with the powerful arrowheads. In Kaphalori, however, I not only was allowed to dance with the weapons but also was approached by a rather shy local farmer, who asked if I would dance with him and offered to teach me the steps. I was nervous about dancing in front of such a large crowd. What if I dropped the arrows? But my friends encouraged me, and soon I found myself whirling around the dancing square, doing my best to mirror the steps of my partner. After we had danced the steps of bathing, worshiping the gods, meditating, and donning our sacred threads, "Dronacharya" stood up in a corner and held out the weapons. My partner grasped a bow and arrow, which he began to shake furiously. Then I danced

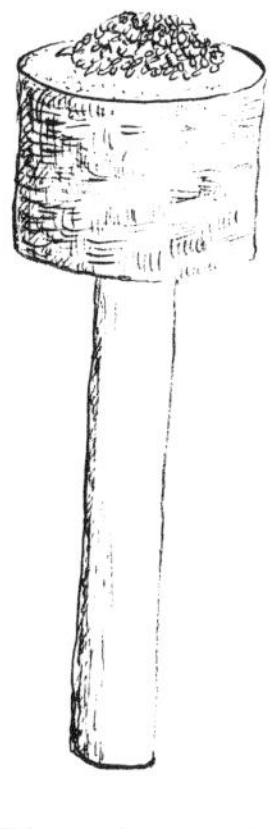

Figure 3. Bhima's club. Drawing prepared by Martin Gaenszle.

over and seized my bow and arrow, and when I shook it, the harness bells bound to it jingled so loudly that I felt as though I were going deaf. I distinctly remember looking up, past the weapons held over my head, to the stars high above, which began to rotate with increasing speed. Then I realized that it was not the stars but I who was spinning around, without willing myself to move! I felt as though I were a passive object, a puppet manipulated by the powerful weapons. As the dance ended, I found myself once again in control of my actions, and my friends told me that I had obviously been in trance. That was the only time I have ever had such an experience.

My assistant Dabar Singh explained the weapons' power like this:

> When the Pandavas' *līlā* begins and they take out the weapons and the Pandavas' scene is set, then the real feeling comes into the dancers' hearts—*ḍhak-ḍhak-ḍhak-ḍhak*—all of creation trembles, and even though they dance barefoot, they are never hurt. You'd think that from dancing in such cold, they would get sick, but nothing happens to them. The Pandavas' *līlā* is such that though their feet are soft, nothing happens to them: that is their magic, their *māyā*.

The weapons with which characters dance in the *pāṇḍav līlā* clearly embody martial power; they do not merely "represent" it. Martial virtues are also exemplified by prominent characters in the drama. One such character is Babrik, who embodies a combination of fearlessness and nonattachment that is specifically recommended for warriors by Krishna in the *Bhagavad Gītā*,[5] though curiously, Babrik is also the victim of Krishna's deceit.[6]

> Babrik's mother was the serpent woman Uccha who lived in the Seventh Underworld [*sātveṃ payāl*]. Bhima was once poisoned by the Kauravas, and his corpse floated down to the underworld, where Uccha was worshiping the Ganges. She had made a dam in the river, vowing to accept whatever it brought to her, and she ended up with Bhima's corpse! Shiva's wife Parvati saw what had happened and felt sorry for the serpent woman, so she persuaded Shiva to revive Bhima. After he awoke, Shiva asked him who he was, and he said that he was the son of Pandu and so forth. He stayed in the underworld with Uccha for some time, and eventually Babrik was born of their union.
>
> Many years later, Krishna, Arjun, and Babrik were looking for a merciless land [*nirdayī bhūmī*] where they could fight the great war. While they were searching, they saw a farmer planting his field, and near the farmer in another field was his son, also cutting grass. The son was bitten by a snake and died. The father thought this was terrible but decided to finish planting before he attended to his dead son. By this time,

5. See earlier remarks by Padam Singh.
6. The following version is an amalgamation of several fragmentary tellings.

the farmer's wife had brought their lunch to the field. She said to her husband, "Call our son to eat his bread." The father said, "He's dead; there's only the two of us for lunch. Let's finish our work first, and then we'll cremate him." When they saw this, Arjuna and Krishna said, "This is the place for the war. Their son has died, yet they continue to eat. This is truly a merciless land—a good place for a war of brother against brother." And so they planted their flag there.

On their way home Krishna asked Babrik whose side he would fight on, and Babrik said, "I will fight on the side of those who were to lose, and cause the winners to be defeated." Krishna said, "You will fight on the side of the Kauravas, even though you are part of the Pandavas' family?" And Babrik replied, "Yes, if the Kauravas are meant to lose, then I will fight with them against the Pandavas."

It was difficult for Krishna to believe such a thing, so he took five leaves from a tree in the name of the five Pandava brothers and placed them beneath his foot. Then he told Babrik to shoot every leaf of the tree. Babrik shot his arrow, and it pierced every leaf, soared into the sky, came streaking down and pierced Krishna's foot. When Krishna saw that Babrik had pierced every leaf, even the one beneath his foot, he said, "Hmmm, this Babrik has spoiled our game. If the Kauravas are to be destroyed, then be destroyed they will. But this warrior will destroy the Pandavas as well."

So Krishna went to Dharmaraja Yudhisthira, whose kingdom it was, and said, "We have selected the battlefield, but it first requires the sacrifice of a warrior with the thirty-two signs.[7] It demands his blood." Dharmaraja Yudhisthira said, "Whom shall we sacrifice? Where can we find him?" And Krishna answered, "Only three of us went to choose the battleground: Arjuna, Babrik, and I. One of us must be sacrificed." Babrik said to him, "Everything the Pandavas do is dependent on you. You are the Lord, you are God. And if Arjuna dies, then all the Pandavas die, because the Pandavas depend upon Arjuna. Therefore I will sacrifice myself, because I cannot die by anyone else's hand. And you must hang my head from a pole, so that I may see the great war." Krishna said, "All right, you cut off your own head, and I will enliven it so that you can see the war."

And that is what they did. Babrik cut off his own head, but Krishna kept the breath of life inside it. By the grace of Krishna, Babrik's head lived on, and Bhima lifted it and placed in on a pole [or, in some versions, on the peak of a mountain], from where Babrik watched the war for eighteen days. At the end of the war they asked him what he had seen, and he reported that all he saw was Krishna's discus whizzing around the battlefield, and Kali's skull, filled with blood.

7. The thirty-two signs (*battīs lakṣaṇa*) are associated with heroic figures: world conquerors like Krishna, Arjuna, and other great kings, as well as world renouncers like the Buddha.

Thus Krishna saved the Pandavas. Had he not tricked Babrik into sacrificing himself, Babrik would have killed them all. And Krishna had already done the same thing to his own brother Balarama. Before the war began, he told Balarama that the great war would happen after eighteen years, and that he should therefore go on a pilgrimage. But they fought the war in eighteen days, so that by the time Balarama returned, it was over. Krishna did this deliberately because he knew that if Balarama fought in the war, he would help the Kauravas to win, since he was Duryodhana's guru, having taught him how to fight with a club. This was another example of Krishna's deceit.

Babrik also appears in Garhwali folklore and religion as the god Jakh. The most notable feature of Jakh's cult is his periodic ritual tours, the last one of which (in 1997) occurred after thirty-six years. The musicians Ram Das and Purna Das from Kujaum village near Gopeshwar possess an illuminated manuscript in archaic Garhwali that gives a detailed history of this deity. I have not seen the manuscript; however, Ram Das provided me with a summary of it in Hindi, which I translate here.

Victory to Vazīr Devatā (Jākh)
The Story of Jakh Devata

When the war between the Pandavas and the Kauravas was happening in Kurukshetra, all the gods came to watch it. And last of all, from the southern part of Tibet [*hūṇḍeś*] came Jakspati (Lord of the *Yakshas*)[8] to watch the *Mahānbhārat* [*sic*] war. He was a very powerful and strong warrior. Not even the gods could defeat him because he had such powerful weapons.

When Bhagawan Sri Krishna saw that King Jakspati had come to see the *Mahānbhārat* war, he asked him what he would do. The king answered that he would cause the losers to win. Then Sri Krishna got worried because the Pandavas were suppoed to win, and he began to think about how he might kill King Jakspati. So he said to him, "If you are such a fierce warrior that your weapons can destroy the whole world in a minute, then let us see them." So the king shot his arrow at the leaves of a pipal tree, but Krishna caused a strong wind to blow. Nevertheless, the king's arrow pierced every one of the flapping leaves and returned to him. But as it was coming back, Krishna tied five more leaves around Jakspati's neck, so that the arrow cut off his head and dropped it in a thick forest. The head began to cry out, "Hey Krishna, you didn't let me see the war!" So Krishna and Arjuna went to the thick forest, picked up the king's head, and hung it on a bamboo pole so that he could see the *Mahānbhārat* war. Then Krishna said, "O king,

8. *Yakshas* are minor deities associated with natural features such as forests, streams, and waterfalls.

don't be angry with us, we will make an image out of your head and take it to all the pilgrimage places in the world of men," and the king was pacified. And he told the king that the image of his head would be worshiped under the name of Jakh in the city where it would be found.

Despite differences in the two narratives, the main features are clear: Jakspati is a valiant warrior who dies as a result of Krishna's deception but is rewarded by being allowed to watch the great war. Under the name of Vazir Devata, he circumambulates his territory in the manner of a Hindu king, and in 1997, at the conclusion of such a tour, the god's entourage performed a rare form of masked drama.[9] The "mythical charter" for Vazir Devata's tour is summarized as follows in Ram Das's synopsis of the illuminated manuscript:

Jakh Devata's Farce (**svāṅg**) *and the coming of Narada*

When the king's head was cut off, he said to Krishna, "Call Narada: he alone will extinguish my zeal [*jośmiṭhānā*]." Then the five gods say, "Who will go to the kingdom of Tibet to call Narada?" And Kunti's son Bhimsen says, "I will go to Tibet to call Narada."

Then Bhimsen reaches Tibet and meets Narada. And Narada says, "Why have you come here today?" Then Bhimsen says, "Krishna cut off the head of king Jakspati in the *Mahānbhārat* war, and the head cried out for Narada to come here, and the five gods sent me here."

Then Narada got ready and reached the assembly of the five gods and began an amusing entertainment [*haṃsī khel*].[10] Then King Jakspati was happy, and his anger subsided, and he said, "You will also be worshiped [lit. "eat *pūjā*"] in the world with me."

The figure of Babrik is unknown in the Sanskrit *Mahābhārata* but well known in the folk traditions of India, for example, in Rajasthan, where he has a temple near Jaipur called *śyāmjī khāṭū*, which is a major religious place for the Agarwal caste.[11] In Telengana, Bhima and Hidimba have a son named Barbareeka, to whom Krishna grants a boon that he will be able to see the eighteen-day war from a mountaintop.[12] According to the folklore of Kurukshetra, Krishna saw that Bhurishravas was invincible, so he disguised himself as a Brahman and requested the boon of Bhurishravas's head.

9. The only study of this masked drama that I know of is Purohit 1993.

10. In the drama, the figure of Narad is a kind of clown who introduces each of the eighteen dancers of the performance. His head and face are covered with a huge mop of yak-tail hair, and he speaks in a very rough voice, corresponding to local stereotypes about "barbaric" Tibetans.

11. Komal Kothari, personal communication.

12. Subba Rao 1976, 272–73, cited in Hiltebeitel 1988, 317.

Bhurishravas conceded this, but only on the condition that his head be mounted on the pinnacle of Krishna's chariot. This was done, and the Pandavas were victorious.[13] There is a Nepalese tradition according to which King Yalambar went to watch the *Mahābhārata*. Krishna asked him which side he would fight on, and when he answered "the losing side," Krishna beheaded him.[14]

The most extensive documentation of such a local tradition has been made by Alf Hiltebeitel (1988, 1995b, 1999) concerning the Tamil figure Aravan. In the Tamil versions, Aravan, the son of Ulupi by Arjuna,[15] has already agreed—as a properly dutiful junior—to perform his act of self-sacrifice for Duryodhana, thus ensuring the Kauravas' victory. Krishna's task is therefore to persuade him to perform it for the Pandavas instead, which he does through a series of complex machinations (Hiltebeitel 1988, chap. 15). The notion of a timely, if deceitful, intervention by Krishna in order to save the Pandavas is common to both the Tamil and the Garhwali versions of this myth, lending support to Hiltebeitel, who, following Biardeau, argues that *Mahābhārata* is a kind of "foundational" bhakti text.[16] For our purposes, the most important aspect of this myth is its representation of the ideal Kshatriya as brave and valiant to the point of self-sacrifice. In the Tamil performances, Aravan's self-sacrifice (he cuts himself thirty-two times) is dramatized, during which he is supposed to remain "stern, brave, and impassive" (Hiltebeitel 1988, 326). The character of Babrik is not so elaborately developed in Garhwal as in Tamil Nadu, nor have I seen or heard of any Babrik-related episodes enacted in *pāṇḍav līlā*, but when he does dance, it is always with a warrior's club and accompanied by his father, Bhima, another exemplary Kshatriya. The narratives about Babrik are remarkably consistent in portraying him as brave and impassive, qualities that are extolled by Krishna in the *Bhagavad Gītā* and cultivated and admired among the Rajputs of Garhwal. One is reminded of Schomer's explanation of the great and continuing popularity of the *Ālhā* epic in north India. The heroes belong to the low castes, she says, and therefore rural audiences identify more with them than with the courtly heroes of the epics. Moreover, these heroes risk all, and lose all, for the sake of their *rājputī*, or "*Rajputness*": "What they are left with at the end is not victory and a kingdom, as in the case of the Pandavas, but dignity and honor in defeat—a goal to which even humble people victimized by the inequities of the Kali Yuga can aspire" (1989, 150).

Such qualities are also exemplified in the Circular Array (*cakravyūha*), a drama enacting the capture and death, in a Kaurava military formation of the same name, of Arjuna's son Abhimanyu. Like Babrik, Abhimanyu is a

13. Cunningham 1970, 99, cited in Hiltebeitel 1988, 317.

14. Anderson 1971, 128, cited in Hiltebeitel 1988, 317.

15. Note that Babhruvahana is the son of Ulupi by Arjuna in the Sanskrit *Mahābhārata*.

16. See Biardeau 1976, 1978, 1981, and the various references at Hiltebeitel 1988, 458–59; also Hiltebeitel 1976.

brave, chivalrous, truthful, but doomed warrior, and once again the agent of his destruction is Krishna.[17] Abhimanyu's story is prominent in Sanskrit *Mahābhāratas* and well known throughout India, but the Garhwali version reproduced in the following adds that in a previous birth he was a demon and Krishna's enemy.[18] The Garhwali version of Abhimanyu's story shares a theme with other *Mahābhārata*-related traditions throughout India, including that of Babrik: that the Kauravas were fated to win, but Krishna intervened and ensured the Pandavas' victory:

> In his previous birth, Abhimanyu was a demon, and he hated Krishna. He knew a kind of extraordinary science, on the basis of which he made a special, beautiful throne out of precious metals. It had a *button system*, so that if you touched a certain button you would be burned to ashes. He planned to kill Krishna in it.[19] So he took it to where Krishna lived, but Krishna was ready. He knew that the demon was coming to kill him. They all knew. So Krishna changed himself into an aged Brahman and went to meet him. He met the demon on the road and asked him where he was going. The demon said, "What's it to you where I'm going? I'm going. I'm an old man, you should help me find the way and not try to stop me." "Yes, but where are you taking that throne?" "I'm going to meet Krishna, that's all." "OK, but what's the throne for?" "He'll sit here, push this button, and be burned up!" "You old fool! What are you talking about? Show me how it works!" So the old man sat down in the chair, pushed the button, and was himself incinerated.

According to another version,

> The demon opened a drawer within a drawer within a drawer. Krishna invited him to enter, and when he did so Krishna quickly closed all the drawers and locked the box from outside. The demon said, "You rogue! I didn't realize that you were Krishna! Look out, *chela!*[20] Perhaps only my bones will remain, but I will surely kill you one day!" Krishna dug a hole, buried the box, and covered it with mud and rocks. Much later he remembered that he had put the demon in the hole, and he went there. By that time, only bones were left, and Krishna brought the

17. Cf. Veena Das's discussion of the "considerable tension between close patrilineal relatives" that existed among ruling Rajput clans in India, largely as a result of primogeniture (1976, 132–33).

18. The version here is compiled from the tellings of Bacan Singh "Shastri" and Dabar Singh Rawat of Toli village, Shri Bhandari from Agast Muni, and an anonymous visitor to the Jabari *pāṇḍav līlā*, 1991.

19. Shri Bhandari is a local dramaturge who has directed some innovative adaptations of *pāṇḍav līlā* and aspires to perform it in Delhi. The detail of the machine with its "button system" is one of his innovations.

20. *Celā* literally means "student" or "disciple," but in colloquial Hindi it refers to the passive partner in an act of sodomy.

demon home and ground his bones into powder. He kept the powder in his house and ordered that no one was even to look at it.

But once when Krishna's sister Subhadra was cleaning his room, she noticed the box. Krishna had told her never, ever to open it, and she had promised not to. But, being a woman, she was unable to control her curiosity. She opened it and gasped in surprise, and the demon's life-breath [*prāṇ*] came out and went inside her, and she became pregnant. Krishna wondered what to do, since according to a prophecy he was doomed to be killed by his sister's son. He told Arjuna to take her away, so the child would be born in his house, and perhaps Krishna would be safe.[21]

Arjuna took Subhadra to Hastinapaur. Once he was telling her about how to penetrate the Circular Array with its seven gates and so forth. She listened as far as the sixth door, and Abhimanyu, who was still in her womb, heard every word. But then she fell asleep, and Abhimanyu didn't hear the secret of the seventh door, and so his knowledge was incomplete. Krishna caused her to fall asleep, so that the Kauravas could kill Abhimanyu later.

During the war, when the Kauravas began to form the Circular Array, Krishna took Arjuna to a place called Satapunji, so that he couldn't rescue his son. The Kauravas called out, "If any Pandava is a hero, then penetrate our Circular Array," and Abhimanyu replied, "I am Subhadra's darling, with hair on my chest!"[22] His uncle Bhima went with him, but when he saw the warrior Jayadratha standing there, he fled because Jayadratha had earlier done asceticism for Shiva and received the boon that he would kill Bhima. So Abhimanyu went alone.

As Abhimanyu entered the Circular Array, he merely knocked out the six gatekeepers. Had he killed them, he might have survived, but it was time for him to die. The Kauravas were frightened of him, and that is why they tricked him. They said, "Listen, son, why are you doing this? We are all brothers—put your weapons down." Very kindly and gently they urged him to place his weapons on the ground. He did so . . . and they killed him! With his dying breath, he called out, "Hey, father Arjuna, if your Gandiva bow has strength, destroy these sinners! Hey, Krishna, my mother's brother, if there is truth [*satya*] in your discus, then kill them! Hey, mother Subhadra, if you are truthful, then witness the death of Jayadratha!"

Then Krishna and Arjuna returned, and as they approached the battleground, the top of Arjuna's crown fell on the ground. He said, "Hey, Janardhana, hey, Krishna, there has been some tragedy in my house." Krishna said, "No, nothing has happened." But Arjuna saw

21. Ever since then, according to Dabar Singh, south Indians have married the father's sister's daughter to the mother's brother's son.

22. A proverbial line: *maiṃ hūṃ subhadra kā lāl, jis kā chātī hai bāl!*

> that his son was dead, and he asked Krishna why he had taken him away when he knew that the Kauravas had formed the Circular Array. If Arjuna had stayed, he might have saved his son.

Abhimanyu is chiefly remembered not only for his bravery, truthfulness, and steadfastness in battle but also for his youthful impetuosity, which may account for why his exclamation about his "hairy chest" is so widely remembered. These qualities are very much in evidence in the performance of the Circular Array. According to D. R. Purohit, several such "arrays" are produced in Garhwal: not only the *cakravyūha* but also the *garūḍavyūha* (bird array), dramatizing the Karuavas' theft of King Virat's cattle and their attempt to trap Prince Uttara, and the *kamalavyūha* (lotus array), a recent innovation involving fourteen "gates" (twice the number found in the *cakra vyūha*), performed in 1991 by research scholars in the Department of History at Hemavati Nandan Bahuguna Garhwal University (1993, 55–79, 89). But the most popular, and certainly the best known, of such dramatized battles featuring stylized military formations is the Circular Array, which is the culminating episode in many village productions of *pāṇḍav līlā*, where, like the Rhinoceros and the *śrāddha*, it metonymically designates the entire performance, so that people say that "a *cakravyūha* is happening" at such-and such a time and place.

In these performances, a level patch of ground (normally a terraced field) is cleared, and dozens of small stakes are driven into the ground in the shape of the Circular Array, which is a kind of maze (see figure 4).[23] Saris are collected from village women,[24] then draped over and secured to the stakes to make the walls of the maze. The result is a very attractive and colorful theatrical "set" [plate 9]. Purohit dates the origin of what he calls this "transformed arena theatre" to 1900 in the Ukhimath area (1993, 76). Wherever it is found, the Circular Array is now associated with increased literacy and the decay of the oral tradition. In performances I attended in the Mandakini River basin, dancers relied on handheld printed scripts, from which they declaimed in a rather stilted fashion, reminiscent of *rām līlā* performances in the plains and in nearby Kumaon. When I asked the old men if they were not able to recite the story from memory, as they do in Chandpur, they said that for them it was a matter of pride that their sons could read from such a script. Why should they preserve their old, illiterate traditions? Perhaps because of its association with literacy, the Circular Array seems to be growing rapidly in popularity and spreading well beyond its original area near Ukhimath, as far as Nandak and the region surrounding Rudraprayag.

23. Purohit was told by an "elderly relative" that this particular shape is a "symbol of the womb in occult rituals" (1993, 77).

24. Purohit mentions a "new-found belief" that those who contribute saris are blessed: the childless with children, unmarried girls with a husband, the poor with wealth, and so on (1993, 90).

Figure 4. Schematic version of the "Circular Array." Drawing prepared by Jarrod Whitaker.

Indeed, in 1993 when I returned to Sutol after seven years to see the *pāṇḍav līlā*, I discovered that a performance of the Circular Array was one of the many innovations that had been introduced in the interim.[25] When I asked my old friend Kunvar Singh why they were performing the Circular Array, he answered that if they performed it a few times and were successful, then the Sutol *pāṇḍav līlā* would become "famous throughout Garhwal."

25. In fact, Sutol was the third village in the upper Nandakini Valley to produce a Circular Array.

Plate 9. The Circular Array in Jabari village, constructed of women's saris. Photo by William S. Sax.

It seemed to me that Sutol's production of the Circular Array was less rigidly scripted, incorporating more dialect and less Hindi, than similar performances elsewhere. After the villagers had constructed the maze and donned costumes and makeup, they began enacting discord among the Kauravas. Duryodhana questioned Drona's loyalties, suggesting that was obstructing the Kaurvas' *policy* (he used the English word), and Drona responded that although he loved both the Pandavas and the Kauravas, no one should have any doubt as to his loyalty. The Pandavas were the enemy, he said, and he would destroy them if he could. Eventually Drona got angry, accusing Duryodhana of having a demonic intelligence (*rākṣas-buddhi*). Duryodhana begged his forgiveness, and Drona said that he would grant it because Duryodhana was his disciple, but that should he again make such an accusation, Drona would resign as general. He then promised to make a Circular Array in which to kill one of the Pandavas. One by one, each of the Kauravas entered the Circular Array and danced to his station within it, to wait for Abhimanyu. Normally, in Sutol and elsewhere, it is only the Pandavas who dance, but in this performance the Kauravas also danced, arrogantly laughing, "Ha! ha! ha!" Their army laughed, too, a pack of ragtag children dressed in dirty, tattered clothes, who raced around and around in the maze, leaping from the terraced fields and rolling in the dust, shouting, "Victory to Duryodhana! Death to the Pandavas!" Their humor was so infectious, and the "evil" laughter of the Kauravas so comical, that the audience was soon caught up in the lighthearted mood of the drama.

Now Drona (played by Padam Singh) called out, "Today in Arjuna's absence, the Kauravas have created a Circular Array. If any warrior knows how to pierce it and kill the wicked Kauravas, then let him do so now!" Abhimanyu volunteered, and his relatives were horrified, but he said to them,

> Why are you so downcast? I, Abhimanyu, will heroically pierce the Circular Array, up to the sixth door. Why are you so sad? What has happened to the strength of your arms? Watch! I will now pierce the Circular Array with my weapon!

Drona called out to Abhimanyu, asking how a sixteen-year-old boy had learned such wisdom, and Abhimanyu answered him. He said that he was the son of a great warrior; he sang songs of praise to Krishna; he boasted that he would destroy the entire Kaurava army. He explained how he heard the secret of the Circular Array while in his mother's womb, and that he knew how to pierce every gate except the seventh and final one. Then Bhima called out:

> Hey, Yudhisthira! It doesn't matter that Arjuna is not here. If we fail to enter the Circular Array today, we are humiliated, and our Kshatriya dharma is gone. So don't worry: if the child Abhimanyu knows the first six gates, then I, Bhima, will smash the seventh.

Next the actors discussed among themselves what they should say, whether they should let the Pandavas attack now or first stage an argument with the Kauravas (the play was being made up as they went along). The Kauravas taunted them:

> Where is your bowman [Arjuna]? Where is your butter thief [Krishna]? Today we see how the Pandavas are helpless without them! Go and drink your mother's milk, you sixteen-year-old boy! Either that or face a shower of Jayadratha's arrows!

"Give me leave!" begged Abhimanyu. "Let me into the Circular Array!" Drona continued to bait him, finally employing the ultimate challenge:

> If you are truly born of the Pandavas' blood, if you are truly born of Subhadra's womb; if you are a Kshatriya hero and know how to pierce the Circular Array, then you may make obeisance to your elder and younger uncles, and enter the maze!

Now Drona thought aloud: "I promised I would kill a Pandava hero, but I didn't know it would be such a young child. What can I do? I have promised: I must fight, I must fight."

Abhimanyu entered the maze and shot three of the guards, who fell unconscious. But now he had run out of arrows and had to fight with his chariot wheel. Still he was victorious, and Duryodhana swore at him. Drona berated Duryodhana and the other Kauravas for their sinful, evil war. But the Kauravas only laughed disdainfully: "Good and evil are all the same to us!" said one. Shortly thereafter, Abhimanyu was treacherously killed in the middle of the Circular Array by his cousins, the Kauravas.

Now the action shifted from the field where the Circular Array was erected to the dancing square in the middle of the village. Krishna and Arjuna were returning on Arjuna's chariot. The mood of the audience was subdued, apprehensive: Arjuna was about to learn of the death of his son. Nandvir Singh, the priest of the village god Dyosingh, honored Krishna with shoots of barley, incense, and a lamp, and so did other respected local men, including the village headman and a Brahman schoolteacher. Only then did Krishna and Arjuna dismount from the chariot. They first honored each of the dancers, touching their fistfuls of barley to the dancer's feet, hips, shoulders, and head. Then the silence was pierced by Arjuna's lament over the death of Abhimanyu. He spoke of his grief, and another dancer consoled him. Life is just a *līlā*, he said, a drama; a *motion picture*. No scene lasts; the drama keeps changing; no one can live forever. "In some future age," he continued,

> perhaps Abhimanyu will be reborn as the father, and you as the son. In your wanderings through the 8,400,000 births to which all are destined, you will meet again in this mortal world. In the eighteen books of the *Gītā*, it is written that one faces many difficulties, and that he is truly a human being [*insān*] who neither falls into despair in the midst of his difficulties nor becomes too eager in the midst of his excitement.

The dancer's speech exemplified the ideal Rajput response to death, as did Arjuna's reply: he vowed to avenge himself on Jayadratha who barred Bhima's entry into the Circular Array, or die in the attempt. Arjuna also quoted the *Gītā*: everyone who is born must die, and the death of the body is only like the changing of a set of old clothes.

Pāṇḍav Līlā as a Sacrifice

So far, I have shown how the weapons and characters of the *pāṇḍav līlā* both embody and reproduce a set of virtues and values that are fundamental to the self-conception of Garhwali Rajputs. In these performances, the Rajputs construct themselves as powerful, brave, self-sacrificing, and impetuous warriors. Of particular importance is their insistence on legitimate descent, an insistence that is perhaps related to the widespread but unspoken knowledge that many local Rajputs are in fact members of the suspect *khaśa* category.

But as I have stressed throughout this book, the meaning of the performance cannot be deduced from the text, not even if that "text" is broadly defined to include additional elements of the performance such as weapons and related mythologies. Attention must also be paid to the context of performance: the processes by which *pāṇḍav līlā*s are produced, the activities that "frame" them, and the overarching metaphors in terms of which they are understood. One of the most important such metaphors is that of the sacrifice (*yajña*). *Pāṇḍav līlā* is analogous to sacrifice, it includes particular sacrifices, and it is sometimes explicitly conceptualized as a sacrifice. This is important because it relates directly to the Rajputs' social position as the locally dominant caste.

Since earliest times, Kshatriyas have been regarded as the preeminent sponsors of sacrifices. In the well-known *Puruṣasūkta* of the *Ṛgveda*, the Kshatriya defends the sacrifice by the strength of his arm (RV 10.90), while the Brahman chants the words of the liturgy. The complementarity of *kṣatriya* and *brāhmaṇa*, respectively, patron and priest of the sacrifice, is further developed in classical Hindu law, where Kshatriyas (and especially kings) are enjoined to sponsor sacrifices and make gifts to Brahmans, while Brahmans are enjoined to perform sacrifices and receive gifts from their patrons. Hindu mythology supports the idea that kings are the preeminent sacrificial patrons, and Indian history confirms that sponsorship of sacrifices was a paradigmatic and political act in historical Indian kingdoms (Devahuti 1970; Gonda 1969).

For classical Hindu kings, sponsoring lavish state sacrifices was a means of maintaining and enhancing their relationships with the deities from whom their power and authority were ultimately derived (Inden 1990, chap. 6). In general, only kings were able to command sufficient wealth and labor to succesfully mount a major state sacrifice, and Hindu myths are replete with descriptions of the difficulties encountered by would-be sacrificial patrons: recalcitrant or avaricious priests, demonic opponents, and especially rival kings.[26] To perform certain sacrifices—in particular the horse sacrifice (*aśvamedha*) and the royal installation (*rājasūya*)—was tantamount to declaring oneself a "king of kings," a universal overlord. The horse sacrifice was, as Gonda puts it, "the most important manifestation of kingship" and "the king of sacrifices" (1969,113–14); therefore, it could not be countenanced by enemies, who would use any means at their disposal to sabotage it. Indeed, Yudhisthira's interrupted royal installation is at the core of the *Mahābhārata* story: Duryodhana would not allow him to complete it, as this would be tantamount to acknowledging Yudhishthira's overlordship. It was at this point, therefore, that Duryodhana arranged the Pandavas' gambling loss and subsequent forest exile.

26. These difficulties are well illustrated by the story of King Marut's *aśvamedha yajña* (found in the Pune edition at 7.55). Interestingly, a Himalayan village named *kalāp* is mentioned in Pauranik versions of this story, and residents of Kalap village in *paṭṭī* Singtur in western Garhwal claim that it is indeed their village that is indicated. They also claim that Singtur will be the only part of India to survive an imminent nuclear holocaust.

Classical royal sacrifices provide a particularly vivid example of how public rituals have both "expressive" and "instrumental" dimensions. To analyze these rituals merely in terms of "belief," without attention to their political and economic functions, would be as inadequate as attending solely to their social and political context, while ignoring the political cosmology (or cosmic polity) that they express. Such sacrifices are both political and theological, "instrumental" and "expressive," and that is why the best scholars have always attempted, with varying degrees of success, to incorporate both approaches in their analyses of them.

But to phrase the issue in this way is to remain impaled on the horns of a dichotomy because we are still speaking of "integrating" two different kinds of analysis. Is there a way in which such rituals can be analyzed nondichotomously, without falling victim either to an idealistic approach that fails to account for the environing effects of history and economics or to a materialist approach that ignores agency and imagination, our most characteristically human attributes?[27] In my view, Bourdieu's notion of symbolic capital is a useful tool for transcending this unhelpful dichotomy. Like all forms of public ritual, classical royal sacrifices may be understood as investments of symbolic capital that, by conspicuously displaying the superior power of the sponsor and his greater access to material resources, also serve his political ends. One of the most important points about the forms of capital enumerated by Bourdieu—material, cultural, symbolic, and educational—is that they are interconvertible (1990, 118–19). Material capital can be converted into educational capital (one can pay for an education), educational capital can be converted into material capital (high salaries for those with higher qualifications), and so on. This interconvertibility of all forms of capital helps us to understand the efficacy of public rituals such as royal sacrifices and *pāṇḍav līlās*, where the display of symbolic capital serves both material and political interests.

For rulers of states based on the extraction of agricultural surplus—including classical Indian kingdoms—lavish displays of symbolic capital (military parades, state rituals, vast sacrifices) could be converted into manpower when necessary, for example, during the periodic labor shortages associated with agricultural harvests, or when there was an urgent need to raise an army. A prudent subject would be more likely to lend his hand to the harvest, or his arm to the army, of the ruler who commanded the most lavish symbolic displays. For such a subject, this, too, was a kind of investment, which might be repaid in the form of a loan, remission of taxes, or (and this is probably the most common case, and one that clearly informs both religious and political language since at least the late medieval period) the

27. A similar point is made by Agnew in his review of the development of twentieth-century social theory: "The mimesis or imitation of scientific discourse in the context of social theory encouraged a strong tendency towards objectification. Instead of sacred symbols and rituals as the expression of collective existence the essence of society is seen to be production and subsistence" (1989, 17).

ruler's "protection." Similarly for the peasants who sponsor a *pāṇḍav līlā*, the display of symbolic capital may be (and is) converted into enhanced marriage alliances, political networks, and the prestige that accrues to the sponsoring village. As Bourdieu puts it, "[T]he exhibition of symbolic capital (which is always very expensive in economic terms) is one of the mechanisms which (no doubt universally) make capital go to capital" (1990, 120).

Garhwalis themselves often compare *pāṇḍav līlā* to a sacrifice. Like other sacrifices, it begins with a *saṃkalpa*, a vow to complete the ritual, which also specifies the recipient(s) of the ritual's fruits. This vow, however, is undertaken not by a single individual but rather by the village *pañcāyat*, or council, which in this instance always consists of five members, as the etymology of the word *pañcāyat* indicates. The village worships collectively, and it harvests the fruits of worship collectively.[28] Many, if not most, *pāṇḍav līlās* conclude with the sacrifice of a goat (often identified with the rhinoceros; see chapter 3), consumption of which is limited to resident high-caste villagers. Because most villages are dominated by a single caste, and also because *pāṇḍav līlā* is so strongly associated with Garhwali Rajputs, this means that the paradigmatic *yajamāna*, or sacrificial patron—the "sacrifier," in Hubert and Mauss's terms—of *pāṇḍav līlā* considered as a sacrifice is the Rajput community as a whole: in brief, the "royal function" itself.

In chapter 3, we saw that *pāṇḍav līlā* is conceived of as the *śrāddha*, or mortuary ritual, of the Pandavas' father, King Pandu. All *pāṇḍav līlās* incorporate some version of the *śrāddha*, and in some areas the term is used metonymically to designate the performance as a whole. Pandu's *śrāddha* is linked in turn to the interrupted royal sacrifice: the latter ritual could be completed (and thus Yudhisthira could be installed as king) only after the wandering ghost of King Pandu was appeased. Here is how Dharman Singh Bisht recited the story in the 1990 *pāṇḍav līlā* in Jakh village:

> I'll tell you now about the royal sacrifice.
> In Indraprastha was the knot of brothers:
> Yudhishthira said, "Today we perform
> the royal sacrifice for Pandu, our father."
> In Indraprastha was a great assembly,
> in a golden pavilion, attended by the gods.
> The divine sage Narada came to this assembly,
> and said to Dharmaraja,
> "Your assembly is splendid."
> To the five brothers he said,
> "Your father Pandu is not yet free."
> They fell at his feet, and asked,
> "What are you saying? We didn't know this."
> They fell at the sage's feet:

28. See chapter 3; also Sax 1991a, 98–104.

"Tell us how we can help our father,
King Pandu, to reach heaven."
Narada the sage paced in the assembly hall.
"You must perform the royal sacrifice,
and then your father will reach heaven.
Here is the method: you must collect sixteen items,
and then you can perform the royal sacrifice.
Krishna must come, and from heaven the wish-granting cow.
Much gold from the city of Lanka,
and a golden pavilion from the deep underworld.
From the king of Manipur, the hide of a rhinoceros,
and from Magadha, the 20,800 captive princes.
These kings, when they escape from Jarasandha's captivity,
will come to Indraprastha.
You must have barley from Barleyton
and Sesame from Sesameville,
and then the royal sacrifice will be complete."

As described in the preceding chapter, Arjuna's hunt for the rhinoceros involves him in a conflict with his son, the enactment of which is among the most fundamental episodes in *pāṇḍav līlā*. But the rhinoceros hide is not the only thing that must be gathered for the sacrifice. Other items are also necessary, and their accumulation can be highly elaborated. In Taintura village in 1990, the dancers were divided into two armies (*senā*), one associated with Bhima and the other with Arjuna.[29] The villagers said that in order to perform King Pandu's *śrāddha*, these armies had to go begging from village to village for the requisite materials. Arjuna's army went only when it was invited, but Bhima's army went begging every day. I was told that these two "armies" collected only from those villages that also perform *pāṇḍav līlā*. The armies thus incurred an obligation to contribute, in turn, to the other villages' performances in subsequent years. They expected to collect from eight to ten kilos of rice, and twenty to twenty-five rupees, from each of approximately five neighboring villages.[30]

In the afternoon, Bhima's army (and sometimes Arjuna's) would return with all the things they had gathered in neighboring villages, and the Das would quiz them to the beat of his drum: "Have you brought the fruit and the grains, the flowers and the incense, and all the materials for the *śrāddha*?" And Bhima would chant in reply, "We've brought the truth of

29. Bhima's army included Bhima himself, along with his son Babrik, plus Phaladu, Malyal, and Kaliya the ironsmith. (I do not recall the characteristics of *malyāḷ* or *phalāḍū*.) Arjuna's army included Arjuna, Yudhisthira, Nagarjuna, Abhimanyu, Sahadeva, Draupadi, Nagarjuni, and Vasanta.

30. A similar custom is practiced at the other end of Garhwal, in the Rawain area, where *pāṇḍav līlā* is known as *sarāddh* (see Sax 1996).

the truth-tellers, the followers of the leaders. We've brought fruits and vegetables, incense and flowers, and all the materials for the *śrāddha*."

When I told my assistant Dabar Singh about this custom, he said that the Taintura villagers must be very poor to have to beg like that, and that obviously *pāṇḍav līlā* was for them a means of acquiring food. Here is a noteworthy difference between classical royal sacrifices and their dramatization in *pāṇḍav līlā*. Whereas classical royal sacrifices, and in particular the *rājasūya*, were preceded by armed raids to obtain the vast quantities of material necessary for the ritual (Heesterman 1990, 102, 104), in *pāṇḍav līlā* villagers gather their materials through a form of ritualized begging. This is because *pāṇḍav līlā* is not about one geographic unit—say, a village or group of villages—asserting its dominance over another. Rather, villages organize their own performances independently and noncompetitively, contributing to the overall reproduction of Rajput dominance in the region. Gathering supplies through ritualized begging serves to reproduce networks of mutual obligation and exchange among Rajput villages, clans, and castes, whose collective dominance is enhanced by the performance. In his spontaneous remarks, Dabar Singh sounded rather like Gary Becker and the so-called rational choice theorists, and such naive (instrumentalist) functionalism is indeed the first line of cultural analysis for the "man in the street," as every anthropologist knows. But the Taintura villagers were not especially poor. In fact, their *pāṇḍav līlā* was the best-attended performance I have ever seen, and dancers and musicians earned a great deal of money from contributions by the audience, which numbered close to a thousand. In a purely "material" sense it was a geat success, and there was no material need for the "armies" to beg for the grain, money, and other supplies, which in any case did not amount to much.

Nevertheless, Dabar Singh's remark does point to the very great difficulties faced by villagers attempting to produce a *pāṇḍav līlā*. In 1991, in Gugali village, the young men said that they had wanted to perform a Circular Array for years but lacked the funds. They earned money by performing other local dramas and saved about 1,500 rupees toward expenses, so that the financial burden on the village would not be too heavy. They constantly complained about how difficult it was for a small village such as theirs to put on a *pāṇḍav līlā*, likening their difficulties to those faced by the Pandava brothers when they wanted to perform the royal installation. During the 1985 *pāṇḍav līlā* in Bhatgwali, my host, Vishnu Singh, fed about 35 people twice daily for the penultimate two days, and about 100 people twice daily on the final two days. His case was typical: he calculated that each village household spent 700 to 800 rupees on the *līlā*, including supplies for its own members and guests, contributions to the collective stores, clothes and sweets for all the village daughters, and a parting "mark" or "gift" (*piṭhāīṃ*) of one rupee to each guest.

This is a huge expenditure for local farmers, many of whom are materially impoverished. A generation or two ago, Garhwalis were perhaps not so aware of their relative poverty, but such an awareness is quickly becoming part of their consciousness. Young, educated Garhwalis (mostly men but now women as well) experience a huge gap between what Marx called the "idiocy" of village life and the modern, technological age that seems to have passed them by. Many—probably most—young Garhwali men are frustrated by the lack of interesting or lucrative employment, and this is made yet more unbearable by social and familial pressure to marry, raise a family, and so forth.

Given such daunting economic problems, why do Garhwalis still go to the trouble and expense of producing *pāṇḍav līlās*? Some villages (like Taintura) develop reputations for superlative performances, and they attract large crowds every second or third year, where costs can be recouped and profits sometimes generated. But they are exceptional. In most villages, *pāṇḍav līlās* are performed only once in a generation, every thirty years or so. It would therefore be a mistake to understand the motivation for *pāṇḍav līlā* in terms of straightforward desire for material profit. But, as Bourdieu teaches us, material capital is not the only kind of capital, and symbolic profits can be converted into material ones. In a *pāṇḍav līlā*, as in any public spectacle, villagers dress in their best clothes, clean and paint their houses, invite friends and family as guests, hire religious specialists, organize transport, provide large feasts, and so on. They show themselves at their best, both to themselves and to their guests, constructing and displaying an idealized self-conception that enhances the prestige—and therefore the prospects—of villagers. *Pāṇḍav līlā* is not literally a *yajña* (even though it includes *yajñas* and concludes with them); however, it is understood in similar terms to the mythical *yajña* of the Pandavas, the interrupted royal installation in which the Pandavas collected a great deal of material capital, invested it as symbolic capital, and thus established themselves as powerful and competent rulers.

Another reason for the strong association of sacrifice with kingship and Kshatriyas has to do with generosity. To sponsor a sacrifice or a *pāṇḍav līlā*, one must control much wealth, which is redistributed to participants in the form of fees, payments, gifts, and so on. Despite the obligatory nature of many of these prestations, actors prefer to gloss them as "generosity,"[31] believed to be an essential characteristic of Kshatriyas. The generosity of the Kshatriya is brought into relief by comparison with the Brahman, who is believed to be characteristically miserly. These stereotypes are ubiquitous: classical Hindu law discusses the Kshatriya's dharma of giving gifts and the Brahman's dharma of receiving them; Marriott (1976) distinguishes between the "optimizing" strategy of the Brahman and the "maximizing" strategy of the Kshatriya; many writers associate the outwardly directed and redistributive practices of the Kshatriya with "politics" and the inwardly directed, fundamentally conservative practices of the Brahman with "religion."

31. This predilection confirms Bourdieu's insistence that much of social life depends on what he calls misrecognition: "Culture is the rite, par excellence, of misrecognition," because to be cultured is to be seen—and to understand oneself—as not motivated by a cynical calculus (even though, inevitably, one is) (1984, 86).

There is an old saying in Garhwal, to the effect that a true Kshatriya always approaches another person with his palm downward (in order to give), never upward (in order to receive). In other words, Kshatriyas do not ask for handouts. Such a notion is common throughout north India, for example, in Rajasthan, where Harlan reports an identical adage. In both Rajasthan and Garhwal, the ideal characteristics of the Rajput center on sacrifice and generosity. One is a Rajput by nature, and this nature is realized through generous action (Harlan 1992, 122–23). Dabar Singh put it with typical bluntness: Brahmans are beggars, and they depend on Rajputs, while the dharma of the Rajput is to worship Brahmans and cows and to protect them.

One demonstrates generosity by being hospitable, and many Garhwali Rajputs strive to be hospitable to guests, while accusing Brahmans of being inhospitable. During the Bhatgwali *pāṇḍav līlā*, the entire company went in procession from the village down through the main local bazaar in Nauti, on their way to uproot the *śamī* tree (see later discussion). But while they were passing through Nauti village, they received no hospitality (*satkār*); that is, no one in the Brahman village offered them tea or biscuits or even a place to sit and rest. Therefore, they refused to stop in the bazaar on the way back up to Bhatgwali, and they even canceled arrangements for 100 cups of tea to be served there. Rajputs often grumble that although Brahmans occasionally perform the *pāṇḍav līlā*, they fail to invite their friends, relatives, daughters, and so forth. "For them," say the Rajputs, "it's like a *rām līlā*, a *nāṭak* [secular drama]."

On those rare occasions when Brahmans do stage a *pāṇḍav līā*, their transactions are strictly limited. They invite neither friends nor relatives, and little or no feasting occurs. Since *pāṇḍav līlā* is considered a Rajput tradition, a Brahman *līlā* is, as one of my Rajput friends succintly put it, a "matter of false impersonation" (*ḍhakosalewālī bāt*). When the (mostly young, male, Brahman) residents of Nauti sponsored a *pāṇḍav līlā*, they invited no guests. Their exchanges were all directed inward, to fellow villagers. In the Brahmans' *pāṇḍav līlā*, preliminary dancing began one evening, and on the next afternoon they "danced" the Pandavas' weapons at the village goddess's temple and sought her permission to perform the *līlā*. On the remaining three days, the same sequence was repeated in every courtyard in the village. Each house had prepared a platter with red powder, flowers, yogurt, an orange, and some raw, husked rice grains. A four-legged stool was placed in the middle of the square, and Bhima held his club upright on it. The village goddess's Brahman priest poured yogurt and then water over the club and marked it with red powder. Then the powder offered by the household was mixed with that in the platter brought by the Pandavas, and this was used to mark all the weapons and drums. Dancers, priest, and visitors were served tea, then left. The village was divided into three sections, and this form of worship occurred in each house in a section, successively on the three final days of the performance. Local people told me that it was done to ensure good crops and weather and general prosperity. They also stressed the mixing of powder from each household, which brought about the union of all villagers, both Brahmans and Rajputs.[32] No Brahmans from outside the village were invited, and to do so would have been faintly ludicrous, since *pāṇḍav līlā* is considered a Rajput and not a Brahman tradition.

The feasting with which Rajputs conclude *their pāṇḍav līlās* does not merely represent their kinglike status as the dominant caste: as an embodied ritual performance, it also reproduces it. The Rajputs themselves consciously relate the practice to *Mahābhārata*, citing two precedents. It is said that after Bhima killed the demon Bakasur, King Naganjit, in whose dominions the demon had been wreaking havoc, rewarded him by feeding him bread sweetened with jaggery and fried in ghee; plain, deep-fried bread; gram-flour cakes stuffed with vegetables and deep-fried in oil; pounded, dry-fried grains; milk; clarified butter; and butter.[33] This is virtually a paradigm list of the "food of feasts" (Marriott 1968), properly fed by Raja Naganjit as an inferior to Bhima his divine superior. A second precedent is even more interesting. It is said that during the Pandavas' forest exile, Duryodhana sent Durvasa and all his disciples to test Mata Kunti's *sat*, her "truth," "goodness," or "integrity."[34] The Pandavas had finished eating when Durvasa and his entourage showed up. What to do? They had finished, and there was nothing left. As a Kshatriya woman, however, Kunti was obliged to feed her guests, especially since they were Brahmans: it was her dharma. She called on Krishna, who saw that there was only one rice grain remaining, instructed Kunti to cook it, and told Durvasa and his disciples to go and bathe in the river while their meal was being prepared. Through Krishna's *māyā*, they felt as though they had eaten more than their fill, and they began burping and farting. When they returned to where Kunti had cooked up the single grain into a potful of rice, they protested that they had no more room in their bellies. Thus Krishna saved Kunti's *sat*, even as he had previously saved Draupadi's by giving her the endless sari. The point is that to be able to feed others is more than a matter of honor and prestige. For a true Rajput, it is a reflection of one's *sat*, of the truth of one's being. To be unable to feed others is to be profoundly inauthentic, like the illegitimate offspring discussed in the previous chapter; to lack the resources to do so is humiliating.

I began this section by showing that patronage and protection of the sacrifice have been regarded as the paramount dharma of Kshatriyas and

32. There were three Rajput households in a village of about seventy households, but the ritual did not significantly vary in them. The lowest castes of the village were also united with their fellow villagers, but in a way that insulated the latter from negative effects. For instance, they received the powder (*lāl piṭhāīṃ*) mentioned earlier but were not invited to contribute it. In all performances I saw, villagers were careful to contribute both raw and cooked grains to the lowest-caste *dās* in return for the latters' drumming, which is indispensable to the *līlā*.

33. *roṇṭ, pūḍī, pakoḍā, khājā, dūdh, ghī,* and *makkhan.*

34. The Prune edition contains a similar story, but with Draupadi as the cook instead of Kunti, since it was Draupadi and not Kunti who accompanied the Pandavas during their forest exile. The testing of Kunti's *sat* is a very important theme (see chapter 5).

kings since ancient times. As Hubert and Mauss (1967) recognized long ago, the paradigmatic sacrifier, or *yajamāna*, is the Kshatriya (in Garhwal, the Rajput)—what we might call the "royal function" itself—while the Brahman is the paradigmatic "sacrificer," the *purohita* or priest. Sacrifice is found explicitly in the *pāṇḍav līlā*: not only are particular sacrifices dramatized, but the performance as a whole is likened to a sacrifice, particularly in connection with the funerary rituals for King Pandu. To sponsor a sacrifice, or to produce a *pāṇḍav līlā*, requires control over people and resources, and this control is an aspect of power and domination. But power is linked to generosity, which is also considered an essential characteristic of both kings and Rajputs. All in all, then, both *pāṇḍav līlās* and sacrifices are closely associated with the self-conception of Garhwali Rajputs, who, as the locally dominant caste, think of themselves as generous sacrifical patrons.

The Theater of Hegemony

If we take the dominance of the Rajputs into consideration, then *pāṇḍav līlā* looks like a very conservative institution, one that perpetuates the Rajputs' dominance by establishing their hegemony. The concept of cultural hegemony was first articulated by Antonio Gramsci, who was attempting to convince Marxists of the Third International that domination is never simply a matter of economic power but always has a cultural, ideological dimension. This comes out clearly in his characterization of hegemony as "the 'spontaneous' consent given by the great masses of the population to the general direction imposed on social life by the dominant fundamental group; this consent is 'historically' caused by the prestige (and consequent confidence) which the dominant group enjoys because of its position and function in the world of production."[35]

As Lears (1985) points out, hegemony is always linked to domination: one or the other predominates in any given social formation. Gramsci's ideas about dominance and hegemony have sometimes been applied to South Asia, for example, by Guha (1997), who in a recent and very ambitious book proposes a logarithm specifying the relationship between the two. But on the whole, anthropologists of South Asia have not often employed these concepts, even though they reflect the same antinomy of values and power presented at the beginning of this chapter, in the debate between Dumont, who rigidly distinguishes the two, and his critics, who support a more nuanced view of their relationship. Just as Gramsci was attempting to counter the vulgar Marxian view that domination is simply a matter of economic power, so

35. Gramsci 1971, 12. The best general discussion of Gramsci's notion of cultural hegemony that I have yet encountered is Lears (1985); see also Bocock, who defines hegemony as "occurring when the intellectual, moral and philosophical leadership provided by the class or alliance of classes and class fractions which is ruling, successfully achieves its objective of providing the fundamental outlook for the whole society" (1986, 63).

Dumont's critics are attempting to counter what they perceive as his mistaken notion that "power" or "force" is a residual leftover in Indian ideology.

It can fairly be said that the revival of interest in Gramsci's thought has centered not on the concept of hegemony per se, but rather on the related notion of "counterhegemony," a space or a process in or by which subordinated groups articulate, criticize, and sometimes resist their oppressors. However, *pāṇḍav līlā* is not counterhegemonic. On the contrary, it would seem to be a particularly clear example of hegemonic technique because, through it, the Rajputs seek to persuade everyone (including themselves!) of their fitness to dominate.

But here we must pause, because as I have argued all along, the efficacy of public rituals generally, and *pāṇḍav līlā* in particular, depends more on participation than on cognition. Other scholars of ritual have also argued that ritual efficacy should not be understood in purely ideological or cognitive terms.[36] The social efficacy of embodied performance is also fundamental. Earlier in this chapter, I have described at length those performative features of *pāṇḍav līlā* that connect it to the self-identity of the Rajputs: the characteristics of the main dancers, the deployment of powerful weapons, the selection of episodes for dramatization, the symbolic displays that "frame" a performance, and its similarity to the sacrifice, of which Rajputs are the paradigmatic patrons. *Pāṇḍav līlā* is not a set of propositions to be rationally evaluated or a "text" to be passively read in isolation. It is neither a list of prescriptive rules authoritatively promulgated nor a schematic "reflection" of society. It is a public, ritual performance that, by obliging the participation of all members of society, helps to reproduce the very system of dominance that it simultaneously represents.

Insofar as its representations are plausible and its enactments persuasive, *pāṇḍav līlā* could be said to contribute to Rajput hegemony, but its social efficacy goes beyond the notion of hegemony as formulated by Gramsci because it depends more on bodily participation than on ideological assent. The low-caste drummer or the high-caste priest who is employed in a performance may not agree with the attitudes embodied in it, especially those concerning Rajput dominance. They may well have other attitudes, even contrary understandings of what *pāṇḍav līlā* means. For example, in his private conversations with me, the Brahman priest who officiated at the *pāṇḍav līlā* in Jakh village was rather dismissive of the whole event, not only of its religious value but also of the authenticity of various forms of "possession" within it. "Actually," he said, "this drama is merely a symbol [*pratīk*], to show the public that the Pandavas did such and such. It is practical [*vyavahārik*], not spiritual [*paramārthik*]." But as the hereditary village priest, he was required to provide ritual services for his Rajput patrons. This was his daily bread (*dāl-roṭī*), he said, and if he refused to participate, the villagers might

36. Bell 1992; Bourdieu 1977; Kertzer 1988; Lukes 1975. This argument is developed at length in the Introduction.

simply ask him to leave the village. Hereditary drummers of the same village evidently had less to lose than the priest: they refused to perform, and organizers were compelled to hire drummers from elsewhere. Both the imported musicians and the local priest participated in the event—for a price. What was purchased was not only their ritual services but also their acquiescence in a system of domination in which Rajputs *are* rulers, though perhaps not their endorsement of the hegemonic ideology according to which Rajputs *should be* rulers. My point is that in order to be effective, rituals do not require ideological consensus, but they do require participation: the best way to sabotage a ritual is simply to stay away. Therefore, when the non-Rajput castes of Garhwal participate in *pāṇḍav līlā*, they are helping to perpetuate a system of dominance with which they may not agree, and that may well thwart some of their interests, while serving others.[37] The drummer drums, and the Brahman prays at the Rajputs' behest, and what goes on "inside their heads" is largely irrelevant to the efficacy of the ritual.

The *pāṇḍav līlā* of Garhwal is thus a conservative performance that represents, and thus reproduces, the dominance of the Rajputs. It seems also to contribute to their hegemony. But there is a problem with this tidy picture, as I shall explain in the following section.

The *Śamī* Tree

What is wrong with the idea that *pāṇḍav līlā* supports Rajput dominance as well as hegemony?[38] To answer this question, one must first be aware of a rivalry between Rajputs and Brahmans that simmers away beneath the placid surface of Garhwali society. Although scholars have dealt explicitly and at length with what one might call the structural complementarity of Brahman and Kshatriya, they have had little to say about their rivalry.[39] In Garhwal, however, many Rajputs are envious or critical of the higher status of the Brahmans. Dabar Singh often accuses his Brahman neighbors of not being "real" Brahmans, of merely parroting Sanskrit mantras without knowing their meaning. On the other hand, he himself claims to have a good understanding of the import of Sanskrit language and ritual, and thus to be more entitled to the respect due a Brahman than are many Brahmans themselves. In fact, he is rather notorious for his habit of challenging Brah-

37. This is likely to be an unpopular claim in some quarters, as was my assertion, in a previous publication, that Garhwali women's participation in some of the rituals associated with the goddess Nanda Devi helps "to reproduce the system of social relations that keeps them in a subordinate position" (Sax 1991a, 206). I was subsequently criticized for failing to acknowledge women's political and cultural alternatives. However, I stand by both claims: religious rituals are indeed implicated in systems of gender and caste, which they sometimes perpetuate.

38. The following section is adapted from Sax 1995.

39. For exceptions, see Berreman 1972 [1963]; Biardeau 1976, 1978; Delige 1992; Dumont 1962; and Heesterman 1962.

mans in an attempt to demonstrate his greater knowledge of scripture and its meaning, and he relates these incidents with obvious relish.

Pāṇḍav līlā provides an opportunity for like-minded Rajputs to demonstrate that they are not inferior to Brahmans, and that in matters of religious learning they are the Brahmans' equal. It might even be said that in these performances, the Rajputs of Garhwal assert that they themselves are Brahmans of a kind. This is mainly done by the competitive, public display of knowledge. One of the more interesting aspects of *pāṇḍav līlā* is competitive bardic recitation of the *Mahābhārata* by Rajput men in the local dialect. One bard challenges another to recall some part of the story; if the man so challenged is unable to recall the detail, he is considered defeated by the challenger. Less often, one bard will "put down" another by interrupting his recitation with a correction, but this is rare because bardic competition is governed by a code of politeness.[40] Typically, the challenger begins by showering the preceding bard with praise, and the actual challenge is issued in such a way that it seems to be almost an afterthought. In Bhatgwali, for example, one bard was challenged by another to answer a specific question, and this was his cue to take over the recitation:

> Come forth, my son, into the assembly of king Dharma awhile;
> and sing the Pandavas' praises.
> Come into the assembly of Dharmanandana Yudhisthira!
> Such is the dharma of those who live on.
>
> *merā beṭā, hājurī ai jāṇo, dharmarāj kī pātī vṛttikā sabhā mā o*
> *ke ghaḍī beṭā, pāṇḍavoṃ kī stutī*
> *Dharmanandana yudhiṣthir kī sabhā mā hājurī hvai jāṇ!*
> *raiyāṃ bacyūṃ go dharam yan huṇ.*
>
> Man dies, but the Pandavas' story remains;
> the bird flies, but the summit remains.
> Blessed, O blessed is a human birth;
> and blessed, O blessed, is a vision of the Lord!
>
> *manakhī mar jāṇ, paṃvāra rai jānā*
> *pañcī uḍ jānī, ḍhayā rai jānā*
> *dhanya ho dhanya ho, manuṣya deī*
> *dhanya ho dhanya ho, haridarśana!*

40. This is remarkably similar to the Purakalli performance of Kerala, which "is cerebral in nature, in which the performers called the Panikkars asked each other questions on the Vedas, Epics and the Puranas as well as the grammar and prosody of the Malayalam language. The skill of the performer lay not in answering the questions but in posing ones of greater complexity. . . . The importance of such an artefact lies in the problems it poses for a study of popular culture. It was performed by lower caste Tiyyas, showed great Brahminical and Sanskrit influence and in its derivation entirely from that tradition was unique among the folk forms" (Menon 1988, 11).

Unions are at pilgrims' places, Badri and Kedar.
Unions are in festivals, in this moonlit silver square.
And how many reunions in the parents' loving lap!

kit bheṭ huṇī badarī kedār ma.
kit bheṭ huṇī tīrathoṃ bartoṃ mā.
colā cāndī cauk māṃ, mā bāpoṃ ke god māṃ!

Yayati, Puru, Ikshvaku, Mirag,[41] Muchkunda, Pratipa, Mahabhish,
the woman named Ganga . . . O my bumblebee messenger,
how many kings from diverse countries have come today! How did
mother Ganga become the queen of King Shantanu?
How did King Shantanu receive the boon that his woman would be named "Ganga"?

yāyatī, purū, ikśākū, mirag, muckuṇḍa, pratīp, mahābīs,
gaṅgānām strī . . . myār bhaṃvar
āj āyāṃ hvala deś deśoṃ kā nāreśa tuma!
ek gaṅgā nām strī gaṅgā māi kan rājā śantanu kī rānī hvae?
raja śantanu ne kahāṃ pāe varadān,
ki terī strī gaṅga nām hvale?

The bard who was challenged answered in the polite language characteristic of these exchanges:

Thank you, O Vyasa, for the wisdom
that has emanated from your mouth!
In the mortal realm of diverse creatures
this conference of gods,
this conference of men,
has been established.
What a happy day it is, there are cheers in the assembly
of Dharmanand, praise, praise to the Pandavas!
Blessed be the lineage of Vyasas,
who have learned the entire Veda
and put it in their hearts;
the four Vedas that Brahma spoke
with his four mouths.
You spoke the Vedas with four mouths,
you told the fundamental truth.
You examined the matter to its very root,
and told us the fifty-six lineages.

41. This name does not seem to belong in the list. My recording is unclear at this point.

He then began to tell the story of Shantanu, and also of Parasara. (Note how the audience is drawn into the performance and likened sometimes to an assembly of men, sometimes of kings, and sometimes of gods.) Before completing Shantanu's story, the bard addressed his audience:

> O brothers, are you listening?
> It is such a long, long story,
> and the frost has reached our knees,
> on this star-filled night, in this assembly of men,
> even the Pandavas who won the Great War are shivering!

Clearly there is a tension between dramatic episodes that emphasize militant and aggressive action, and competitive recitation, which is nevertheless characterized by a decorous politesse. Although they are public performers, bards are expected to show humility and not to take overt pride in their learning. The most accomplished bard in Chandpur, Bacan Singh Rawat of Toli village, exhibited this combination of knowledge and humility in both his public performances and his private pronouncements. But although bardic displays of knowledge are indeed competitive, they are more characteristic of a peaceful debate than a violent battle: in short, bards behave more like scholarly Brahmans than warlike Kshatriyas.

Heesterman (1964) has asserted that along with the Upanishadic interiorization of the Vedic ritual, the dominant religious question in Hinduism came to be "Who is the true Brahman?" and that it was answered in terms of possession of esoteric knowledge. It is precisely this sort of knowledge that is tested and displayed in *pāṇḍav līlā*. The very terms of address for bards are ones that are normally reserved for Brahmans: *śāstrī*, *vyās*, *paṇḍit*. Bacan Singh is called "Shastri-ji" offstage as well as on, despite the fact that he is unlettered. He has in some sense achieved the status—and certainly the respect—due to a Brahman. Another bard, Padam Singh Rawat of Sutol, interspersed his narration of the story with much edifying material, thus appropriating the preceptive as well as the pedagogical role of the Brahman. And he often recited in Sanskrit, a language normally associated with Brahmans. For these reasons, he was proudly referred to by his fellow villagers as "a real pandit." It seems clear, therefore, that through these displays, Rajputs are saying that they are the Brahmans' equal, that they are as worthy, as learned and controlled, as Brahmans ought to be.

This conflation of Brahman and Kshatriya qualities is not without precedent. One recalls that the Kshatriya king Janaka became a Brahman after winning a verbal contest. The *vrātyas* studied by Heesterman (1962, 1964) are a mirror image of the Rajput bards of *pāṇḍav līlā*. Whereas the Rajputs become, at least for the duration of the *līlā*, quasi Brahmans by virtue of their knowledge, the *vrātyas* were a group of knowledgeable priests who became quasi Kshatriyas by virtue of their participation in violent cattle raids.[42] So long as legitimate violence is associated exclusively with the Kshatriya and religious preceptorship with the Brahman, things are fine. Ambiguities result when the Kshatriya takes on the role of teacher, or when the Brahman engages in aggressive violence. Of course *Mahābhārata* itself supplies a precedent for the blurring of *varṇa* distinctions. I am not thinking so much of Drona, the Brahman who became a great soldier and general, but of the five Pandavas, who unite in their persons the powers of both *braḥman* and *kṣatra* (Hiltebeitel 1976, 80 n. 4, 159; 1988, chap. 8; 1991, 50–51). By now it should be obvious that their putative descendants, the bards of *pāṇḍav līlā*, do so as well.

Within the "playful" frame of *pāṇḍav līlā*, the Rajputs of Garhwal temporarily become Brahmans, who dance and recite the story of that other set of famous Brahmans, the Pandavas (!). Once again, the Rajputs' submerged identities as Brahmans are parallelled in the Sanskrit *Mahābhārata*: Hiltebeitel suggests that the "deepest" identities of the Pandavas were revealed during their final year of exile, which they spent in disguise at the court of King Virat (1980, 147–48).[43] Just as *pāṇḍav līlā* confirms Hiltebeitel's intuition of the identity of Draupadi and Kali,[44] so it also confirms his suggestion regarding the identity of the Pandavas. The Pandavas frequently disguised themselves as Brahmans, for example, in the city of Ekacakra before killing the demon Baka, and at Draupadi's *svayaṃvara*, where Arjuna assumed the guise of a Brahman. Moreover, Arjuna's father Indra is said to have won Shri from Prahlada while disguised as a Brahman (Hiltebeitel 1976, 159), and the Pune edition of *Mahābhārata* identifies Draupadi as an incarnation of Shri, so the pattern is precisely repeated. Dhritarashtra and Pandu, sons of the same Brahman father, each had Kshatriya mothers, and as the Brahman-like deities Dharma, Vayu, and the Ashvins fathered Yudhishthira, Bhima, Nakula,[45] and Sahadeva on the Kshatriya women Draupadi and Madri. And just as I am contending that the bardic "narrators" of *pāṇḍav līlā* are Brahmans of a sort, so written versions of *Mahābhārata* are narrated by the Brahman sages Vyasa and Vaishampayana. Of course the best-known example of the Pandavas' Brahmanical side occurred during their year in hiding at the court of King Virat, when Yudhisthira, Bhima, and Sahadeva disguised themslves as Brahmans. Perhaps their Brahmanical qualities were more evident because during that year they had consigned their royal power to the *śamī* tree by hiding their weapons in it.

42. According to Heesterman, the *vrātyas*, generally seen by scholars as a group of "fallen" Aryans, in fact occupied the interstices of an as-yet-unsolidified *varṇa* system, between Brahmans and Kshatriyas. He speculates that endogamy and prescriptive exchange came later, along with the development of the classical sacrifice.

43. In Garhwal, King Virat's realm is identified with the region just north of Lakha Mandal, itself said to be the location of the attempted assassination of the Pandavas in the "lac palace."

44. See chapter 5; also Sax 1991a, 289–90.

45. Note, however, that according to the Garhwli folk tradition, Nakula was the biological son of Pandu, by Madri (see chapter 3).

Plate 10. The Pandavas' "army" dancing around the śamī tree in Bhatgwali village. Photo by William S. Sax.

The equivalence of Rajputs and Brahmans is unambiguously expressed in this myth, which is associated with the important *śamī* tree *līlā* (also called *koḷyūṃ kauthīk*, or the "pine tree spectacle"), an episode that is especially well developed in Chandpur. In this *līlā*, a pine tree without blemish is selected and carefully uprooted, ritually enlivened, delimbed by Bhima with his club, and carried to the dancing ground, where it is proudly erected.[46] Bards sing to it, weapons from the previous *līlā* are placed at its base, dancers joyfully circumambulate it [plate 10], and on the final day it is "buried" together with the sacred weapons at a nearby water source. Its needles are distributed to all villagers as the true *prasāda*, or "edible grace," of the *pāṇḍava līlā*.

When I asked villagers about the significance of this drama, they usually cited a well-known incident from the *Mahābhārata*. They said that when the Pandavas left for their exile, they were required under the terms of their agreement with the Kauravas to leave their weapons behind. They sought a place to hide them in Vishnu's heaven, in the mortal realm, and at Krishna's fortress-city of Dwaraka, but no one was able or willing to keep them. Finally the *śamī* tree, which was growing in a cremation ground, split open its own stomach and hid the weapons inside. But it made a condition,

46. It is uprooted rather than cut, and its limbs are knocked off by Bhima rather than sawed off, because cutting or sawing it would be "disrespectful."

saying, "I will protect your weapons, but later you must protect me." The Pandavas left their weapons in the tree and proceeded into exile. After many years they retrieved their weapons from the tree and proceeded to win the great *Mahābhārata* war. When the *śamī* tree is carried to the Pandavas' dancing square and joyfully erected, participants say they are fulfilling the agreement made between the original tree and their ancestors, the Pandavas.

The *śamī* tree *līlā* is clearly a celebration of the Pandavas' military victory, and indeed the *śamī* tree has long served as an icon of victory in Indian culture. For example, Beals (1955) describes a Mysore village where the annual worship of weapons "reaches its peak with a procession of the village deity, Gopalaswami, to the outskirts of the village and the shooting of an arrow through the branch of the Sāmi [*sic*] (Prospis spicagara) tree in memory of the actions of the Pandavas when they regained their arms after their exile and prepared to make war upon the Kauravas." This is hardly surprising, since the king of Mysore himself worshiped a *śamī* tree on Victory Tenth (*vijayadasamī*), the annual pan-Indian military festival (Fuller 1992, 116). O'Hanlon reports that in Maharashtra on Victory Tenth, "the men of the village cross over the village boundary and take some leaves from the *shami* tree; these leaves represent 'gold' on this day. They are 'looted' by the men and brought back in triumph to the village. This day was also considered the most auspicious time among Maratha chiefs for starting a campaign" (1985, 159).[47]

But the *śamī* tree is not only a sign of victory in war. In Garhwal, it has other meanings, too. When I asked Bacan Singh Shastri about its significance, he told a story that established the equivalence of Brahmans and Rajputs by asserting that they, the rhinoceros and the *śamī* tree are all members of the same lineage.

> Once upon a time there was a Brahman named Atmadeva, the father of Vidyadhara. He was an old man, and he had a cow named Kaila. Someone shouted at him that his cow had just given birth to a calf. Atmadeva cut some fodder and brought it, and the calf began to suckle from its mother.
>
> When Atmadeva pulled the calf away from its mother in order to milk it, the calf leaped up and struck the old Brahman on the forehead with its hoof. He was knocked down, and he died.[48] The cow said, "O calf, you've killed a Brahman. You are guilty of brahmanicide. You may not drink my milk."

47. For more on this topic, see Gupte 1994, 180–83; Underhill 1921, 56–57.

48. Note that this is the same Brahman priest Atmadeva whose son Vidyadhara killed the cow in anger and was reborn as a demon, then again as the rhinoceros. Now, at a later point in the story, Vidyadhara is killed by the calf. This story makes Goldman's Freudian (Oed-Epic?) interpretation (see chapter 3) even less plausible, since here it is the cow that is guilty of brahmanicide.

Now originally, Brahma had five heads. But one of them spoke with a bad voice, like a donkey, and Shiva cut it off. So Parvati said to Shiva, "You are now guilty of brahmanicide. Don't come to my door." She told him that near Varanasi there was a river called Gomati, and that the sin of brahmanicide could be erased by bathing in it.

The cow also told its calf that he should go bathe in the Gomati and his brahmanicide would be expiated. So Atmadeva's cow's calf went and bathed in the Gomati River, and was liberated, and was reborn as a snake. He lived as a snake for many thousands of years. One day the divine bird Garuda came along and killed him. Now Atmadeva's cow kept her calf's portion of milk at Khimi Karani pond. She used to say, "This is your portion, O calf." When Garuda killed the snake, he dropped it into the pond of milk, and from its bones, the *śamī* tree was born.

Meanwhile, Atmadeva's eldest son, Dharmishtya, returned from his studies in Kashi. His guru said, "You are returning home. If you've learned your Sanskrit correctly, then you should not crush any living being beneath your feet." But as he was going along he stepped on a stone, beneath which were nine ants. The nine ants were killed. They said, "Go! You also will have nine children, and they also will die!" When he returned home, he married the Brahman girl named Shanta Rishesvari, the daughter of Garga Muni. Their first child died, and then the second, and the third, and so on, until eight sons had died. None escaped.

One day, Nar-ji[49] was wandering about, and he came to the home of Dharmishtya the Brahman. The Brahman and his wife were grieving. Nar-ji asked why, and they said, "What can you do about it?" He said, "Tell me anyway; perhaps I can help." They said, "Eight boys have been born, but they have all died. Now the ninth is about to be born." Nar-ji closed all the doors and windows [of the birthing room] with his arrows, so that no ghosts or demons could enter. Nevertheless, the child was stillborn, and Dharmishtya said, "Until today they were at least born alive! But today he was born dead—and you said you would protect us! Get out! We have no faith in you! I will give you *brahmaśūl* [the Brahman's blade/pain]!" And from his four interior fires he put the *brahmaśūl* into Nar-ji's stomach. Nar-ji began to scream with pain and searched for Dharmishtya's dead son but could not find him. So he decided to immolate himself on a pyre, to be rid of his pain. When he lit the pyre, he called out, "Hey Janardhana, hey Madhusudana [names of Krishna], today I am being burned because Dharmishtya's son." Then Vishnu manifested himself. He took Nar-ji's hand and said, "You tried to save Dharmishtya's son by your own strength. You didn't call upon me first. Had you done so, I would have helped, and his son

49. *Nar* means "man," and one of the names of God, *nārāyaṇa*, is derived from it. The pair Nar and Narayana are said to have taken birth many times, including during the Dwapara age as Arjuna and Krishna.

would have lived. Go! Across the seven oceans is a banyan tree, beneath which Dharmishtya's nine sons are sitting. Go there and bring them back." Nar-ji did so and received a blessing from Dharmishtya: "You have brought my nine dead sons back to life. Now if you die, so many times will you be revived."

And in the Dwapara age, Nar-ji was reborn as Arjuna. And every time that he was killed, he was revived. And since that day, the Brahman was weakened. He gave of his four fires to the Kshatriya, who now has eight, while the Brahman has only four. So the Kshatriya is stronger than the Brahman.

Bacan Singh concluded this part of his story with an abbreviated version of the myth of the eight Vasus. Briefly, Dharmishtya had nine divine sons. Along with his wife and sons, he began to dwell in heaven, but as a result of stealing the Brahman Vasistha's cow, eight of the sons were cursed to be reborn among mortals. The ninth was born as the son of King Santanu, who grew up to become Bhisma, the "grandfather" of the Pandavas. Thus Atmadeva's cow's calf became first a snake and then the *śamī* tree. And his grandson became Bhisma. Atmadeva's second son, Vidyadhar, who killed the cow with the golden scythe, became the rhinoceros. And that is the reason, according to Bacan Singh, that the *śamī* tree, the rhinoceros, and the Pandavas are worshiped together: because they were all descended from the same Brahman ancestor.

This is a rich and interesting myth, which could be analyzed on many levels. Like the Rhinoceros Tale, it is a superb example of the mythological imagination at work, making connections among different levels of story and narrative. For the master storyteller Bacan Singh (as indeed for many of the redactors of India's numerous *Mahābhāratas*), the primary device for making connections is genealogy: disparate characters from different epochs are brought into relation by the simple expedient of genealogical connection.

I explained in the previous chapter that genealogy and the purity of descent are extremely important principles for Garhwali Rajputs. And yet in this story, just as in the Sanskrit *Mahābhārata*, the Kshatriya protagonists turn out to have Brahmans among their ancestors. Thus the assertions implicit in the performance—that Rajputs are the equal of Brahmans—are "proven" by genealogy. Moreover, the ostensible differences between learned, self-controlled Brahmans and violent, impetuous Kshatriyas are undermined. Brahmans are violent and quick to anger, like Dharmishtya when he gave the *brahmaśūl* to Nar-ji, whereas Kshatriyas such as Nar-ji are self-controlled, learned, and compassionate. In the end, the superior qualities of the Kshatriya are rewarded. The Brahman "gave of his four fires to the Kshatriya, who now has eight, while the Brahman has only four. So the Kshatriya is stronger than the Brahman." And in *pāṇḍav līlā* at least, the Kshatriya is also more learned than the Brahman.

The story and performance of the *śamī* tree thus signify the dual themes of this chapter. On the one hand, the erection of the tree in the central dancing square is a joyous, auspicious event celebrating the victory of the Pandavas over the forces of evil, and their fitness to rule as kings. On the other hand, close examination of the myth reveals a secondary, "submerged" claim to Brahmanical status.

Dominance and Hegemony Reconsidered

If the Rajputs of Garhwal secretly wish to be Brahmans, or perhaps more accurately, if they secretly wish to be regarded as equal to Brahmans, then should we not say that hegemony belongs to the Brahmans and not to the Rajputs? I want to suggest that although *pāṇḍav līlā* does indeed reinforce the dominance of the Rajputs, it also and at the same time reveals the ultimate hegemony of the Brahmans. As noted earlier, *pāṇḍav līlā* is for Rajputs an instrument for strengthening dominance, and in this sense it is a conservative institution. However, to borrow from the title of Ranajit Guha's most recent book, this Rajput dominance is, in a certain sense, a dominance without hegemony. In short, I am suggesting that in Garhwal the Rajputs are dominant (in both Gramsci's and Srinivas's sense), whereas the Brahmans are hegemonic.[50] But to justify this assertion, I must reformulate Gramsci's notion of hegemony (which is rather inchoate in any case) in a more culturally sensitive manner.

Recall that hegemony is what we call it when the ruling class obtains the consent, indeed the approval, of those over whom it rules. If we stay with Gramsci, we might view the Rajputs of Garhwal as a "historical block," that is, a group that has developed a worldview that appeals to a wide range of other groups within the society, that has, indeed, convinced those other groups that the Rajputs' interests are those of society at large. *Pāṇḍav līlā* would then be one of the means by which such a hegemonic worldview is constructed. To a degree this is true, and in the first part of this chapter I suggested how *pāṇḍav līlā* might be analyzed in such terms. But there is still a problem with how we conceptualize the relationship between Brahmans and Kshatriyas in Indian culture. To address this problem, we must make a brief excursus into the anthropological and historical literature.

The relationship between an order of castes headed by the Brahman and a form of sovereignty focused on the king has been called "the central conundrum of Indian social ideology" (Trautman 1981), and Raheja rightly notes that "[v]irtually all of the major contributions to the anthropological, Indological, and historical study of Hindu South Asia have been concerned in some fashion with this relationship" (1988a, 497). Dumont (1970 [1966]) set the terms of the debate with his assertion that what is most distinctive about Hindu society is caste, which can be explained in terms of

50. This situation is reminiscent of Gramsci's discussion of the "contradictory consciousness" of the "man-in-the-mass," whose activity unites him to his fellow workers but whose ideology binds him to the past (1971, 326–27, 333).

the opposition of the pure to the impure. At every level of the system, this opposition generates a superior (purer, higher) and an inferior (more impure, lower) term. The content of a term can be multiple, as, for example, the three "twice-born" classes (*varṇa*) who are collectively opposed as high/pure to the low/impure *śūdra* class that is prohibited from studying the Veda, wearing the sacred thread, and so on. Likewise, Brahmans and Kshatriyas can be jointly opposed to the other two classes, or Brahmans alone can be opposed to the three lower classes. The content of the terms varies according to the relevant level, but the form of their opposition—pure versus impure—remains constant. In the final analysis, the immense complexity of India's caste system is to be explained according to this simple opposition. Caste is therefore an intellectual structure, a "state of mind," and because the opposition of sacred to profane is a "religious" opposition, we must therefore understand religious values to be hierarchically superior to political values in India, just as the Brahman priest is superior to the Kshatriya warrior and king (Dumont 1970 [1966], 34, 66, 74–75, 196). Caste is the key to Indian society, and the "religious" value of purity is the key to caste.

Dumont insisted that his theory of hierarchy was fundamentally Indian, and he conscientiously drew upon classical Hindu legal, political, mythological, and ritual texts to confirm it. However, he minimized the fact that the authors of such texts were nearly always Brahmans, members of the highest class, so that their writings, and thus Dumont's theory itself, tended to represent a Brahmanical perspective, a view "from the top," by those who were culturally hegemonic throughout much of South Asian history. By "hegemonic," I mean that Brahmanical norms and values set the standard against which persons and practices were measured. Because Brahmans were normally considered to have the highest status, these norms and values were often uncritically accepted, even among anti-Brahmanical movements or among low-caste groups that reproduced a version of the same hierarchical system among themselves (see Moffatt 1979). Although it is evident that the Brahmanical point of view was (and remains) disproportionately consequential for India's cultures, still it was not the only one. Insofar as Dumont claimed to have discovered the single, generative basis of caste, he therefore in some sense had to be challenged, and the challenge came, as it were, on behalf of classical Hindu kings.

King-centered rather than Brahman-centered theories of Hindu civilization were of course nothing new. Among the most noteworthy was that of A. M. Hocart (1968 [1950]), who argued that caste and castelike systems from South Asia to Polynesia derived from similarly structured royal cults focused on the king as guarantor of "life," prosperity, and well-being. Dumont made use of Hocart's insights but accused him of paying too much attention to the separation of castes, thereby failing to adequately emphasize the underlying "form" of their distinction, namely, the opposition of pure and impure (1970, 29–30, 48–49). Like Hocart, Raheja (1988a, 1988b, 1989) stresses the ways in which locally dominant castes reproduce the royal function, so that in many contexts, the order of castes is best understood not as a Dumontian linear hierarchy but rather as a set of exchange relationships with the dominant caste at the center and other castes (including Brahmans) at the periphery. More recently, Inden (1990) has tried to shift the Indological focus away from Brahmans and caste, and instead toward kingship and the state, arguing that an earlier focus on caste was part and parcel of an "Orientalist" conspiracy designed to make the traditional Indian state look weaker than it actually was.

Dirks has provided what is perhaps the most elegant solution to the "central conundrum of Indian social ideology." Based on his historical research on a south Indian Hindu kingdom ruled by members of the Kallar caste, he argues that "while the brahman was superior to the king as Kallar, he was inferior to the Kallar as king. The so-called material dependence of brahmans on kings, which countered against their spiritual dominance, was not upheld in the domain of temple honors, which itself can be seen as neither exclusively spiritual nor exclusively material" (1987, 291).

He argues that caste was embedded in a political context of kingship; that the prevalent ideology in precolonial India was not a religious one centered on purity and pollution but rather a political one based on royal authority and honor; and that Brahmans became key figures in Indian society only during the last two centuries, when they were employed as cultural mediators for the British, who had "decapitated" the Indian state (Dirks 1987, 1989). The real focus of traditional Indian religion, politics, and ideology was not the Brahman but the king. As several commentators (e.g., Fuller 1992, 81) have noted, this approach risks merely replacing Dumont's Brahman-centric system with a king-centric one.

What is most fundamentally at stake in this complex discussion is the relationship between power and values, of which the relationship between dominance and hegemony is a kind of parallel subset. As Quigley (summarizing Dumont) puts it, "The fact that brahmans are everywhere superior in status though often materially dependent makes nonsense of the theory that status follows on from power and can therefore be explained in terms of it" (1993, 35). But Dumont's notion that power is merely a residue in Indian ideology is also unacceptable, as his critics have repeatedly shown. In my view, the most potent criticism of Dumont—and one that bears directly on the material in this chapter—is that in traditional India, politics and religion were neither distinguished nor clearly distinguishable. Dumont himself recognized this point as early as 1962, in his article on kingship, but he failed to develop it. Dirks acknowledges the point in an important footnote,[51] but he promptly forgets it; Quigley seems to have missed it alto-

51. "Indian society, indeed caste itself, was shaped by political struggles and processes. In using the term 'political' I am of course conscious of imposing an exogenous analytic term on to a situation in which, as I will argue, ritual and political forms were fundamentally the same. However, I must stress the political both to redress the previous emphasis on 'religion' and to underscore the social fact that caste structure, ritual form, and political

gether. But I would insist that we cannot even begin to describe Indian society and history—to say nothing of analyzing them—if we continue to think of religion and politics as separate, bounded realms, and this is as true of contemporary Indian politics as it is of classical Indian society.[52] *Pāṇḍav līlā* is a case in point. If my argument is sound, then religious ritual serves dominance and therefore has an important political dimension, while politics—that is, the struggle over the distribution of power—is thoroughly ritualized.

But let us return to the issue of dominance and hegemony. It is clear that *pāṇḍav līlā* reinforces the dominance of the Rajputs by obliging all the other castes to participate in a public ritual that defines the Rajputs as dominant. Its ritual efficacy therefore derives from the politics of performance. But I have also said that there is an important sense in which *pāṇḍav līlā* reinforces the hegemony of the Brahmans. What do I mean by this?

For Gramsci, both domination and hegemony ultimately depend on a particular kind of political and economic rationality: an employment of appropriate means toward the end of power. But it would be a mistake to view this rationality as either universal or natural. It, too, is a particular cultural and historical product, and it must be understood as such, rather than employed as a yardstick to measure other cultures. Here we are well advised to follow Bourdieu, who, in the discussion of symbolic capital adumbrated earlier, urges us not to limit our analysis to conventional notions of economic rationality. "Economism," as he puts it, "is a form of ethnocentrism" (1990,112), but the solution to this ethnocentrism is not to renounce economism but rather to expand it, and to ask in all cases what it is that people live for (and, perhaps more important, what they die for), because what people live for and what they die for are precisely those things that conventional—which is to say, economistic—social science ignores: honor, prestige, love, family, nation, religion, and so on. All of these are nonmaterial things; they are "symbolic" items, the most important of which is prestige.

In the societies of "the West," prestige is associated with economic and political power, and we have a corresponding notion of domination as founded upon politics and economics. Hegemony is the ideological side of domination, and the two of them together relate to the particular economic rationality of the West. But we must not generalize this particular rationality, which is after all a social and historical product, to all of humankind.[53] Indeed, in

---

process were all dependent on relations of power. These relations were constituted in and through history; and these relations were culturally constructed. And it is on the cultural construction of power, in the final analysis, that I rest my case" (Dirks 1987, 4–5).

52. See Sax 2000a.

53. As Agnew puts it, a "hedonistic calculus" is taken to be a universal by market theory (and, one might add, by much social theory): "In this respect, theory naturalizes what is in every other respect a radical disruption and restructuration of needs and their mode of gratification via the market" (1986, 5).

rural India it seems to be the case that the greatest prestige is accorded not to wealth or political power but to high rank in the system of castes.[54]

Just as Gramsci was trying to sensitize his fellow Marxists to the ideological side of domination, so we must sensitize Gramsci to the cultural construction of value. We must in the first instance look to what is culturally valued within a given social formation. In many parts of rural India, we find that what is most valued is neither political power nor wealth but rather rank within the system of castes. In this sense, hegemony is exercised not by the Kshatriya but by the Brahman because the Brahman is the universal point of reference for prestige-seeking behavior, and *pāṇḍav līlā* is a case in point. This is shown not only by the fact that the Rajputs attempt in some sense to construct themselves as Brahmans within the performance and its related myths but also, and more important, by the fact that once the performance is over, the feast begins, and this feast must be prepared by high-ranking Brahmans. Here, the playful aspect of *pāṇḍav līlā* ceases, and the serious work of arranging marriages, confirming alliances, securing votes, and strengthening kinship networks begins. It is at this very point, where the dominant caste must show itself to be powerful and in control, that it acknowledges the superiority of the Brahmans.

Dumont's critics will say that I am mistaking the single axis of purity and pollution for the entire system, that other axes are just as important. My reply is that the actors themselves confirm my argument by their prestige-seeking behavior, which clearly shows that high rank is valued over political power and wealth. As Swami Vivekananda, the great Indian nationalist, was fond of pointing out, Hinduism is a religion of the stomach, and in the final analysis the caste system boils down to matters of food. And that is why, despite their pretensions to Brahmanical rank, despite their displays of learning and wealth, in the end the Rajputs, *despite themselves*, must acknowledge the hegemony of the Brahmans by asking them to cook their rice and serve it to their friends and relations. Once again, it is neither the cognitive nor the ideological content of ritual that is important but rather differentiated participation in it. It is as if the Rajputs acknowledged the hegemony of the Brahmans without even intending to do so, which is of course precisely what hegemony is all about. Dominance is intentional, overt, and sometimes spectacular. Hegemony is unconscious and covert, passing unnoticed as a "natural" state of affairs: simply the way things are.

In this chapter, I have tried to show that religious values cannot be separated from politics, nor culture from power. *Pāṇḍav līlā* simultaneously reproduces both values and power, the hegemony of the Brahmans as well as the dominance of the Rajputs. Politics has important religious dimensions, and religion has clear political effects. In the next chapter, I expand this analysis to the politics of gender.

54. The situation may very well be changing, especially in cities and other sites where people are exposed to world media and advertising on a massive scale. However, this is not the case in Garhwal—at least not yet.

5

Violent Women

Draupadi and Kunti in the Pāṇḍav Līlā

Goddesses, Wild and Tame

Wild goddesses such as Kali and domestic goddesses such as Lakshmi seem to have little in common.[1] Kali wears a garland of freshly cut human heads and earrings made of human infants, while Lakshmi is benign and beautiful, holding a lotus. Judging from a range of characteristics—iconography, diet, self-control, marital status—the two goddesses seem opposed to one another. Kali and her wild sisters Chandika, Chamunda, and the rest are bloodthirsty, terrifying, and uncontrolled by any male, while Lakshmi, Sita, Parvati, and similar goddesses tend to be gentle, married vegetarians, a kind of divine sewing circle, "breast mothers" versus "tooth mothers," as A. K. Ramanujan (1986) put it. Many scholars have seen this distinction as evidence of a deep-seated split or contradiction in Hindu conceptions of femaleness, with sexuality, blood, and pollution on the one hand opposed to chastity, purity, and self-control on the other.[2] The "split" model has important implications for the construction of gender and for relations between men and women. For example, the wild goddesses are seen as representing raw female power (*śakti*), autonomous and dangerously out of

1. This chapter is adapted from Sax 1996.

2. E.g., Bennett 1983; Das 1976; Dumont 1975; Fruzetti 1982; Jacobson 1977, 1978; O'Flaherty 1980; Wadley 1977. Smith's remarks are typical: "The epic world is essentially a male world [a footnote reads: 'Save for the female-centered sacrificial epics described in the Introduction to this volume.']: performance is normally both by and for men, and epic attitudes towards sexuality consequently reflect men's attitudes. The pattern which emerges from the narrative reveals a powerful sexual fear (cf. Carstairs 1957; Beck 1980; O'Flaherty 1980); women as mothers are strong and courageous as are many sisters and wives; celibate women and widows are dangerous and often destructive; women as sexual beings are a direct threat to men's source of strength" (1989, 188).

control, while the domestic goddesses, tamed by their male consorts, are more dependably auspicious and benevolent. It is claimed that, by extension, South Asian Hindu women are caught in a double bind: the dominant ideology requires that they be chaste, submissive wives, even as it recognizes that their dangerous and polluting sexual powers are indispensable for the reproduction of households, lineages, castes, and larger communities. The "split" model is useful because it clarifies a number of salient distinctions in the iconography, myths, and rituals of Hindu goddesses that might be summed up under the classical distinction between fierce (*ugra*) and peaceful (*śānta*) forms of the goddess. But to make the leap from distinction to contradiction, or to speak of a "paradox," is unwarranted not only because it flies in the face of most Hindu exegesis, according to which all goddesses are ultimately one, but also because recent empirical studies throw doubt on the idea that Hindu women's self-image is contradictory.[3]

In the *pāṇḍav līlā*, these two contrasting images are incarnated in the figures of Draupadi and Kunti. The elderly, maternal Kunti is associated with motherhood, sexual modesty, nurturance, and especially virtue, while the dangerous and sexually active Draupadi is explicitly identified as Kali and is sometimes the recipient of dramatic blood sacrifices. Daughter-in-law and mother-in-law embody both sides of the distinction between the fierce, bloodthirsty goddess and sexually active female, on the one hand, and the benevolent, vegetarian goddess and nurturing, nonsexual mother, on the other. Draupadi and Kunti are the most important female characters in *pāṇḍav līlā* (and indeed in the *Mahābhārata* story), and so a comparative analysis of them can contribute greatly to our understanding of the cultural construction of femaleness in Garhwal. But this analysis must not be limited to the "text"— neither the text of *Mahābhārata* (in any of its versions) nor the text of *pāṇḍav līlā*. For an adequate analysis we must leave our texts and attend to the social contexts and ritual performances in which these divine female figures are invoked and embodied. When we do so, we will find that they have something important in common not only with each other but also with the women for whom they are paradigms of identity. What they share is a concern for personal and familial honor. Ultimately, cults of the goddess are social products, and we must look beyond myths and liturgies, we must look carefully at the social contexts of their actual use, if we are to understand how distinctions are employed and contradictions are avoided in practice.

The Dangerous Wife

Female characters in *pāṇḍav līlā* include Draupadi, Kunti, Subhadra (who is both Arjuna's wife and Krishna's sister), and Nagarjuni the sister of Nagarjuna. Of these, Draupadi and Kunti are the most important. Through-

3. See Babb 1976; Erndl 1993; Gold 1994; Hansen 1988; Kurtz 1992; Nicholas 1982; Raheja and Gold 1994; Robinson 1985; Sax 1993, 1994.

out Garhwal, Draupadi is explicitly identified with Kali. Although this identification is not made in Sanskrit versions of the epic, it is paralleled in the cult of Draupadi in Tamil Nadu (Frasca 1990; Hiltebeitel 1982, 1988, 1991, 1995a, 1999), which is the only other comparably elaborate tradition of performance of *Mahābhārata* in South Asia. It is a commonplace among Hindus that the *Mahābhārata* war was fought because of a woman, because the Kauravas' public humiliation of Draupadi in the midst of the assembly was one of their most repugnant acts, and one that demanded revenge. She was menstruating at the time, and in various written and performed *Mahābhāratas* there are complex symbolic links between her blood and the blood of her enemies, in which she finally washes her hair in the gruesome scene following the battle (see Hiltebeitel 1981).

In Garhwal, however, the links between Draupadi and Kali are not merely "symbolic." Draupadi is unambiguously believed to be an incarnation of Kali, who brought about the *Mahābhārata* war in order to slake her thirst for blood.[4] It is commonly said that "Draupadi incarnated eight times; the Kali of Kailash did Kurukshetra" (i.e., caused the war).[5] Here is how Padam Singh Negi, chief bard in Sutol village, put it when he chanted the ritual summons commanding Draupadi to appear, at a performance I recorded in 1986:

In Satyug, the woman of five brothers stayed with Rama, incarnate as Sita.
In Treta Yug, drummer, she stayed with Shiva, and her name was Parvati,
In Dwapar Yug, drummer, she incarnated as Draupadi in the home of Drupad Raja.

pañjāpratā nārī dropati satajug māṃ gā raiī rāmā gā dagaṛ hvalī sītā avatār hvayā.
tretā yug māṃ śiv gā śaṅg dāsā tūṅgo pāravatī avatār chayā.
dwāpar yug māṃ gā hvayo tūṅgo dropat rājā ke ghar māṃ dropatī avatārā dāsā.

She was born from the fire pit, drummer, and she wears a burning headcloth,
and in Kaliyug, drummer, she incarnated as Kali, the mother of four yugas
and the dangerous wife of five brothers.
I have sent my bumblebee messengers, O drummer, and a pair of escorts.

aginī kuṇḍo dyeke hvaī ār dropati avatārā dāsā tū gā pās aginī pāṭ sāṛ chayo
ār kaliyug māṃ hvayo tūṅgo kālī avatārā dāsā to cāroṃ yug kī mātā
ār pañcapratā dūrānārī duropatā.
yab bhaṃvar bhedwāḷ bheje ār dāsā moharī jauḷiyā

4. Smith (1990, 12) discusses a Rajasthani "folk-*Mahābhārata*" in which the goddess offers to take birth as Draupadi in order to bring about a great war and annihilate the Pandavas. This is a typical motif, also found in the *Pābūjī* and *Devnārāyaṇ* epics (Smith 1991; Malik 1999), in which the goddess incarnates as a woman in order to destroy the heroes.

5. *Āṭho avatār duropati līno, kālī ke kavilāś kurukṣetra kīno.*

All major characters in *pāṇḍav līlā* are summoned by chanting such a *birad* (Skt. *vṛddhi*, "growth, enhancement"), during which they become possessed by the character in question and begin to tremble, roll their eyes, and exhibit other conventional signs of possession. Each character has a distinctive weapon and/or dance; for example, Arjun dances with the bow and arrow, Kunti stands in the midst of her sons with her hands raised in blessing and Bhima dances with a club.[6] Draupadi's weapon is the scythe (*darānti*) used by Garhwali women to cut grass, and assimilated in this context to Kali's sword. After saluting the drummer, Draupadi circumambulates or otherwise honors the fire that is always kept burning in a corner of the dancing square, because she was born from the fire sacrifice of King Drupad. But when the drummmer plays the drumbeat of war, she becomes Kali, and her sinuous dance movements become more violent. In Sutol village, she raises her arms above her head and crosses and recrosses her wrists, signifying conflict and strife.

Draupadi's association with Kali was explained by another well-known local bard, Bacan Singh Rawat of Toli village, in terms of the popular tradition (as found in the *Rāmacaritamānasa* of Tulasi Das) that it was only a "shadow" Sita who was sent to Lanka with Ravana, while the "real" Sita stayed hidden. This "shadow" Sita, he explained, was later reincarnated as Draupadi.[7] When I asked if she had any incarnations before that, Bacan Singh said there were many, and he recited a mantra identifying Draupadi with numerous forms of disease, including jaundice, bile, sore throat, measles, fatal snakebite, and whooping cough.[8] He told me that she takes all these disease forms in order to destroy her enemies.

Like Kali, Draupadi craves blood, as illustrated in local tellings of *Mahābhārata*. A holy man in Singtur at the headwaters of the Tons River in far western Garhwal, for example, related that once when Krishna was testing his sword to see how sharp it was, he cut his hand; Draupadi sucked

6. It should be noted that, pace Wadley (1977, 128), women frequently dance in *pāṇḍav līla* performances; see chapter 2.

7. See Doniger 1999 for many other versions.

8. *Prathame rūp devī gandhkā* (The goddess's first form is sulfur)
Dūjo rūp devī caṇḍikā (Her second form is the fierce goddess Chandika)
Tab rūp devī hiṅgolā (Then her form is Hinglaj Devi [?])
Tab rūp devī piṅgolā (. . . jaundice)
Tab rūp devī ḍāṅkhiṇī (. . . bile)
Tab rūp devī śāṅkhiṇī (. . . sore throat)
Tab rūp devī cūṛī (. . . bangle)
Tab rūp devī camārī (. . . f. leather worker)
Tab rūp devī chaṛāmukhī (. . . stick-face[?])
Tab rūp devī pataṅgarī (. . . flyer[?])
Tab rūp devī dadorā (. . . rash)
Tab rūp devī śītalā (. . . smallpox goddess)
Tab rūp devī mṛtīnāgalā (. . . fatal snakebite[?])
Tab rūp devī andhī (. . . blind one)
Tab rūp devī locaṛī (. . . whooping cough).

the wound before binding it, in return for which Krishna said he would some day rescue her.[9] According to the bard Bacan Singh, Draupadi was born in order to kill the Kauravas. She was not actually the Pandavas' wife but rather their protector, an incarnation of the goddess. This theme was clearly brought out in a story he recited at a *pāṇḍav līlā* in Jakh village in 1991. The story is set during the Pandavas' thirteenth year of exile, when they were in disguise in the court of King Virat:

> When the Pandavas were in the city of Virat, someone came to Kanka [Yudhishthira] and said, "Your hairdresser [Draupadi] goes to the burning ground every day, eats the flesh of corpses, then bathes, washes, brings water, and cooks your food. Why do you keep such a dirty woman with you?"
>
> So Arjun sent Vallabha [Bhima] to check and see if the story was true. Bhima went to the river and saw that Draupadi was indeed eating human flesh. When she had finished, she bathed and washed, filled her vessels, and began to carry them home. Bhima took the form of Shiva and sat along the path where she could see him. When she reached there, she said, "Hey, Bhima, why have you taken the form of Shiva today?" He was astonished that she had so easily recognized him, and asked her how she had done it.
>
> She said, "O Bhima, you think that I am your wife. But I am the Power of God [*bhagavan ki śakti*]. I am not your woman [*strī*]. Lord Vishnu has sent me to protect you. I also protected you when you were exiled to the forest, and that is why you had no sorrow for twelve years." She opened her mouth, and inside it Bhima saw the sun and the moon, the earth and all its rivers, and so on. He saw it all and was astonished.[10]

The most vivid and dramatic identification of Draupadi with Kali that I have seen takes place by means of a ritual that occurs in the far west of Garhwal, near the headwaters of the Tons River, in a *paṭṭī* that is "ruled" by Karna as a divine king (see chapter 6). Here, *pāṇḍav līlā* is normally called *sarāddh* (Skt. *śrāddha*), which is also the name of the obligatory annual Hindu ritual honoring patrilineal ancestors (see chapter 3). Unlike many public rituals, a *sarāddh* is sponsored by a single individual, usually to repay the Pandavas for some particular blessing.[11] This local version of *pāṇḍav līlā* has many interesting continuities with and differences from the *pāṇḍav līlā*s in eastern Garhwal, but here I will concentrate only on the culminating ritual, where a woman possessed by Draupadi/Kali sucks the blood from a goat kid.

A woman who performs this ritual does it in order to complete a fast (*vrat*) that lasts for three months or for three lunar fortnights. The fast may

9. For more on Krishna's cut finger, see Hiltebeitel 1988.

10. Cf. Draupadi's *viśvarūpam* in Hiltebeitel 1988, 85, 291, 293.

11. My host in 1994 was the late Kirti Singh "Kapti" Panwar, who sponsored the *sarāddh* in celebration of the birth of his son Puran Singh Panwar.

be voluntarily undertaken for some desired end (e.g., to conceive, or to cure disease), but more often it is performed in response to Kali's command. If a woman attends a festival where Kali is present, then the goddess may be attracted to her; or the woman may, either intentionally or not, come into contact with Kali's shield (*churrā*) or sword (*kaṭār*), as a result of which the goddess becomes attached to her and demands that she complete the vow. During the vow, the woman must remain celibate and avoid intoxicants and red foods (e.g., meat, chilis, red lentils); if anyone mentions something offensive while she is eating, she must get up and leave her food.

On the culminating day of the *sarāddh*, the sacrifice is offered to Draupadi/Kali. In a performance I witnessed in January 1994, an unusually large number of women were dancing in the bodies of their female "beasts" (*pasvā*; Hindi *paśu*). These included Draupadi, Subhadra, Runiya the leatherworker,[12] Chungka, Ghasiyari the grass cutter (Arjuna's concubine), and Kaliya Luharin, wife of the Pandavas' weaponsmith Kaliya Lohar, who "danced" on the ground on her knees. One by one the women went and stood before the drummer Bhuli Das, and when they began to tremble, the men dancing the parts of the Pandavas would come and loosen their hair, which the women would then toss wildly about, while the intensity of their dancing increased.[13] Up to nine goddesses were dancing at once in the square to the pounding drumbeat—an electrifying sight! They would come out of trance only when they were seized by the hair and forcibly seated by one of the Pandavas. The ritual was of course focused on Draupadi/Kali. Usually her "beast" wears a large silver necklace with an elaborate image of the goddess inscribed on it. This is called an "amulet," or a "seat" or "sign" of the goddess.[14] Sometimes such amulets are made collectively and pass from Draupadi/Kali's recognized village "beast" to the next. If they are made by an individual, then they stay with their owner.

In the 1994 performance, some very interesting problems arose in connection with these amulets, ones that nearly led to the ritual being aborted. To understand these problems, one must first be aware that one of the chief purposes of the performance is to firmly identify the dancer as a member of his or her lineage, thereby enhancing lineage solidarity. This is indicated not only by the name of the performance—*sarāddh*—but also by the ritual with which it begins, one in which the dancers circle burning incense over the heads of the Pandavas, then offer it in the name of Yudhishthira, eldest of the Pandava brothers.[15] Subsequently they offer incense in the names of their mother's father, their village, their extended family, the "five-named

12. Rūniyā Camārī; a *camārī* is a female of the untouchable leatherworkers' caste (*camār*).

13. For the importance of loosened hair in female possession in the western Himalayas, see Erndl 1993; for Draupadi's hair, see Hiltebeitel 1981; for womens' hair generally in South Asian culture and religion, see Obeyesekare 1981.

14. *tābit* (from Urdu *tābīz*?); *āsan*; *niśān*. The last term is commonly used in Garhwal to refer to material representations of deities, such as weapons and processional icons.

15. However, as they say locally, "Dharamaraj (Yudhishthira) doesn't dance in this valley," because it is so strongly associated with the Kauravas (see chapter 6).

gods" (*pañcanām devatā*), the place where the ritual is performed, and finally in the name of Karna, their divine king (see chapter 6). Then the drummer plays and the dancers dance for a long while, and once more they offer incense and rice to their ancestors. Next they "bathe" their respective weapons in incense and then offer incense to the Pandavas. Following this, the sponsor of the ritual applies yellow pine dust (evidently a substitute for turmeric) to all the silver goddess amulets worn by the dancing women.

The ritual was going according to plan until one of the dancers slated to take a goat-kid sacrifice—I will call her "Kali One"—began to seem uncertain about her identity. Throughout the afternoon, she identified herself inconsistently while in trance, sometimes calling herself Draupadi and sometimes Subhadra. The drummer and other (mostly male) participants in the ritual tried a number of auguries to determine her identity (these involved correctly choosing one of four sticks or small piles of rice), but here, too, she was inconsistent. As it turned out, she had recently married outside the village and had taken her paternal grandmother's Draupadi amulet when the old lady offered it to her—but this was improper, as it is believed that a new bride ought to embrace the gods of her husband's home and leave her old gods behind (see Sax 1991a, chap. 1).

Meanwhile, the woman who was slated to take a second goat-kid sacrifice—I will call her "Kali Two"—had married into Kali One's natal family and therefore should have received the amulet that Kali One was wearing. Like Kali One, Kali Two had also been offered an amulet by her paternal grandmother, but she had judiciously and properly refused to accept it. She wanted only the amulet of her husband's place, but that amulet was (improperly) being worn by Kali One! The drummer Bhuli Das, explicitly (and surprisingly, given his low caste) regarded as "guru" by his Kshatriya patrons, said that, should it prove necessary, a silver rupee could be punctured with a nail and Kali could be invoked in it, and it could then serve as an amulet for Kali One.

Throughout the afternoon, the difficulties mounted, with Kali One sometimes identifying herself as Draupadi, sometimes as Subhadra. This was especially disturbing because Subhadra is regarded as a vegetarian, and yet Kali One was preparing to accept a blood sacrifice! Bhuli Das identified another possible origin of the problem: during her thirty-day fast, she had inadvertently cleaned a glass that had liquor in it, thus polluting herself. Later in the afternoon the Pandavas went on a begging round from house to house, and at every house Bhima chanted the following blessing:

May your children prosper, young and old!
May your married couples prosper!
May your lineage and family prosper!

rāju raiyā tere choṭe baṛe bacce!
rāju raiyā tere joṛī-javānī!
rāju raiyā tere kuṭumbh-parivār!

Eventually they arrived at the house of Kali One. Her husband was drunk and weeping; he begged the Pandavas' pardon for all the trouble, and they told him to return to the dancing square, where all his questions would be answered. The Pandavas reached the square, but the goat sacrifice was delayed while they prepared a new amulet by puncturing a silver rupee. The husband was fined for giving his wife a polluted glass to wash, and then the Pandavas proceeded to a nearby stream, where they performed a local version of *piṇḍa-dāna*, the feeding of the ancestors. Then all the dancers returned to the central square.

As the sun dipped toward the mountain peaks on the horizon, Arjuna put a bit of yellow pine dust on each "beast's" amulet. Meanwhile, a small tentlike structure had been set up in one corner of the dancing square, in which two men crouched with the goat kid stretched between them. Kali became entranced for the last time, passed by the fire burning at one side of the dancing square, and raked up a bare handful of coals. Just as the sun set, at a signal from the drummer the men inside the tent slit the goat kid's throat, Arjuna scattered yellow pine dust on everyone, and Kali leaped into the enclosure and began sucking the blood from the kid. It took her several minutes to do this, in silence and shielded from everyone's eyes by the walls of the tent. Later the victim was butchered: its head and rear foot went to the drummer, its foreleg went to the man dancing the part of Bhima, and its heart went to Draupadi and Arjuna. When Kali was finished, the dancers each took up a blanket and formed a cloth wall around the fire, where they sacrificed a second kid by throwing it onto the coals. After the ritual was complete, the crowd sat silently, sated by so much blood. Meanwhile, the men were very solicitous toward the young woman who had been possessed by Kali. They helped her to wash her hands and face, and they fed her fried breads and semolina sweetmeats (*purī-prasād*). She sat very quietly. It seemed to me that once again, she had become a shy young woman, amazed to have played such a part in the ritual. As I watched her, a man turned to me and said, "Now her thirty-day vow is complete."

This *sarāddh* ritual exemplifies in a graphic way what everyone in Garhwal already knows to be the case: that Draupadi is Kali. Draupadi demanded the blood of her enemies, the Kauravas, to avenge the insult she suffered at their hands, and in this sense she was the bloodthirsty "cause" of the *Mahābhārata* war. The sacrifice of the goat kid is itself linked back to Draupadi's bloodthirstiness. As one village man related:

> Draupadi's five sons were killed by Duryodhana. She said, "The fire in my heart will be quenched only by blood." Bhima said, "A second *Mahābhārata* can't be fought; where will the blood come from?" So he threw his club up in the sky, and it landed on his chest. Blood rushed from his mouth and fell on the fire pit from which Draupadi had been born, which had burned continuously until that moment, and extinguished it. So they sacrifice the goat kid in memory of Bhima.

I began this chapter by suggesting that there were two apparently opposed types of goddesses. The first is associated with blood and sexuality, and clearly Draupadi/Kali fits that model: it is but a few short steps from the blood of Draupadi's vengeance to the blood of sacrifice to the blood of Kali's victims. Draupadi is also thought to exhibit a kind of hypersexuality. Throughout Garhwal, women appeal to Draupadi, the sexually active wife, and not to Kunti, the aged mother, when they wish to become pregnant.[16] She is, after all, the common wife of five brothers, and although the epic poets were clearly embarrassed about this, they could not ignore it (see Hiltebeitel 1988, 267–69). Garhwalis tell different stories to explain how it is that Draupadi managed to end up with five husbands. Most of these have to do with her actions in a previous life, and most of them equate polyandry with an excessive sexual appetite. For example, it is said that in a previous life Draupadi practiced extreme asceticism for a very long time in the Himalayas, until Shiva finally appeared and granted her a boon. Well, it was cold up there, and she was lonely, so when she finally got a chance she blurted out, "I want a husband, a husband, a husband, a husband, a husband!" And she got her wish.

These associations are particularly strong in the upper Tons valley, where fraternal polyandry is still practiced.[17] Outsiders believe that women from this area are sexually insatiable, and travelers are warned not to eat food from their hands, lest they be drugged or bewitched and compelled to become sexual slaves (see chapter 7). Local women are aware of these outrageous stories, and they joke privately about them. But virtually everyone in the area regards the existence of polyandry, which was previously widespread, as proof of the fact that the Pandavas were their ancestors.

With such strong associations with blood and sexuality, Draupadi embodies one of the poles with which I began this chapter: the bloodthirsty, dangerous, and sexually active wife. Clearly she is an incarnation of female power, but so is the Pandavas' mother, Kunti, to whom I now turn.

The Truthful Mother

If Draupadi is the dangerous, blood-drinking wife, then Kunti is the virtuous, food-giving mother. Wherever *pāṇḍav līlā* is performed, one of the eldest and most respected women in the village plays the part of Kunti. Even in those many villages where the parts of Draupadi, Subhadra, and other women are now danced by men, the part of Kunti is invariably still played by an elderly woman. According to Garhwalis (and unlike the Pune edition of *Mahābhārata*), Kunti accompanied the Pandavas on their thirteen-

16. In Kaliphat, between the Mandakini and Alakananda Rivers, women who desire children tie coins into the hem of Draupadi's shawl when she possesses her "beast" during *pāṇḍav līlās*.

17. See Majumdar 1963; Rao 1992.

year exile. During this period of hardship, and especially during the first twelve years when the brothers roamed through the jungles and mountains of Garhwal, Kunti fed and protected them and rescued them from many dangers, all through the power of her *sat*, her "truth" or "virtue."[18] So closely is Kunti identified with truth and virtue that the normal epithet for her is "Truthful Mother Kunti" (*satī mātā kuntī*), or sometimes "Devout Kunti" (*dharmā kuntī*), and her "truth" is even objectified, becoming a kind of ritual object (see later discussion). Kunti is also associated with service (*sevā*)—in particular, she serves the gods in order to obtain her five sons.[19] Every bard tells a slightly different version of the birth of the Pandavas. Here is one told by the drummer Dharam Das, of Sutol village:

O greatest of gods! In king Santanu's line
in Citra and Vicitra's line, in Hansurai's line,
in Kunjarai's line, hey five Pandavas:
I will forget, but you mustn't forget!
In Mahabharata's line, in Kurukshetra's line,
in king Gudha's line, in old Pandu's line,
in king Dharma's line, in king Indra's line,
O greatest of gods! I will call the Pandavas today
and send them away tomorrow to Victory Palace in the plain.
The burning wood hisses! My heart jumps!
I will send a pair of honeybees to take an invitation.

o parameśvar devatā! to rājā santan ke pāṭā
citra-vicitra ke pāṭā, haṃsurāī ke pāṭā
kuñjarāī ke pāṭā, to he pāñc pāṇḍavo
maiṃ bhauḷā jaulā, tum bhulā na jaiyā!
mahābhārat ke pāṭā, kurūkṣetra ke pāṭā
gūḍhā rāj ke pāṭā, būḍhā pāṇḍū ke pāṭā
dharmarāj ke pāṭā, rājā indra ke pāṭā
parameśvar devatā! to nyūtī bulaulā
bhauḷī paiṭyūlā syalī jaintī bārau.
maiṃ pahoḍī parājā, hīḍā bhāḍulī
moharī rebārā bhauṃryā jauḷyā bhejulā.

In king Santanu's line, O greatest of gods!
The truthful mother got her boon children,
the five Pandavas. The truthful Kunti,
How she served the Ganges for twelve years!
How she served the god Indra for twelve years!

18. Cf. Flueckiger's (1989) discussion of *sat* in the *Lorik-Candā* epic; also Harlan 1992, 124–26.

19. Garhwali oral versions of *Mahābhārata* have little or nothing to say about the conception of Karna by Surya, which was effectively a rape.

How she served the lord Dharma for twelve years!
How she served the god Brahma for twelve years!

to rājā santan ke pāṭā, paramesvar devatā!
satyevantī mātā, to bart ge putra ju chayā
ye pāñc pāṇḍav, satyakuntāmātā ne
bārah varas kain gaṅgā jī kī sevā!
bārah varas kain indar kī sevā!
bārah varas kain dharamarāj kī sevā!
bārah varas kain barmājī kī sevā!

She served old Pandu. Serving and serving,
her hair turned white as the khasa grass.
She was bent in three places like a lock from Banaras,
and her petticoat was torn to the knee.

to būḍhā pāṇḍū kī sevā. sevā karte karte
muṇḍalī phūlaigī khāṃsā beṭūlī.
tiguḍī nyūḍī banārasā tāl
ghāgarā phāṭī kvaṇyūṃ māthā.

She served the gods with a necklace-shaped brazier.
She served the gods with a golden pitcher.
O greatest of gods! She took laughing barley and speaking leaves[20]
and entered the assembly of gods.

devatoṃ kī sevā par hār kī dhūpyāṇī.
sovan kā gaḍuvā paramesar devatā.
haiṃsaṇ juṇyāḷo bulānī pātī
devatoṃ kī sabhā par cal gaī satī kuntī mātā.

Then true mother Kunti said, "Hey, five-named gods:
How I've served the Ganges for twelve years!
How I've served King Dharma for twelve years!
But there's no boon for me!"
O greatest of gods! The five-named gods said,
"True mother Kunti, you go home today.
Tomorrow morning, on the eighth Sunday, step out of your door
and come to the assembly of Gods, and a boon will be given to you."

satī kuntī mātā, he pañcanām devatāo
bārah baras kain gaṅgājī kī sevā!
bārah baras kain dharmarāj kī sevā!
to merī vāstā koī varadān nī hvaiyā!

20. See chapter 1, note 7.

to parameśvar devatā, to pañcanām devatāl bol
saccī kuntī mātā, to āj ghar lauṭī jā
bhauḷ sube bārā, āṭhoṃ etwārā, bāharoṃ dvārālo,
to devatoṃ kī sabhā par āyā, terī vāstā baradān deī jālo

But on the day of the boon, mother Kunti got a fever.
So the woman Gandhari ("Come here, woman!")[21]
Gandhari arose, took water and incense,
a golden jug, the laughing barley, and the speaking leaves
and went to the gods' assembly.

to satī kuntī mātā, var kā dīno, jaur ai gāyā.
to kuntī gonārī—yakh aiyo nārī!—
to gonārī uṭhī, ārag dhūpyāṇī
to devatoṃ kī sabhā par cale gaī.

And just at that moment the five-named gods
gave Gandhari the boon of the 6000 Kauravas.[22]
She took that boon and returned
to Victory palace in the plains.

to pañcanām devatoṃ ne vaī bagat
gonārī gā vāstā saṭhya sau kaurav ko bar jo denā.
to saṭhya sau kaurav ko var laikanī
parameśvar devatā, śailī jaintī bārā jab āī.

I'll speak of that time: Gandhari arose and came laughing,
and true mother Kunti said, "Hey, little sister, why are you so happy?"
And Gandhari answered her, "Hey, elder sister, today
the five gods gave me a boon of 6000 sons!"

to te bagat bolo, to gonārī uṭhī, haiṃsaṇ haiṃsaṇ āī.
kuntī mātā ne bolo, ki he merī bhulī, terī vāstā āj kī kusī gujarī?
to gonārī boṇ baiṭhī, he merī dīdī, merī vāstā āj
to pañcanām devatoṃ ne bar jo deyo, saṭhya sau putra ko var.

So true mother Kunti said, "Tomorrow I'll go."
And early next morning she went to the Ganges to bathe.
On the bank of the Ganges she removed her five garments and bathed.
Then she got dressed, put on sandalwood paste,
took water and incense, a golden pot, the laughing barley,
and the speaking pole, and went to the gods' assembly.

21. Here the drummer directs a member of the audience to step forward and assume the part of Gandhari.

22. The Kauravas are often asserted to have been 60 in number, not 100 as in the Pune edition of the epic. Here "6,000" is hyperbolic.

to kuntī mātā bolaṇ baiṭhī, bhauḷ sube bārā, suberī bagat
to suberī bagat, kuntī mātā gaṅgā snān cale gaī.
gaṅgāre kināre par pāñc kapaḍyūṃ kholī, isnān lai.
kapaḍyūṃ jo pairī, candan jo pairī, tai bagat par
ārag dhūpyāṇī, sovan kā gaḍuvā, haiṃsaṇ juṇyāḷā,
bolan pātī lejai, devatoṃ sabhā par cale gaī.

O greatest of gods, in the great gods' assembly
the five-named gods said "True mother Kunti,
yesterday was your day for receiving a boon,
why do you come again and again?"

parameśvar devatā, so devatoṃ sabhā par
to pañcanām devatā ne bolo ki, he kuntī mātā,
byelī terī vāstā bar deṇ. to hameśā hameśā
bar ke vāstā kyūṃ auṇ lagyūṃ chau?

Then true mother Kunti said "Hey five-named gods,
Kunti and Gandhari have identical faces.
I've gotten no boon. I had fever the day of my boon."
Then true mother Kunti said "Give me my boon now"
And the five-named gods said "True mother Kunti,
bring a pot of hailstone water, paddy that ripens in a day,
laughing barley and the speaking leaves.
Bathe in it, and you shall obtain your boon."

to kuntī mātā ne bolo, he pañcanām devatā bala,
kuntī gonārī yak aunārī chau.
merī vāstā koī bar nī milo. yo mī bar kā dīn jvarā ai gayā.
ve bagat kuntī mātā boṇ baiṭhī, merī vāstā baradān dyaḷo.
pañcanām devatoṃ boṇ lāgyāṃ chau, tū saccī kuntī mātā chau.
auṃsī ghaḍlo pāṇī, byāḷ būtā dhānoṃ,
haiṃsaṇ juṇyāḷā, bulānī pātī lyo.
yū sī isnān lailī, to terī bāstā var milalo.

So true mother Kunti went into the forest.
In the heat of the summer, the crow doesn't speak and the mouse doesn't scamper.
The crow simply sat there, and Kunti went to a cool grassy clearing
with red rhododendrons. She chanted the mantra of truth:
"If I've truly served you, O five-named gods.
I will bathe in a pot of hailstone water, and paddy that ripens in a day."
She bathed in it, with the laughing barley and the speaking leaves.

saccī kuntī mātā jo chī, cale gaī raṇ-vaṇ jaṅgal par.
jeṭh-vaiśākh ke ghām, kāg nī karkaṇī, mūs nī barkaṇī.

syaḷo-myaḷo kāg jakh baiṭhaṇ lagyāṃ cha, to saccī kuntī mātā cale gaī,
rāṃsī-burāṃsī unyāḷī pātal par. satasvara jaupā:
he pañcanām devatā bala, saccī holo mī tumārī sevā karaṇ lagyūṃ
to merī vāstā auṃsī ghaḍo pāṇī byāḷ būtā dhānā. kuntī mātā ne
yūsī isnān leṇ. yo haiṃsaṇ juṇyāḷā bulānā pātī asnān laigī chā.

She began to bathe, and just at that moment,
Crow Minister went there and saw Kunti naked.
He saw Kunti naked, that simple crow, and true mother Kunti said,
"Hey Crow Minister, none has seen me naked before.
Today for the first time, Kagbhusundi[23] has seen me naked—
may your face be black!" At that very moment, O greatest of gods,
with the mantra of truth [she cursed him],
so Kagbhusundi went to the five-named gods
and said "I was fair, but today I've become black!
O five-named gods, I saw the pot of hailstone water,
and I saw mother Kunti!" The five-named Gods said
"Crow Minister, the festival time will come,
there will be rituals and worship, and food will be made for you—
is she not true mother Kunti?"

ve bagat par gaī kāg devāno, to kāg devān ne kuntī mātā gā aṅg jo dekho.
to syaḷo-myaḷo kāg jo dekho. kuntī mātā ne bolo,
he kāg devāno, mero aṅg kail nī dekh cho.
āj se kāgbhuṣuṇḍ ne myaro aṅg dekho,
to tero kālo mukh hvai jāyā! veī bagat par, parameśvar devatā,
satasvaura jāpā. to kāgabhuṣuṇḍ jo cho, pañcanām devatā kā pās āyo.
to ve bagat boṇ baiṭho, mī bilkul dhauḷo cho! āj myaro kālo mukho hvaiyo
he pañcanām devatoṃ bala, to mīla auṃsī ghaḍo pāṇī dyakhaṇ,
kuntī mātā dyakhaṇ lagāyo. pañcanām devatoṃ ne bolo ki,
he kāg devāno, bār tivār ālo, bārah pūjā holī, terī vāstā agyārī ban diyā jāl
yo saccī kuntī mātā che ki nī cho?

Then true mother Kunti filled the pot with hailstone water
and bathed in it, and to the five-named gods
she took leaves, and paddy that ripens in a day.
She gave the water and paddy to the five-named gods.
And they gave her five boon-sons:

to ve bagat par, saccī kuntī mātā chau, auṃsī ghaḍo pāṇī bharaṇ laigīṃ cho.
auṃsī snān leṇ laigīṃ chau. byāḷ būtā dhān lyūṇī chā
sākhinī pātal lyūṇī chā, pañcānām devatoṃ kā pāsā.
to saccī kuntī mātā jo chī, auṃsī ghaḍo pāṇī, byāḷ butā dhānā.
to pañcanām devatoṃ ne pāñc putra gā var jo dinā.

23. *kakabhuḷuodi*, from the famous crow-narrator in Tulasi Das's *Sriramacari-tamanasa.*

She served the king Dharma, Yudhisthira was born.
She served the god Indra and Arjuna was born
She served the king Bhuva[24] and Bhimsen was born
She served the god Brahma and Sahadev was born
She served old Pandu and Nakula was born.[25]
She received the boon of five warrior sons
in the Pandava lineage, O greatest of gods.
The Pandava boon-children, in Victory palace in the plains.

to dharmarāj kī sevā kana, yuddhiṣṭhir paidā baṇyūṃ hvoyo.
to indar kī sevā kana, arjun paidā baṇyūṃ hvoyo.
to bhuvākhān kī sevā kana, bhīmsen paidā hvoyo.
to baramā kī sevā kana, sahadeva paidā hvoyo.
būḍhā pāṇdu kī sevā kana, nakul paidā hvoyo.
to pāñc putra gā var jo mīlo, chetrī vaṅgś jo cha,
pāṇḍav vaṅgś jo cha, parameśvar devatā
he pāñc pāṇḍavo, to baradānī putra hvai ke, śailī jaintī bār para.

Here the idea of service is paramount: Kunti serves the gods and receives the five Pandavas in return, as a boon. Her virtue, or *sat*, is highlighted not only by the contrast with Gandhari's duplicity but also by her sexual modesty in the incident with the crow. Later it is tested by the gods, and these tests are a major theme in the oral traditions surrounding the Pandavas' twelve years in the forest. In the upper Tons valley, a character called "Crafty Narayan" (a multiform of Krishna) is introduced, who persistently but unsuccessfully attempts to destroy Kunti's *sat*. In the following song, recorded live in performance,[26] it can clearly be seen that Kunti's *sat* is inextricably linked to her honor, and the honor of her family:

> All the gods came to the assembly. Shiva came from Kailash, Krishna came from Dwarika, Rama and Lakshmana came from Ayodhya, bearing the wealth of the world. They had their meeting in Dwarika. When all these gods had gathered together, they began to argue among themselves about who was the greatest, about who should sit where. Then Shiva said to them, "Who is the greatest god? None of you! No, it is that mother who is a font of truth [*satudhārī mātā*], the mother of the Pandavas. She doesn't let anyone go hungry; instead she goes without. She doesn't let anyone go naked; instead she herself goes naked, the mother of the Pandavas. She indeed is an ocean of truth, a knower of dharma. She worships the five Pandavas. She does difficult *tapasyā*."

24. Bhuvarāj is Vāyu, the wind god.

25. This telling was inconsistent with the usual Garhwali version of *Mahābhārata*, according to which Nakula was born from the Ashvins, and Sahadeva was born to Pandu and Madri. (And the Garhwali version is in turn inconsistent with the Pune edition, according to which both Nakula and Sahadeva were conceived by the Ashvins, while Pandu had no biological offspring.)

26. *Pāṇḍav jāgar* sung by Rudra Das of Jakhol village in December 1993.

The gods said they would test her *sat*. They all arose and went to the Pandavas' house, to their spacious audience hall. They arrived and set up their assembly. Mother Kunti saw them from her verandah. Then she brought sandalwood paste, flowers, water, and so forth in her platter. She offered them incense in her incense burner and went to where they were seated. Mother Kunti put her five fingers in the platter, got the sandal, and applied it to the foreheads of the five gods. And they said, "What nerve! What audacity!"[27] And when she had done this, they all took her food.

In her heart, Mother Kunti began to worry that some god might still be hungry. They said they were very hungry indeed, and so she prepared her kitchen. She made grain for the grain eaters, incense for the incense eaters, and so forth. She distributed all these fine foods in her platter: milk for the milk eaters, rice for the rice eaters, and so on. But in no time at all, Crafty Narayan made trouble. The rice turned to worms, the milk turned to blood. The gods said, "Old woman, what kind of food have you fed us? Hey mother-in-law! Who in the world eats maggots and blood?" Mother Kunti's own son-in-law has come to test her *sat*. He says, "What person or god in this world has eaten such food?" She was utterly humiliated and said, "Yes, I see, I don't know how . . ."

"You have so much *sat* you make the flowers rain."[28]

"What is the problem, Mother Kuntī? What's happened to your flowery *sat*? Why can't you do anything?" Their words were so harsh, it gave her a backache. My mother, the font of virtue, ran off crying. She went to Arjuna and said, "Son, they've come to defeat my *sat*. The five-named gods are demanding that I make it rain flowers." Arjuna said, "Only Indra can do this. . . . How can we reach him in his city? There is someone named Gopichitra at Indra's palace; he has power over flowers." The five Pandavas began to weep: "Our mother's *sat* is being stolen."

Sahadeva said, "Mother, why, after all, was I born? Gopchitra is my father—you did his *tapasyā* and I was born.[29] I will go to Indra's stronghold and ask him for it." Sahadeva got ready to go: he took a bath and spread sandalwood paste on himself. He dressed to go and did obeisance to his mother, and she and his brothers kissed his cheeks and sent him on his way. She also slipped him a letter and told him to give it to her husband, Gopichitra. Inside was written: "Oh, my husband, I am in great trouble here in Hastinapur. I did your *tapasyā* for twelve long years: listen to my plea. If you're my husband, please make it rain flowers. If you do this, I will worship your feet. I will recite your name morning and evening. If you are happy with my service, make it rain flowers."

27. The gods are surprised that Mother Kunti would be so bold as to apply these marks herself, since this threatens them with pollution from her. The point seems to be that her virtue is so great that she cannot pollute the gods even by touching them.

28. This line is a *kaḍī*, a formulaic phrase used by musicians.

29. Note that this is a different telling (and a different region) than the preceding story about Gandhari stealing Kunti's boon.

> Sahadeva took the road to Indra's stronghold. When he reached there, Gopchitra was sitting in the assembly. He looked at Sahadeva and thought, "Who is this? Why has a mortal come here?" As soon as Sahadeva reached there, he gave the letter to Gopichitra. Gopichitra read the letter: "The five-named gods have come here to steal my *sat*. I salute you with my right hand. I have done your *tapasyā*. Save my honor [*lāj*]. If you are happy with me, please make it rain flowers. These gods are demanding it of me: give it or I will be humiliated. The bearer of this letter is the fruit of your boon; this Sahadeva Pandit has your very form." Gopichitra took out a mirror and sat Sahadeva next to him. He looked at their reflections and saw they were truly of one form. "This must indeed be my own boon-child. Hey Pandit—you are my son!" Gopichitra embraced Sahadeva, who said, "Ask for whatever you want from my lower world—but I can't return empty-handed." When he said this, all the different kinds of trees in the world began to fly up toward heaven. Gopichitra said, "Hey, my beloved! You must indeed be someone, who can make these trees fly up from below! But please don't make the whole mortal world fly up here! You are a great, learned, powerful, perfected [*siddh*] man, at whose command the trees fly up! You needn't do so much—take the flowers—they suit you. I can't deny your mother, who did twelve years' *tapasyā*—take them!" Sahadeva did obeisance to his father and departed. Before leaving, he devotedly worshiped his father's feet, then went back to Mother Kunti. Ahead went Sahadeva, and behind came a rain of flowers. In two minutes, all the mountains were covered with many kinds of flowers. Greatest of all is the Brahma Lotus, which grows among the peaks. Then snow began to fall; it fell so fast that the birds were covered with it. And when Sahadeva went to where the gods were sitting, he saw that they, too, were covered with snow. Then Shiva asked them, "Why did you do this? Hasn't she proven herself now? Hasn't she done as you demanded?"
>
> She always thought that the naked should be clothed before she herself was, and should be fed before she herself was. The gods' place was filled with snow. Crafty Narayan said, "One more thing, mother-in-law: bring me the flower of the sun from atop the serpent Shesh's head . . ."

This and other stories revolve around various gods' attempts to destroy or somehow defeat Kunti's *sat*. Fundamentally, it is her honor and prestige that are at stake, as her own comments and those of her sons make clear. But the gods are unable to defeat Kunti's *sat* because she is so pure. She is an ideal mother, always serving others selflessly, and this service most often takes the form of offering food. Kunti feeds her children, and she also feeds the audience during *pāṇḍav līlā*. For example, on the first day of a performance in Taintura village in Lobha Chandpur in 1990, the old woman playing the part of Mother Kunti made some fried breads and grain and offered it at the shrine of the Pandavas. This was referred to as her *sat*. After the day's performance was over, the villagers brought similar foods, from which five sweet breads were selected in the name of the Pandavas. These were placed in a small platter and spun about dramatically by the dancers, who would hold the platter upright on their palms and then spin it around in wide circles. The fact that the bread did not fall from the platter was attributed not to centrifugal force but to Mother Kunti's *sat*. Some of the food was given to a drummer and an ironworker who were present, while the rest was distributed among the crowd. Kunti's fried foods were blended with food the villagers had brought, and the mixture was distributed among spectators, who took it home.

Clearly, Kunti is understood as a supremely virtuous, benevolent, and self-sacrificing mother, as distinguished from Draupadi, who is represented as dangerous, bloodthirsty, and destructive. Kunti feeds others, while Draupadi/Kali feeds *on* others. But another story, told by Bhuli Das of Dyora village, calls into question the distinction between these two figures:

> Usal, Dusal, Dronacarya, and Duryodhana, the king of them all, began to feel a rivalry with the Pandavas in their youth, because even then Bhimsen was such a mighty warrior that he could kill thousands with his left hand and thousands with his right. Lakshmi flowed from Duryodhana's hand as water from a stream; that's what it was like in his capital. Bhimsen fought with such a man.
>
> Mother Kunti said, "My Bhimsen has struck enmity with Usal, Dusal, Dronacarya, and the king of them all, Duryodhana. What will happen now? There will be a great war. Who wins and who loses will be decided at a meeting of the yoginis at the *śāl* tree. One can only hear the result by hiding in the belly of the tree.

I served the wind god for twelve years—might he help me save my sons?
I served the sun god for twelve years—might he help me save my sons?
I served the sages for twelve years—might they help me save my sons?
I served King Pandu for twelve years—might he help me save my sons?
I was born from the strength of the sages—will they help?
How will my five sons be saved? One of them has three eyes—how can I save him?"

> Once she had remembered all this, she sent her five sons to summon Pandits from all the countries. When the Pandits arrived, Mother Kunti asked them how the five Pandavas could be saved: "Usal, Dusal, Dronacarya, and the king of them all, Duryodhana, are the sons of Lakshmi, goddess of wealth; the kings of the earth are under their sway, and the five Pandavas are all alone. There will be a war, and the sixty-four yoginis will decide who will lose and who will win.[30] Tell me how one may go there to hear their decision."

30. A standard phrase: *kis kā khay, kis kā jay*.

They began to roll their dice.[31] First the Pandavas were below, and the Kauravas were on top. Then the Kauravas were below, and the Pandavas were on top. The Pandits said, "First they lost, but we asked our die, Mother of Wisdom [*vidyāmātā*], a second time, on the basis of your *sat*. Don't worry—we'll tell you how to go there. Tell your three-eyed son to bathe inside, in a copper tub, and when he comes out, tie a silver coin on his head. He was to have been killed, but we've asked Mother of Wisdom, and if you do this ritual, he will be saved. This will protect him: when he descends the steps to the square, sacrifice a black and white billy goat to him as he mounts his horse. And put a mark of its blood on your son's head. He was marked for death, his head was to be severed, but the sixty-four yoginis will eat the goat's blood instead." Mother Kunti demanded a promise [*dharam*] from the Pandits, that their words were true. They said, "Don't take one promise, take seven: your sons will be saved."

The Pandits said, "We don't know where this *śāl* tree is. What will Arjuna eat there? What will he wear? When will he sleep? This will be a very difficult journey for your three-eyed son; none of the comforts of home, you know." She made all sorts of food and sweets, and gave them to Arjuna along with warm blankets that would protect him from the wind, rain, and cold.

Mother Kunti said, "I don't know anything about this place. You tell me." The Pandits said, "There is a huge tree there; no one knows how old it is. It is the yoginis' tree. It is hollow inside, but no one knows that. If your son Arjuna goes there and takes your name and the names of the five gods, and shoots his arrow, then it will open by itself."

Mother Kunti told Arjuna, "You should avoid anger, you should just listen to what the yoginis say, but if you get angry your weapons will not work. It will be difficult there. The first watch [*pahar*] is of men: the sick and the lame will come. The second watch is of ghosts: all kinds of strange ones will come. But keep on taking the name of the five Pandavas. The third watch is the watch of lions, the fourth is of leopards, the fifth is of wind, and the sixth is of fire. Don't go outside: just accept it and listen to what they say. Pay attention only to what the sixty-four yoginis say, and come back and tell me. And then my heart will be at peace. Listen to all that they say: don't ignore anything."

They did as directed. Arjuna bathed inside, in a copper tub, and when he came out of the bath they tied a silver coin on his head. And when he descended the steps to the square and mounted his horse, they sacrificed a black and white billy goat and marked his forehead with its blood. When they sacrificed the goat, Arjuna felt ill at ease. He thought, "We used to sacrifice goats at people's arrival, not at their departure. Why has the Pandit advised us to do this backward wor-

31. A common form of augury, especialy in the upper Tons basin.

ship? Who knows whether I shall win or lose?" He touched his mother's feet and left. Along the road, he thought that perhaps they had sacrificed the goat because Duryodhana was such a sinner.

It took Arjuna months to reach there. He found the tree. It was a huge tree, filled with huge ghosts, and he couldn't see how or where it was hollow. He took his mother's name, and then he took the name of Bhimsen, who kills thousands of men with his right hand and thousands of men with his left. Arjuna thought, "Bhimsen could hurl this tree if he wished. But why is he such a strong man? It is because of Mother's *sat*."

He took out an arrow, called on Mother Kunti, and fired it. "If I am your true son, then the door will open. My horse must also go inside!" He fired his arrow, and the door opened. The tree said, "Arjuna, come inside my belly," so Arjuna went inside with his horse and the door closed behind. He tethered his horse, sat down on his shawl, and the first watch began, and then the second, and then the third. There were faint noises outside. During the fourth watch, a strong wind began to blow. The tree began to shake, and the wind howled in Arjuna's ear. The wind was so strong that he feared the tree might fall and break, that he would die inside and not be able to fight the Great War [*mahābhārata*]. "I'm stuck in here," he thought, "and I can't even fire my arrows." He was really frightened, so that his whole body shook. But he remembered his mother, who had told him to listen to everything, and he thought, "Why am I so frightened? Even if I die, it's all right, because I am following Mother Kunti's orders. I'll just remember my mother's orders." The sixty-four yoginis began to arrive, and Arjuna could hear the flapping of their wings. One after another they came, in the shape of vultures. They came in by the thousands and took their respective places, according to rank, on twigs and branches. Some were like Chandi, some had skulls, some were bloody, some were like mothers or sisters, some ate the living, some ate the dead. The eldest was an old mother, and she sat at the best place. She was of a high caste, religious and learned and well-spoken. She said, "The war [*bhārat*] is about to commence. You are all gathered together here: now tell me who should lose and who should win."

One hag,[32] who was also known as Kali, stood up and said, "Let the Pandavas lose and the Kauravas win!" A second hag fought with the first one: "How can you say such things?"

With their beaks they fought their way down to the base of the tree, biting and striking each other. The second hag returned and said, "Hey, elder sisters! What nonsense this is! How can we be satisifed by

32. The word for hag, *pañcālī*, is very interesting. It means "bird" (Hindi *pakṣī*) or "hag" and can refer to any or all of these sixty-four birdlike yoginis, but it especially indicates the bird that speaks second in the story. Pāñcālī, "daughter of the Pāñcāla king," is one of Draupadi's names.

the blood of only five brothers? If the sixty Kauravas die, then all our stomachs will be filled. So, my mothers, arrange the Pandavas' victory and the Kauravas' defeat!"

The old lady said, "You are all my own children. To you of such eloquent speech I say, "Well done! You are worthy of being an adviser. It was useless to give birth to the rest of you. You are the real hag adviser. I've called all of you "hags" until now, but from now on you are the real hag. And when we take birth as humans, you will be my daughter-in-law. If we had eaten only the five brothers, we would have been hungry, but now we will eat the sixty Kauravas, and our stomachs will be filled!

The old yogini certified that the Pandavas would win the war and that the Kauravas would lose. All the witches agreed and were happy. And the morning broke, my brother-in-law.[33] Day came, and the witches flew away. Arjuna was peeping through a hole in the tree; he didn't wish to be seen. When he came, he had split the tree with his arrow, but how could he now emerge, the three-eyed one? He took Mother Kunti's name. "I was happy with what you've said, I've done as you instructed, now I can escape only by taking your name. Otherwise, I can't." In no time the tree opened, and the three-eyed Arjuna emerged. Over and over he said, "Well done! Hooray for your honor and your dharma, your dharma which makes for such a drama!" The tree slowly opened, and Arjuna emerged along with his horse. He rode all the long way back to Jayantapuri, went straight to his mother, and touched his head to her feet, that three-eyed one, and said, "The stars in the sky and the stones on the earth" [are few, compared to the greatness of your name].[34] He fell at her feet and said, "I've seen the whole world, but nothing is greater than your dharma. There was an old mother sitting there among the yoginis who was like you. She was just like you!"

Mother Kunti said, "Tell me quickly, what did the yoginis say?" and Arjuna replied, "Listen, my mother, I think that this whole affair is your doing! You are the taker, you are the eater, you are the one who has done this Kurukshetra. I already told you, there was an old woman there just like you. Why are you asking me? You already know! You are both of female caste—I think it was you! Even the casting of the dice that you arranged was matched by what they said there: first we were to lose and the Kauravas were to win, but later the Kauravas were to lose and we were to win. You made me lose the first throw, and you made the Kauravas lose the second one! You also made Dronacarya lose.[35]

33. *bhenā*, (Hindi *jījā*, elder sister's husband), who was present during the performance.

34. *Ākāś kī tārī, pātāl kī gārī.*

35. Here Arjuna is speaking of the final decision of the yoginis. The name used for Dronacarya is *rathacūlya dev*.

Mother Kunti said, "I don't know anything about that, but I can tell by your face that you are happy with the news. So if you're happy then you must write a letter saying you are ready for war.

In this story, differences between Draupadi and Kunti are effaced. They have kept their true identities secret from the Pandavas, who innocently regard them as wife and mother. But in reality both of them are dangerous, bloodthirsty hags, jointly responsible for the carnage of the *Mahābhārata* war. No doubt this "truth" can be accounted for in terms of male projections according to which all women are by nature bloodthirsty. After all, as Arjuna himself says, both Kunti and the elder hag are "of the female caste" (*jāt*)! But even if it is true that this vision of Kunti owes much to male imaginings, it is also true that something more is going on.

In fact, the elder and younger hags in this story are not evil; rather, they are the protectors of the Pandavas, who ensure that the worst carnage of the war will be suffered by their sons' and husbands' enemies. The whole thrust of the story is to show that, through the intercession of these two females, the Pandavas managed to escape their fated death. Indeed, this is the leitmotif throughout all the songs and stories presented in this chapter: Draupadi is seen as the incarnation, in Kaliyug, of the goddess who appeared in earlier ages as Parvati and Sita, both faithful consorts; when Bhimsen sees her in the form of Chandika near the river, she explains that she was "born to protect" the Pandavas; many stories tell how Kunti drew upon her *sat* to feed and protect the five Pandavas during their exile. Ultimately, the Pandavas owe their victory in the great war to these two women, and in this respect Draupadi and Kali are not unlike the innumerable fierce (*ugra*) goddesses who have served as protectors of Hindu kings throughout Indian history.[36]

The point I wish to stress is that by protecting their menfolk, Draupadi and Kunti safeguard their caste honor, an exaggerated concern for which is typical of Kshatriyas, both male and female. Seen from this perspective, the bloodthirsty goddesses are not so extreme as they might at first appear; instead, they can be seen to embody conventional values. Kali/Draupadi and Kunti, like the women who play their parts, are good Kshatriya women. This explains much about what happened during the sacrifice to Draupadi of the goat kid. The problems and mistaken identifications, the ritual faux pas, and the persistence of the "real" Kali and her supporters all related to questions of family honor. She was determined to do the right thing and thus to safeguard her own honor and that of her family. To understand why she engaged in such a bloody ritual, we need neither probe the depths of her psyche nor speculate about the "reality" of the possessing goddess. We need only realize that in the ritual context, she was motivated chiefly by a concern to safeguard her honor and prestige, as these were defined relative to a certain social structure and set of ritual practices.

36. See Schnepel 1995, 1997 for fruitful discussions of this issue.

The problem with the debate over split goddesses is that it is all too often represented as a choice between competing essentialisms. A contradiction arises when it is claimed that the "essence" of the goddess (and, by extension, women) is at the same time "fierce" (*ugra*) and "peaceful" (*śānta*). Here is where a perspectival approach can help: goddesses (and women, too) are sometimes fierce and sometimes peaceful, depending on the goddess's actions and the perspective of the worshiper. Women (and goddesses, too) are sometimes fierce and sometimes peaceful, sometimes angry and sometimes benign.[37] The selves of women, like the selves of men, are not frozen essences: they shift and change according to context. And as we shall see in the next chapter, the same is true of the gods as well.

37. See Bacchetta 1993, 48, along with the other excellent articles in this special issue.

6

A Divine King in the Western Himalayas

In an isolated valley near the headwaters of the Tons River in Uttar Pradesh, Karna from the *Mahābhārata* story rules as a divine king.[1] The local people regard him as their ruler and call him "King Karna" (*rājā karaṇ*). He is served as both a king and a god by the local castes, which are defined in terms of their various relationships to him as priests, ministers, patrons, soldiers, and servants. Like a Hindu king, he jealously (and sometimes violently) protects his territory from incursion by rival, neighboring divine kings. Important local decisions are made in Karna's temple compound by a council of elders and must be ratified by his oracle. He has the power to appoint and dismiss officers, confiscate property, and levy fines. He hears civil and sometimes criminal cases and then, through his oracle, enforces his judgment, usually by compelling disputants to reach a compromise.

Karna is not only a divine king but also a renouncer. When he possesses his oracle to settle disputes and dispense blessings, he appears not as a wealthy and powerful sovereign but rather as a poor, ash-smeared renouncer. His folk songs call him a "yogi," and he is famous for his poverty and detachment, the paradigmatic qualities of a renouncer. But that is not all: in certain respects, Karna is also a Brahman. Not only must the oracle whose body he regularly possesses be a Brahman, but many of his directives and policies are clearly oriented toward promoting various kinds of Brahmanical reform.

This presents us with a set of puzzles. The first has to do with the sheer implausibility of worshiping such a figure. Throughout India, Karna is regarded as a tragic figure, strongly associated with inauspiciousness and defeat. In most parts of Garhwal, the devout will not even open the Sanskrit

1. Parts of this chapter appeared previously in the *Journal of Indian Philosophy* 28(3):295–324 (2000).

Mahābhārata's "Book of Karna" without first sacrificing a goat, for fear that calamity will strike. How is it, then, that the people of the upper Tons basin worship him as a divine king? This puzzle is made even more intriguing by the fact that an adjacent region higher up in the valley is similarly ruled by Duryodhana, regarded by many Hindus as the very embodiment of evil. Why would anyone worship such beings? I will address this question in the final chapter of the book.

A second puzzle has to do with oracular possession, which is common in the western Himalayas. Some readers may be disturbed by the fact that I write about Karna as an authentic agent who speaks and acts much as a human being does. Such readers might not object were I to describe him as a "fictive" person, a collective representation, or a "symbol" of something else; however, the idea of attributing agency to him is bound to evoke resistance in some quarters. One might even speak of a "gulf" between the understandings of local actors, on the one hand, and the conventional analytical frameworks of Western intellectuals, on the other. As an anthropologist, I am thus presented with a problem. I have known the people about whom I write for years, and some of them are among my dearest friends. How can I write about their culture and religion, according to which the presence of this divine king in their midst is a self-evident fact, without making them appear backward and superstitious to my readers? How can I analyze the way in which they construct a world of meaning and significance—a world in which embodied deities are part of the fabric of daily life—without dismissing their understandings as mystified or deluded?

One way to address the problem is suggested by Ronald Inden's notion of "complex agency." Inden's overall goal is to "restore" agency to Indian actors,[2] while at the same time developing a theory that can account for more complex, collective agents: familes, councils, sects, and, above all, polities (1990, 23–26).[3] He relies on historical evidence to describe the processes through which the complex agency of early medieval Indian polities and their constituent groups was articulated. In so doing, he explicitly confronts the problem of treating deities as agents:

> But I will also be dealing with some agents, to wit, the gods Vishnu and Siva (3.4.1), whom some might wish to dismiss as agents. I am going to assume, however, that such agents, whose very existence may

2. Of course, Indian actors never really lost their agency. Inden's goal is actually to inculcate an awareness of the agency of Indians among historians, social scientists, Indologists, and other students of Indian civilization.

3. Inden's project contrasts with mainstream anthropological analyses of kingship, both divine and secular, which subordinate human agency to a reified superagent called "society." Such a view is exemplified by Evans-Pritchard's classically Durkheimian analysis of divine kingship among the Shilluk: "In my view kingship everywhere and at all times has been in some degree a sacred office. *Rex est mixta persona cum sacerdote*. This is because a king symbolizes a whole society and must not be identified with any part of it. . . . It is the kingship and not the king who is divine" (Evans-Pritchard 1948, 36).

> be contested, may in a sense be real. The persons and institutions of a community may indeed attribute a great deal of or even a determining power to a god or gods, ancestors, ghosts, to the state, to reason, to law, to the market, to society, to the party, to the crown, to the people. We may take such agents to be real to the extent that complexes of discursive and nondiscursive practices constitute and perpetuate them, even if some would deny their reality. Indeed, some of the most important quarrels in history have been about such larger-than-life agents. (1990, 27)

The notion of complex agency should not cause any alarm. It is rather similar to Foucault's notion of intentionality without a subject, strategy without a strategist (see Good 1994, 69). As the philosopher Tuomela (1995) has shown, such an idea is consistent with a theory of social action that is both realist and individualist.[4] Tuomela himself, who has elaborated the idea of "group intentions" at great length, is a strict individualist; for him, groups have no ontological status beyond the sum total of their individual members. Another philosopher, John Searle, also insists that some notion of complex agency is required for a realist theory of culture and society, and once again this is hardly a mystical endeavor, as Searle is a self-described materialist. His aim

> is to assimilate social reality to our basic ontology of physics, chemistry, and biology. To do this we need to show the continuous line that goes from molecules and mountains to screwdrivers, levers, and beautiful sunsets, and then to legislatures, money, and nation-states. The central span on the bridge from physics to society is collective intentionality, and the decisive movement on that bridge in the creation of social reality is the collective intentional imposition of function on entities that cannot perform those functions without that imposition. (1995, 41)

Searle, too, is interested in describing how human beings create worlds of meaning and significance and navigate through them, and he finds that such processes cannot be coherently or convincingly described without recourse to a theory of collective intentions. It is perhaps worth noting that,

4. Tuomela maintains that intentions can realistically be attributed to groups. "However, it should be emphasized that neither the notion of group-intention nor the notion of group intention (viz., an intention ascribed to a social group) will on my analysis ontically involve more than social psychological attitudes ascribed to agents, singly or jointly" (1995, 113). Joint intentions "centrally figure in agents' social practical reasonings: They pose new problems and restrict available action alternatives; they serve to initiate and guide joint action and thereby effect coordination; and, as commitments to action, they have a normative impact on the agents' thinking and acting" (114). Also noteworthy is Tuomela's discussion of an "authority system," in which he shows how individual wills are transferred to the group will for collective disposal (174).

according to Searle, people who participate in collective institutions need not realize what they are doing. Indeed, they may have a false theory about the derivation of their institutions, and predictably for Searle, the paradigmatically false theory is the "religious" one (1995, 47–48).[5]

Let me hasten to add that I subscribe neither to Tuomela's methodological individualism nor to Searle's materialism. My point is simply that the idea of complex agency is consistent with—and, according to some, required by—a range of philosophical positions that are neither mystical nor religious. In fact, we have dealings with complex agents all the time. Universities, trade unions, and bridge clubs are all explicitly designed by their constituencies to accomplish collective purposes. If business corporations can be legally defined as "persons" despite the regnant individualism of the business community, then surely we can consider deities as complex agents, despite the personalistic theism of the Hindus! Such an understanding would not be identical to Hindus' religious ideology, but neither would it contradict it. After all, the kings of Garhwal used to appoint local deities as their agents, occasionally devolving administrative and judicial powers to them.[6]

It will be objected that an agent must have consciousness or "mind," and that the gods of Rawain, even if they do somehow enact collective intentions, do not count, since they are nonempirical beings. Such a refusal to take seriously the ontologies of non-European cultures is precisely the sort of arrogance that anthropology is designed to resist. Beyond that, one could argue that the attribution of consciousness to the gods of Rawain is entirely consistent with certain recent developments in cognitive science and the philosophy of mind, particularly those associated with the work of Daniel Dennett. Dennett is opposed to what he regards as the destructive influence of the Cartesian mind-body dualism. "Its central mistake," he writes, "is in supposing that the work of consciousness is a distinct sort of work, different from the work done by the merely unconscious information-processing modules in the brain; work done by a distinct faculty, a salient 'add-on' that might in principle be 'subtracted,' leaving a cognitively competent but entirely unconscious zombie" (1995, 8; cf. 1991).

In other words, consciousness exists, but it is not localized; it cannot be found in the pituitary gland or anywhere else. In Dennett's words, consciousness has no specific Medium. Rather, it is distributive, which I take to be Dennett's central point. Without involving myself in a discussion of the subtle differences between "agency," "mind," and "self," I would simply like to suggest that a complex agent such as Karna exhibits a form of con-

5. For more on collective intentionality, see Bratman 1992; Gilbert 1989; Tuomela and Miller 1988.

6. One of the last kings of Garhwal delegated the settlement of particularly difficult local disputes to the demon-cum-deity Pokkhu (Ravat 1991, 15), whose temple is very close to Karna's, who shares the same *vazīr* (chief minister) and is often identified with Karna's "bodyguard" Shalya (see later discussion).

sciousness that is not radically dissimilar to human forms of consciousness with which we are more familiar. One difference would be that a complex agent's consciousness exists at a higher level of integration. If human consciousness is the articulation of a vast number of "information-processing modules in the brain," then the consciousness of the complex agent would consist in the articulation of the consciousnesses of a number of human agents. We even evaluate both kinds of agency in similar ways: by asking questions, gauging intentions, and then analyzing the degree to which the two match up. The god's anwers to my questions may sometimes be unclear, I may not always be able accurately to gauge his intentions, and there might seem to be endless opportunities for dissimulation and deceit. But this situation is in principle no different from the situation I encounter in attempting to evaluate the consciousness of another human being.

In earlier chapters, I attempted to show that the empirical "selves" of Garhwalis are multiple and to illustrate how these multiple selves are articulated and realized in *pāṇḍav līlā*. In other words, even those human beings whom we recognize as paradigmatic agents are not simple persons but rather complex entities. Once again, this idea is neither radical nor particularly postmodern. I myself am composed of numerous entities, and I experience myself (and am experienced by others) variously as son, brother, father, husband, lover, friend, teacher, rival, and so on. As Inden (following Collingwood) puts it, "[P]ersons as agents are themselves composed of entities that *overlap*," and therefore "[a]gents compounded of more than one person are no more to be seen as inherently unified than are persons themselves" (1990, 24–25, 26; emphasis in original). One advantage to this way of construing social agents is that it obviates the perennial argument among social scientists over whether society is to be seen as a collective entity or as a set of individuals. If, following Inden, we apply Collingwood's "scale of forms" to, say, particular human agents and complex divine agents, we will see that the difference between individuals and collectivities is one of degree and not of kind. In other words, the selves of both humans and deities are multiple. I suggest that the regional gods of the western Himalayas can also be fruitfully analyzed as complex agents, and I hope one day to analyze the processes through which they are so constituted, and their constituents' collective intentions are defined, pursued, contested, and sometimes thwarted.[7]

7. It should be noted that my argument has little in common with Gell's provocative discussion of art and agency. He asserts that "the whole interpretative enterprise is founded on the strict separation between 'agency'—exercised by sentient, enculturated, human beings—and the kind of physical causation which explains the behaviour of mere things." But because he can therefore not accommodate collective agency within his model, he is compelled to make a distinction between the primary agency of sentient human beings and the secondary agency of his real object of analysis: artifacts, including idols and works of art, through which primary agents exercise their agency (1998, 19–20). In fact, Gell does not

In this chapter, I will confine myself to a third puzzle, one that is perhaps of greater relevance to students of South Asia. This puzzle relates to my assertion that Karna is simultaneously king, Brahman, and renouncer, the three most prominent figures in learned discussions of Indic civilization.

King, Brahman, and Renouncer

In chapter 4, I summarized the ongoing debate regarding the relationship between king and Brahman, what Trautmann (1981) calls "the central conundrum of Indian social ideology." On one side are Dumont and his supporters, who claim that Indian social reality and especially caste are fundamentally a matter of values, which find their apotheosis in the Brahman. On the other side of the debate are Dumont's critics, who argue that he has paid insufficient attention to power, and especially to the role of the king in classical Indian civilization. In effect, one side argues that the Brahman is the "key" to Indian civilization, while the other side argues that it is the king who is central.[8] Many, if not most, of the participants in this discussion assume that king and Brahman are mutually exclusive roles, but in this chapter I wish to call that assumption into question with the counterexample of Karna, who is both at once.

The situation is complicated by the fact that Karna is also a "yogi," and this leads us to the third leading candidate for "master symbol" of Hindu culture, the renouncer, who has also been characterized as pivotal in the development of Hindu civilization (e.g., Dumont 1960). The Indologist Jan Heesterman argues that over the centuries, there was a pervasive shift in Hinduism toward the value of renunciation, especially among Brahmans. It is not that renouncers replace Brahmans; rather, Brahmanhood culminates in renunciation. As Heesterman puts it, "(t)he ideal Brahman is the renouncer" (1985, 43) because only by renunciation can he be completely emancipated from his onerous social and ritual obligations. Over many centuries, the "preclassical" warrior's sacrifice was transformed into the renouncer's ritual, thoroughly rational and rationalized but divorced from the world. Indeed, according to Heesterman, India's uniqueness lies in the

---

mean "agency" in any strong sense, but simply the human habit of attributing agency (by which he seems to mean something rather close to "intention") to inanimate objects, such as cars and art objects. He refers to this as "the kind of second-class agency which artefacts acquire once they become enmeshed in a texture of social relationships" (1998, 17).

8. Although the householder is also crucial to the ideological structure of Indic civilization (see, e.g., Madan's 1965 work on Kashmiri householders, and his 1987 discussion of "non-renunciation as a value"), it is also widely recognized that the king is the paradigmatic householder, in effect "encompassing" the householder within his royal function.

fact that its highest value is renunciatory and therefore asocial (1985, chaps. 2, 10, 12).[9]

The differences among Heesterman, Dumont, and his critics are not simply about whether king, Brahman, or renouncer is paramount in Hindu civilization. At a deeper level, they have to do with the relationship of values to power, and the question of whether Hindu civilization's structuring principles are religious, political, or some combination of the two. For Heesterman, the religious value of renunciation is primary, providing an apolitical ideology that orients the entire system.[10] For Dumont as well, religious values are paramount, though the system must come to terms with political power, which it "encompasses." For Dirks, by contrast, the system is more transparently structured by political economic considerations: the dominant ideology accommodates itself to power, rather than the other way around. Raheja notes that Dumont and Heesterman concur in postulating an "absolute distinction between religious values and secular power" (1988a, 503),[11] a distinction that she herself, along with Shulman (1985) and others, seeks to undermine. And upon closer reading, even Dirks's apparent reification of the distinction fades.[12]

But despite their differences, all the theorists mentioned have this in common: that in advancing their arguments, they focus on a single figure who either epitomizes the entire system or is its pivotal figure. For Dumont's purity/pollution theory, that pivotal figure is the Brahman; for Heesterman's Indological theory, it is the renouncer; and for the historian Dirks, it is the king. But why should a single figure be a metonym of the entire system? Ancient India, no less than medieval and modern India, was composed of diverse communities, languages, customs, interests, and agendas.[13] Why should a single one of the trio of Brahman, king, and renouncer be privi-

9. Heesterman's order is inherently and in principle unstable. The king cannot rule without occasional (ritual) recourse to the transcendent authority of the Brahman, but that authority is divorced from the world (cf. Bloch 1987). To the extent that the Brahman is co-opted by the king, he loses his religious power and authority. The solution to this is the division of powers between Brahman and Kshatriya (Heesterman 1986).

10. However, if we equate 'religion' with 'dharma', then we should not qualify reununciation as "religious." Rather, we have the parallel series politics:religion:renunciation :: *artha*:*dharma*:*mokṣa*.

11. This focus on values and ideology is in marked contrast to early anthropological studies of divine kingship, which did not take beliefs very seriously (Feeley-Harnik 1985, 280–81). Interestingly, Feeley-Harnik's learned and informative essay has very little to say about Hindu kingship. This is puzzling, since, although her focus is admittedly on Africa, she does discuss Southeast Asian kingship at some length.

12. As Dirks puts it in a footnote, "Ritual and political forms were fundamentally the same. However, I must stress the political both to redress the previous emphasis on 'religion' and to underscore the social fact that caste structure, ritual form, and political process were all dependent on relations of power" (1987, 4–5).

13. Cf. Heesterman's assumption that the texts ought to provide a "consistent theory" of kingship (1985, chap. 8), and his evident frustration that in fact there is no single, consistent, indigenous theory.

leged over the other two as constituting a master trope for understanding Hindu civilization?

We should not forget that in India at all times, as elsewhere, there were and are many perspectives, each operating in complex fashion with the others.[14] This was recognized by Das (1977), who argued that the "conceptual order of Hinduism" could be grasped through an analysis of the relations among these three categories; and also by Burghart, who showed that kings, Brahmans, and renouncers have distinctive ways of achieving and evaluating power and prestige, so that the "brahman claimed his superiority according to the hierarchy of the sacrificial body of Brahma; the ascetic claimed his superiority according to the hierarchy of the cycle of confused wandering; and the Hindu king claimed his superiority in terms of a tenurial hierarchy which was derived from his lordship over the land" (1978, 520–21).

Both Das and Burghart rightly emphasize the polyphonic character of Hindu civilization: Das stresses the relations among kings, Brahmans, and renouncers, and Burghart gives "equal time" to all three. Nevertheless, both writers assume, along with Dumont, Heesterman, and Dirks, that the roles are mutually exclusive. Just as Heesterman and Dumont see an opposition between Brahman and king, "sacred" and "secular," so Burghart adds a third oppositional term (the renouncer) but does not consider how the three might be compatible with each other. For Das, the Brahman mediates between antithetically opposed renouncer and king.

In what follows, I will draw upon ethnographic evidence of the coexistence these three roles in the "same" person to argue that they are not mutually exclusive.[15] My evidence derives from the cult of Karna, a deity who rules as a divine king in a remote part of the western Himalayas but is also regarded as a Brahman and a renouncer. Karna simultaneously embodies all three roles, and he does so unproblematically, because they are not mutually exclusive essences but rather relational strategies, transient forms determined by action (cf. Sax 1993, 2000b). In other words, the form of the deity depends on the strategic imperatives of the situation, which may be political, economic, ideological, or some combination of the three.

In Karna's Realm

The people of Singtur *paṭṭī* near the upper reaches of the Tons River regard Karna as their divine king. They call him King Karna (*rājā karaṇ*),

14. In my view, the only theorist to do justice to this complexity is Marriott (1976, 1990), who has attempted to characterize South Asian culture at the maximum level of abstraction, in terms of the fluid variables he calls "mixing," "marking," and "matching."

15. Bruce Lincoln, following a Dumezilian line of argument, argues that the coronation ceremonies for Indo-European kings "had as their chief goal the creation of a new social identity for the future king, not as a warrior but as one who integrated within himself the essence of all three classes" (1991, 4). I am indebted to Claus-Peter Zoller for this reference.

and the geographic as well as the social organization of Singtur are predicated upon his kingship. In the *Mahābhārata* story, Karna mediated between the opposing sides because he was at one and the same time the unrecognized brother of the Pandavas and the faithful ally of the Kauravas. Likewise, Singtur is divided into two subregions, respectively associated with the Pandavas and the Kauravas, and once again Karna mediates between them because his temple is located in the geographic and ideological center of the district. The Pandavas dwell in the lower (downstream) half of Singtur, while the Kauravas live in the higher and wilder regions.[16] Each of these subdistricts is again divided in two, and King Karna's temple is located where all four land divisions come together, in the village of Dyora in the "Middle Land" (*mājī thok*) (figure 5).

Local social structure is constituted by actions at Karna's temple at the center of the realm. The local caste system is relatively simple. It consists of Brahmans; two castes of Rajputs or Kshatriyas (aristocratic Rawats and *khūnd* warriors); the Naths, also known as carpenters (*mistarī*); Das musicians and genealogists; and the lowest caste of Kohlis. Distinctions between and among these castes are expressed in daily rituals centered on the divine king. Every day, his Brahman priest worships Karna, who is embodied in a metal image inside his temple. The priest must be a Nautiyal, that is, a member of the highest local Brahman subcaste, and must reside near the temple. Very few of these priests live outside the village because the god will not allow them to do so, and many stories are told of the disasters that befell those who defied his orders by accepting employment elsewhere. The office of chief minister, or *vazīr*,[17] is hereditary and is associated with the aristocratic Rawat caste of Rajputs. The clarified butter required for Karna's daily worship is provided by a Rajput patron, normally from one of the lower-ranked subcastes, who are also known as "warriors" (*khūnd*). The temple fire is tended by a Nath, who is also the god's messenger. The musician caste (*dās*) provides drummers who play thrice daily for the god. Members of the lowest caste (*kohlī*) are excluded from this daily routine, except when they are required to provide wood for special offerings by their Rajput masters. Thus, distinctions among the castes find concrete expression in the daily rituals for King Karna, while still finer distinctions occur during periodic festivals. In these ways, Karna is (at least partly) constituted as king by the actions of his subjects.

In addition to Karna, there are several other deities inside the temple, including Shalya, Karna's charioteer from the *Mahābhārata* story, and two goddesses, one of whom, known as Renuka, or "the Maiden of Nagarkot," was brought from nearby Nanai village at some time in the past. Karna's

16. The Pandavas are called *pāṃsyā*, while the local name for the Kauravas is *ṣāṭhī* (sixty, Skt. *ṣaṣṭi*); the Kauravas are locally believed to have been 60 in number, not 100. The *paṭṭīs* of Panchgain and Adaur, adjacent to but higher than Singtur, are ruled by Duryodhana (see chapter 7 and Sax 1999).

17. This Perso-Arabic term is used by cults throughout the region.

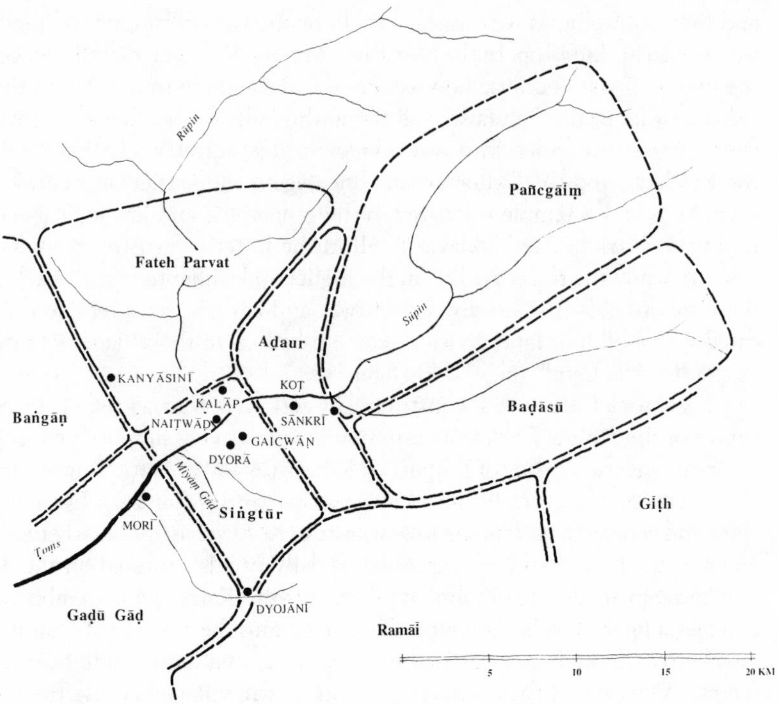

Figure 5. Schematic map of the Upper Tons River basin. Drawing prepared by Niels Gutschow.

Brahman oracle (see later discussion) compared this system to the sun circled by nine planets; when I asked why the goddess had come from Nanai, he answered that Karna had "established his kingdom here and brought other local gods under his sway." This type of sociospatial organization parallels the "central-peripheral, 'royal' models of intercaste relationships" that Raheja (1988b) finds to be of such importance in Pahansu, and that Marriott (1976) has claimed are typical of Kshatriya transactional strategies.[18] The presence of the goddess Renuka inside Karna's temple, and of a temple dedicated to his son Vikhāsan/Visāsan/Vikarṇa in a nearby valley, confirms that Karna is also a householder, but this aspect of his person seems to be encompassed by the kingly function, and I have not treated it separately.

Karna's actions are most kinglike with respect to territory. This is a characteristic that he shares with other nearby deities, who also rule as divine kings. Concern for territory is a fundamental aspect of Hindu kingship (Lingat 1973, 212) and is exemplified by the real and legendary history of this region, which is punctuated by numerous confrontations,

18. It is also reminiscent of Gesick's (1983) summary of the distinctive features of Southeast Asian kingship.

skirmishes, and outright battles between competing gods. Typically, these occur when a deity's image is taken in a palanquin by his followers, who attempt to penetrate the border of a rival deity. It should be noted that palanquin journeys of gods and goddesses, usually accompanied by a procession of their followers, are very common in the central Himalayas—so common, in fact, that they are locally regarded as an icon of Garhwali culture (see chapter 2). These journeys are variously conceptualized: for example, as visits between siblings[19] and surreptitious rendezvous between lovers.[20] However, they are most often understood as somehow defining royal territory, either by the journeys of subordinate deities to pay obeisance to a divine sovereign,[21] or as processions by a ruling deity or his representative through his territory.[22] The latter type is well illustrated by the following two accounts, one legendary, and another based on recent local events.

The legendary account is based on a local folk song. It concerns a contest between King Karna and his demonic rival, the god Mahasu. The song is performed during Karna's festivals and is well known, being a variant or parallel version of a similar song, performed by Mahasu's musicians, in which Mahasu is the protagonist and Karna his rival.[23] There are in fact four Mahasu brothers, one of whom resides permanently at the cult center in Hanol on the banks of the Tons, while the other three perpetually circulate in the region to the west of Karna's realm.[24] According to the song, it was one of these three itinerant gods, Chalda (whose name comes from the root "to move"), who attempted to take over Dyojani, "the eastern border" of Karna's realm. The following is a translation of a version that was narrated to me by an eminent local musician, Bhuli Das of Dyora village:

> Chalda Mahasu left his headquarters with great fanfare, covered with silver, gold, and diamonds: after all, he was a king. On his first night in Karna's realm, he stayed in the midst of four neighboring villages, but those four villages didn't even have enough coals to fill the hookahs of his huge entourage, to say nothing of feeding them![25]
>
> . . . On the fourth day Chalda Mahasu reached Dyojani, and once again the people of that place wondered how they could possibly

19. Raha 1979; Sax 1991a, chap. 3; Sutherland 1988.

20. I have attended three separate Garhwali festivals (*melā*), all of which occurred on or near the spring festival of Baisakhi, where the focal event was a meeting between male and female deities (or deified humans) conceptualized as illicit lovers. These were in Gair Sain, Kulsari, and Duni villages.

21. The best-known examples in Himachal Pradesh are the fairs of the god Madhoraoji in Mandi on Shivaratri, and of Raghunathji in Kulu on Dassehra.

22. Ibbetson and Maclagan 1919; Sax 1991a, chap. 5; 2000a; Sutherland 1998.

23. Claus-Peter Zoller, personal communication.

24. For more on Mahasu, see Ibbetson and Maclagan 1919; Sutherland 1988.

25. When one of the Mahasu brothers arrives in a village, the residents must provide for his worship, feed his entourage, and grant their numerous requests, under penalty of divine sanction.

entertain the thousands of people in his entourage. But somehow or other they did: some gathered wood, some collected cloth, others cooked food, and in order to defeat Mahasu they managed to gather all the necessary things. Now there was a Rajput named Bagadu Audyan from the village of Aur in Dyojani, and he thought to himself, "We can put up with this for a year. But what about next year, and the next? Who can take up such a heavy load? I must go and seek the help of King Karna. He'll get rid of this god." So in the middle of the night he filled his sheep pack with gold and left for Karna's temple in Dyora. And when he reached the temple, he made himself a bed of stinging nettles and a pillow of thorns.[26] And he said, "Suryavanshi,[27] we are being troubled by a god who takes four days to reach Dyojani. But you can arise and reach there in time to take your meal! Shall I be the subject of a god who takes four days to reach my village, or of one who reaches there in time to take his meal?"

King Karna went to confront Chalda. He took Shalya with him, along with Lapaura from Gaichwan village as his minister of speech, Jati Surau as his highborn minister, Dadan and Daragan as his fighters, and the Sunchyans as his wealthy patrons. He took Daurpati Dauraim, the people from Adaur. He took Thani Harcan as his priest, the Dangauda priests with the reversed caps, and Harapatti Haravan, Shalya's greatest champion, from the village of Kanyasini.

Chalda Mahasu was waiting in a field outside Dyojani, because unless and until he took control of the area, he couldn't be seated in a house. But King Karna went straight to the house of one of his subjects, who attended him. Now Chalda Mahasu had eighteen two-headed drums of pure silver, in addition to his other instruments. When they played, how the ground shook! But King Karna didn't have any instruments, only a small, single-headed drum called a *ḍhāk* and a gong. Now the *ḍhāk* makes a special sound: "*vhoo-vhoo*." And Mahasu said, "Who is this *vhoo-vhoo* person?" The people told him it was King Karna. So Mahasu said, "OK, the ritual of worship will decide the case; no shame in winning or losing."[28] And King Karna said the same to him: "The ritual of worship will decide the case; no winner or loser. I am a king. You, too, are a king. Let's just see who is greatest, no shame in winning or losing."

Those eighteen silver drums used to play in the evening for that four-horned king. And when Karna's bodyguard Shalya heard all this noise, he was furious: "Wow—what a lot of noise!" So he said, "O my guru, I don't care what you tell me to do, I am ready to fight and to

26. Karna's petitioners flagellate themselves with stinging nettles in order to attract his attention and sympathy (see later discussion).

27. *sūryavaṃśī*, literally "(he) who is of the solar lineage," a typical royal epithet, and one appropriate for Karna, the son of the sun.

28. *pañc pūjya karolo kāj, hārī jīti na lāj.*

die for you. If you tell me to die for you, I will. Please give me permission to fight."

And King Karna said, "I gave my word: no winner, no loser. He is a king, and I am also a king. . . . But you know, those drums really bother me. I am a yogi: they disturb my meditation. So if you want to do something, you have my permission to take care of those drums." After getting the order, Shalya left Dyojani and went to Mana, which is now known as Mori. After that he went along the river, straight to where the ghosts and ghouls live in Naitwar. It is a cremation ground, and our elders say that the ghosts are Shiva's devotees. So Shalya collected a lot of Shiva's followers there: some were tall and some were short, some had one eye and some had three, some had three heads, some had four hands. He put nine ghosts in an iron basket, and then he collected the ghosts of nine boys who had died in childhood, and put them in the basket, and returned to Dyojani. He reached there at sunrise, and he placed the eighteen ghosts in Chalda Mahasu's eighteen drums, and returned to his lion-skin seat. When Mahasu's priests went to the drums, they couldn't even lift them because the demons were in them, and they were too heavy. When Chalda Mahasu found out about this, he said to Karna, "Have you bewitched my drums? What kind of a black magician god are you?" And Karna said to him, "The ritual of worship will decide the case; no winner or loser. I am a king. You, too, are a king. Let's just see who is greatest; no shame in winning or losing. Just as you said, we'll do it on the basis of worship. And neither will be embarrassed if the other wins."

Thus King Karna silenced Chalda's instruments. And that morning he called together all his subjects from Singtur, and said, "Look, I'd fight him, but with what can I fight? I have only small instruments." What were they to do? How could they manage to make a two-headed drum in such a short time? So all the men took off their copper thumbrings, and they gathered them up and took them to a coppersmith in Uttarkashi, and they made a drum slightly larger than a *ḍhauṃs* but smaller than a *ḍhol*. And because it was made in the time of Bagadu Audyan, it was named "Bagadu's Call" [*bagaḍū kī dhād*]. After they named it, they gave it to the musicians, who began to play. Now this was the month of *jeṭh*, and the women were harvesting the wheat. All the women in the field began dancing, with their scythes in one hand and their sheaths of wheat in the other. And the bundles of wheat that they had tied began dancing in the fields behind them. Chalda Mahasu said, "Hey King Karna, you're some kind of magician! It's one thing to make the women dance, but even the bundles of wheat are dancing!" And King Karna said, "Look, you're a king, and I'm a king. You show your power, and I'll show mine. There's no shame in winning or losing."

When Chalda Mahasu saw that he was losing the contest, he said, "All right, let's make one final wager: whoever has the most gold will rule Dyojani." Now king Karna doesn't have any gold: he's carefree [*phakkaḍ*]. But Chalda Mahasu had so much gold that he spread a blanket on the ground and winnowed gold, right in front of King Karna. Now Karna was in trouble! Where was he to get so much gold?

So King Karna commanded two of his warriors—one from Dargan village and the other from Pasa—to take two great skins, go to the riverbank just below Mori, and bring back both of them filled with sand. They said to themselves, "King Karna is a yogi; he puts ash on himself when he possesses his oracle. Who knows what he's planning?" They were embarrassed to do such a silly thing, you see: to carry two bags filled with sand up the steep slope. But they went anyway, because the god had commanded them to. They went and filled the bags and brought them back. And then what did King Karna do? He emptied the bags out on to the ground and told them to winnow the sand. And as the sand fluttered to earth, it turned into gold! Then Chalda Mahasu said, "You are quite a magician of a god, who can turn sand into gold! Look, whoever has *real* gold will win this place, and whoever has false gold will have to leave. He won't be worshiped here." So they took equal amounts of the gold to the goldsmith in Uttarkashi and asked him to test the gold and see whose was real.

When they went there to test it, King Karna demonstrated his power. He did some magic, and his gold was judged to be pure, but Chalda Mahasu's gold came out as black as iron. Four from each side went to Uttarkashi; eight in all. Four of them came back happy, and four came back defeated. And Chalda Mahasa began to retreat. But King Karna said, "I am a king, but he is also a king. Since he's been defeated, I should offer him a little hospitality." So he stopped him and said, "Hey Mahasu, you are also a king, I am also a king. You are upset now because you've been defeated and I have won, but I would like to offer you something before you leave." He did this in the spirit in which one offers a token [*piṭhāīṃ*] to a departing guest. He said, "I will never set foot in Kharsari village. It is yours. The incense for your *jāgar* ritual in Hanol will come from Kharsari. Only the musicians and the priests of Kharsari will stay with me." And, indeed, Mahasu has a storehouse in that village to this very day.

Control over territory is clearly the main issue in this story. And in classical Hindu thought, royal control of territory and of people are mutually entailed. One of the seven elements of the classical Hindu kingdom is "the country" (*janapada*, *rāṣṭra*), and as Dumont (following Bhandarkar) points out in his classic study of kingship, the term "connotes at the same time territory and population" (1962, 73). The song suggests an organic relationship between king and country that is widely found in South Asia and elsewhere but has perhaps been forgotten in the modern West. This is why Karna's subjects object to being ruled by Chalda Mahasu: the problem is not that he is a demon but rather that he lives at a distance of four days rather than half a day. Thus, Karna's follower Bagadu rhetorically asks, "Shall I be the subject of a god who takes four days to reach my village, or of one who reaches there in time to take his meal?" Chalda is an outsider, and so he cannot be "seated" (i.e., his processional icon cannot halt) in the intimate domestic space of a villager's house until he conquers the territory, whereas Karna goes straight to the house of one of his subjects. These details reflect local practices regarding the accommodation of guests at large public festivals. "Foreign" visitors from outside the region are provided public lodging and food, while local guests are housed privately and bring their own food and supplies, or are entitled to a share of their relatives' food (see Ravat 1991). Chalda's strategy was to be acknowledged as sovereign—that is, as a king organically related to his territory and people—by being invited into the home of a local person. However, by publicly feeding Chalda and his entourage and thus defining them as guests, Karna's subjects defined him as an outsider and denied him the kingship. This is an example of how the king is partly constituted by the pragmatic actions of his subjects.

The second example of territorial skirmishing, like the first, has to do with a deity whose territory adjoins that of Karna. Remarkably enough, that deity is Duryodhana, Karna's patron and ally from the *Mahābhārata*.[29] Although Karna and Duryodhana were friends and allies in the epic, in this part of the Himalayas they have been rivals for as long as anyone can remember. Local folklore celebrates the victory of one side or another in their many violent confrontations. The most vividly remembered of these took place in the 1970s in Sankari, a village claimed by both Duryodhana and Karna (figure 5). Sankari is disputed territory, strategically located at the spot where a major road crosses the boundary between their respective "kingdoms." Some people from Sankari had invited Karna to visit them on one of his ritual processions, but Duryodhana's highland followers stopped Karna's palanquin from proceeding. Karna's subjects retaliated by refusing to allow Duryodhana's palanquin to follow his customary route through their territory on one of his periodic processions. There was a standoff lasting several years, until Duryodhana's followers decided they would once again try to pass through Karna's territory. When Karna's subjects heard about this, they took his "bodyguard" Shalya on his own palanquin and tried to prevent Duryodhana and his entourage from proceeding. But they were outnumbered, and after being severely beaten by Duryodhana's followers, they turned and fled down the hillside in disarray, to where a rough bridge had been constructed by the shepherds of Duryodhana's *vazīr*, Sundar Singh. Karna's followers crossed the bridge to the opposite side of the bank, where Sundar Singh's men were grazing his sheep, destroying the bridge behind them. The shepherds' retreat was cut off, and the men from Singtur took dozens of their sheep, slaughtering so many that they fell into the river and

29. The identity of the god in question is controversial. Many of Duryodhana's subjects insist that he is actually Someshvara, a form of Shiva. See chapter 7.

were swept away. They went from village to village in Singtur, happily feeding Sundar Singh's best animals to their friends and relatives.

By now, the human oracles, wooden palanquins, and processional icons of several local gods had congregated at Karna's temple. The musicians began to play victory songs, and there was such a jubilant commotion that, as they say, "even the sheep were dancing." Some time later, Sundar Singh came demanding restitution, and the local leaders in Singtur had to admit that he was entitled to it. He went from village to village, handpicking the very best animals, which were given to him "with respect": two sheep for every one of his that had been stolen. He paid a fine of 1,000 rupees to King Karna for blocking his procession, and it was agreed that in the future, Duryodhana would be allowed to travel to Kanyasini village via Singtur.

Clearly, disputes over control of territory are not limited to folklore. Real confrontations have occurred within living memory over the attempts of one god to penetrate the territory of another, with competing factions composed almost entirely of territorial coresidents.[30] No doubt there are material interests at stake,[31] but the idiom of competition emphasizes above all the honor and prestige of the ruling divinities of these tiny "kingdoms." It provides yet more evidence of the inseparability of religion and politics in traditional Garhwal society.

Disputes between deities are common in this region, and numerous examples could be recounted.[32] For now, I wish to focus on the fact that these deities all figure as divine kings, with sovereign rights over their respective territories and subjects. Their kingship is constituted not only by their actions with respect to territory but also by other actions. For example, the first court of appeal for many local disputes is king Karna's temple. I witnessed one such adjudication during my second visit to Karna's temple town of Dyora, in 1991. I was with the god's *vazīr*, Raj Mohan Singh Rangad, when word came that someone was flagellating himself with stinging nettles in front of the temple. The man's brothers, with whom he shared the ancestral home, had been sexually harassing his wife, and he had come to ask for justice, gaining the god's attention in the customary way. I followed the *vazīr* to the temple courtyard, where the man was waiting. Karna's messenger was dispatched to summon the brothers by showing them his *gaj* (a small iron bar, bent at one end). Had the brothers refused to come to the courtyard, then the messenger would have hung Karna's "sign" (*niśān*)—a yak-tail whisk—on their house. The villagers say that no one has ever refused such a summons, since the house of one who did so would spontaneously burst into flames, the customary punishment of King Karna. In any event, it

30. Sax 1991, chap. 5, for a discussion of territorialism in relation to the "Royal Pilgrimage" of the regional goddess, Nanda Devi. More recent research has confirmed the salience of territorialism in Garhwali culture, history, and folklore (Sax forthcoming a).

31. Competition for control over high-altitude summer pastures may be of particular importance.

32. See Sax 1991a, 1999, 2000b, forthcoming a.

proved unnecessary to send this "sign" because the brothers responded to the first summons. Soon a small crowd had gathered, including the god's oracle and the aggrieved woman, who sat at some distance. After lengthy discussion and debate, mediated chiefly by the *vazīr*, the brothers one after the other grasped the *gaj* and swore to stop harassing the young wife; in return, her husband agreed to repay an old debt. Karna and his officers often settle domestic disputes in this fashion.

King Karna is also resorted to during times of drought because he is believed to have the power to bring rain. A prolonged dry spell in the autumn of 1997 was widely attributed to the "demonic" deity Pokkhu, who was thought to be punishing his subjects for their failings. Several times during the months of September and October, I watched as local women visited Karna's temple and implored him to intercede with Pokkhu and bring rain. Other neighboring deities such as Duryodhana and Mahasu are also believed to possess the power to bring rain; indeed, it is perhaps the most widely recognized characteristic of divine kingship cross-culturally, and is certainly prominent in the Hindu tradition.[33] And Karna has still more qualifications for kingship: he is a Kshatriya noble, born of the union of Kunti with the sun god; he is known for his benevolence; and he is generous. As his *vazīr* put it,

> King Karna doesn't harm anyone. He sends Shalya his champion to do his dirty work.[34] King Karna himself says, "Have compassion on your family, feed your guests, and give them a place to stay." The god tells everyone to give charity, not to take. And if one does so, then everything one needs will be provided. He even tells us to give our daughters in marriage, although bride-price is the custom everywhere else around here. [see later discussion]

In the *Mahābhārata* story, Karna's generosity was legendary, and in Singtur as well, local folklore tells of his magnanimity. Normally when deities in this region go on ther royal palanquin tours, they demand money from their worshipers, but Karna distributes wealth during his processions. In the late 1980s, when he went to the regional headquarters of Uttarkashi for a scriptural recitation, he gave away eleven cows and some gold and sponsored a public feast for pilgrims.

To summarize, King Karna is constituted as a divine king by the actions of his subjects and by his own actions: defense of territory, adjudication of disputes, control of rain, beneficence. His royal nature is well summed up in the chant recited by his drummers at the end of his daily worship:

33. "A brahmana associates rain and law: rain and order, disorder and drought go together (Śat. Br., XI, I, 6, 24). Later, in the legend of *Triśaṅku* (or Satyavrata, above) as in that of *Devāpi*, the rule of an illegitimate sovereign is signalled by drought. In the Jatakas, the king is rainmaker, and there is an appropriate royal ritual" (Dumont 1962, 60).

34. This point is well illustrated by the folktale recounted earlier, where Shalya's hotheaded willingness to fight contrasts with King Karna's equipoise.

All the gods are awake, and the maiden from Nagarkot.
The music is playing, the priest is worshiping with food, with wealth.
Hari Haridwar, Badri Kedar, the Ganga and the Bhagirathi,
the five Pandavas, the sixty Kauravas, the great and powerful
  Parashurama:
all worship the son of the sun, the prince of the sky,
the king of three worlds, the son of Kunti.
They offer gold and milk-giving cows to the virtuous king.
May your dominions grow, may your temple grow!
May your lion-skin throne be rich![35]

A Renouncer King

Although Raja Karan is clearly a king, he is also a renouncer, an ash-smeared yogi who has no gold and is detached and "carefree" (*phakkaḍ*). This poses yet another puzzle because Karna is not normally depicted as a renouncer in Sanskrit versions of *Mahābhārata*, and when I asked local men about this, they related the story of how he became a disciple of Rama Jamadagnya, from whom he obtained the invincible "Brahma Weapon" with which he hoped to destroy his rival Arjuna. The dreaded Rama Jamadagnya was a Brahman warrior who had exterminated the Kshatriya class to which Karna belonged twenty-one times over; he was also known as Parashurama, or "Axe Rama."[36] One day, a worm began to bore a hole through Karna's leg while Parashurama lay asleep with his head on Karna's lap. Karna bore the pain without flinching so as not to awaken his guru, but when Parashurama arose from his sleep and saw what had happened, he was furious. He knew that Karna had deceived him, since only a Kshatriya could bear such pain in silence, and so he cursed him that on the day he tried to use the secret weapon, Karna's memory would fail him and he would forget the spell used to activate it. And, indeed, in the climactic battle, Karna forgot his special knowledge, and Arjuna, urged on by his charioteer Krishna, unchivalrously slew Karna while the latter was repairing his chariot wheel. Raja Karan's subjects say that when he became a disciple of Parashurama, he also became a renouncer. He is further connected with renunciation by the story

35. *jāge saval sañjā, nagarkoṭ kanyā*
rāg sañjā, bhog sañjā, dhan kī pūjā
hari haridwār, badrī kedār, gaṅgā bhāgarathī
pāñc pāṇḍav, ṣāṭh kaurū, baḍā śakti pharasarām
siri sarjkā rājkvāṃr sāgal māṃ,
tīn talāī ko rājā suraj gā kuntī ko jāī
savāsan manas, dhinālī gāṃv, dharmī rājā
rājbaḍhe, chatravās baḍhe
siṃhāsan ko dhanī!

36. Note that Parashurama is invoked in Raja Karan's mantra above. See Goldman 1977 for a major study of Parashurama.

of the arrival of his image in Singtur. It is said that a wealthy local landlord named Lapavara traveled to "Thati Champavat,"[37] where he lived for several years disguised as a renouncer. Having gained the local peoples' trust, he stole Raja Karan's image and was able to return to Singtur, abandon his renouncer's disguise, and live on without being caught.

Local people see no contradiction in thinking about Raja Karan as both king and renouncer.[38] I once overheard my friend Rajmohan's classificatory "grandmother" compare Raja Karan to Mahasu Devata. She said that Mahasu Devata's servants—his priests, musicians, dancers, quartermasters, and so forth—frighten people into giving him offerings (*dān*), while Raja Karan's servants do not. Mahasu Devata demands meat, wine, and dancing girls, while Raja Karan is a renouncer. He says, "Fine, if Mahasu likes those things, let him have them. But I'm not interested." In the old woman's view, Karan was clearly the morally superior deity.

Raja Karan's dual character as both king and renouncer is strongly associated with his oracular function, which involves him publicly and visibly "possessing" his oracle in order to settle disputes and answer questions.[39] The procedure for this is simple: the oracle listens for a short while to Karan's special drum[40] and gong, then removes his shirt, takes a handful of ash from the fire burning outside the temple, and smears it on himself (plate 11). Hindu renouncers also smear their bodies with ash, especially those who are worshipers of Shiva, the ash-covered lord of renouncers. Ash signifies that the renouncer has undergone his own funeral rites and is "dead" to the world. In Raja Karan's temple, the ash is taken from a renouncer's fire (*dhūnī*) that is kept burning just outside the temple door. This fire is normally tended by the temple watchman (*ṭhāṇī*), who is a member of the Nath caste, which has strong links to Shaiva renouncers, but during my visit in 1993, it was tended by an actual *sādhū*.

Raja Karan's oracular pronouncements normally occur when the complex agency of the village is confounded, for example, when elders are unable to reach a collective decision regarding some delicate or politically sensitive decision. In such situations the cool, dispassionate evenhandedness of the yogi is precisely what is called for, and Karan manifests himself in that form, entering the body of his oracle and smearing himself with renouncer's ash. He announces his presence with the statement "I have nothing," and in subsequent exchange with his petitioners, he invariably

37. Champavat is the old capital of the neighboring Hindu kingdom of Kumaon. Oakley (1991, 226) writes tantalizingly that some of the kings of Champavat were deified after their deaths.

38. "[M]any origin myths in Rohru-Bashahr represent tutelary deities as wandering through the landscape of the human world in the physical form of an ascetic (*sādhu rūp mem*) [*sic*] before they establish themselves as 'rulers' (*rāja*) [*sic*]" (Sutherland 1998, 33).

39. The god's oracle is called a *mālī* (lit. "gardener"), a common term in the western Himalayas. The verb used for inducing possession is *jhulānā*, literally "causing (the god) to swing."

40. The *ḍhāk* mentioned in the ballad above, the one that makes the "*vhoo-vhoo*" sound.

Plate 11. Kamaleshvar Prasad Nautiyal, the mālī *(Brahman oracle) of King Karna, in trance. Dyora village. Photo by William S. Sax.*

claims to be quite disinterested in worldly events and can only be persuaded to intervene by much pleading and cajoling.

This association of Raja Karan's oracular activities with his identity as a renouncer is also evident in a more recent confrontation with Mahasu Devata. After the dispute between Raja Karan and Chalda Mahasu recorded in the earlier ballad, it was agreed that neither should enter the other's territory, and so when Chalda Mahasu periodically visited his cult followers in Bhitari village, in the territory of Fateh Parvat adjoining Singtur, he had to cross the river at Miya Gad and proceed upstream on the right bank. But when the state government constructed a jeepable road on the left bank of the river, Chalda Mahasu's followers began to have second thoughts about this restriction. They argued that times had changed and that the government road should be open to all. It would certainly be much easier for them to reach Bhitari if they were able to use it, rather than clambering through the bushes and along the cliff tops on the right bank of the river, as they had done for generations. They said that Raja Karan's followers had no right to prohibit anyone from using a public road, and in 1996, for the first time in living memory, they broke the old prohibition and processed through the Naitwar bazaar to Bhitari, quickly and very quietly, so as not to create a fuss.

Raja Karan's followers did not immediately respond because they indeed had no legal right to prohibit others from using the road. But they were worried that if they did not ask the god what to do, he might blight them with a curse—after all, it was their responsibility to defend his territory. So they asked him several times what to do, and through his oracle he told them that times were changing and they should not fight, as they would have in the old days. He said he would take care of the problem, that he would give a sign of his *śakti*, or power, to Chalda Mahasu.

At that time, Karan was in the village of Pokhari, on his annual tour through his dominions. Karna's subjects prepared his messenger, Bharat Nath, to make a formal embassy to Chalda Mahasu. They bound Bharat Nath's head with a ceremonial turban and draped him with a long sash and a silver medallion, "just like a policeman." They took four packets of rice to Raja Karan, who empowered them with magical spells, and they gave these to Bharat Nath, with instructions to take them to Mahasu's camp in Bhitari. When Bharat Nath arrived there, people from throughout Fateh Parvat assembled, including many local notables. They even came from nearby Bangan, when they heard that Raja Karan had sent the ensorcelled rice with his messenger. What should they do? They were frightened by the sudden appearance of Raja Karan's representative.

As Rajmohan tells it, Raja Karan did indeed show them his power: the son of one of their quartermasters went mad. They took the boy to Mahasu's court in Bhitari once or twice, but the god could not cure him. They took him to see doctors and traditional healers, they sacrificed a goat to the goddess, but nothing helped. They were frightened that things might get worse, that Raja Karan might afflict them even more. Meanwhile, the people from

Singtur consulted Raja Karan, who informed them that he had given Mahasu's followers a small indication of what could happen to them. If they would now compromise, he would end the affliction, but if they did not, who could say what might happen?

So Mahasu Devata's followers decided that they should come and negotiate. They sent a letter to Raja Karan, saying that they would visit his temple in Dyora in late March 1997. They did not say anything about the young man going mad—they wanted to keep it a secret. They asked the leaders from Karan's territory to assemble when they came, and so they did. Karan's followers wanted to meet in Naitwar because the disputed road is located there, but Mahasu's followers insisted on meeting Raja Karan face-to-face, to be certain that they had the god's agreement. And so both parties met in the courtyard in front of Karan's temple in Dyora. All the important men from the two territories were there: lawyers, politicians, landowners, and government officers.

When this group of dignitaries reached the temple, they were met by representatives of Raja Karan's warrior lineages, the *khūnd* of Singtur. The warriors wanted to show their hospitality to the guests from Bangan by sacrificing a few goats, bringing out the liquor, and commencing what Sutherland calls the "serious political work" of drinking (1998, xxii). At this point, says Rajmohan, he had to call his own meeting behind the temple and instruct his *khūnd* to calm down. "We'll discuss the matter seriously," he said, "and your job is to listen seriously, but not to make such a fuss. First let's see what the outcome is, then we'll show them our hospitality." He told them that three or four representatives from each side would sit together and take turns discussing the issues, and that there would be none of the usual business of everyone waving their arms and shouting at the same time.

Rajmohan told the delegation from Bangan that Raja Karan's followers were glad they had come, and he welcomed them sincerely. "But we feel rather hurt," he continued, "because when you went to Bhitari through our territory, you didn't tell us you were coming. Instead you tried to show your strength; you invoked the law." He turned to Mahasu's *vazīr* and said, "If I was such a foolish *vazīr* as you, then on that day I would have had half of you killed, right there in the market in Naitwar. Don't doubt it: half of you would have ended up in the river. But I thought, 'One fool is enough. We don't need two.' And then you went up the valley to Bhitari village, but when you decide to come back down, we can easily ambush you and defeat you. However, we don't want to fight."

The two groups talked at some length, then summoned the two gods' oracles, who had their own entranced debate, which lasted for three long hours. The gods became angry with each other—so angry that Rajmohan thought there was going to be a battle between them, right then and there. Neither would give an inch. In the end, it was as if the events of the folk ballad were repeating themselves. Raja Karan announced that, as a gift to Mahasu, he would revoke his prohibition on the latter traveling through his domain. He sent the messenger to fetch a leaf from the wild cherry tree (*payyāṃ*), a very sacred plant for Garhwalis. He held the leaf in one hand and some soil in the other, and he asked Mahasu which one he wanted, the leaf or the soil. In other words, Mahasu could accept the sacred leaf, thereby indicating his continued observance of his old vow, or he could accept Raja Karan's gift of land. Now, both gods are kings—"You're a king; I also am a king"—and this was a kingly dispute, which echoed their many disputes, from the time of their contest at Dyojani. Raja Karan was admonishing Mahasu to regard it as a royal matter, and not to go back on his word, because one who breaks his word cannot truly be a king. But if he chose, Mahasu could take the soil instead: that is, he could accept Raja Karan's permission to pass through his territory. However, this would involve accepting a gift from Raja Karan, which is also something that a real king would never do (see pp. 115–16). So Mahasu was trapped! He accepted neither the leaf nor the soil. And Raja Karan said, "Tell me which one you want! You and I agreed ages ago at Dyojani, but if you have decided to go back on your word, then so be it! Take the soil: I give you leave to travel through my territory as a gift! You're a king—I also am a king."

The way Rajmohan tells it, Mahasu's *vazīr*, his lawyer, and all those notables in his entourage had to "grasp their earlobes" (a conventional gesture of shame) and admit they were wrong. They begged Mahasu to accept the gift, because if he did not, they would be unable to leave Bhitari. Mahasu was furious. He insisted that he, too, was a generous giver of gifts; that his influence extended all the way to Delhi; that he had mountains of silver and gold, while Raja Karan, that renouncer of a god, had nothing of value to give. Raja Karan acknowledged that he was indeed a yogi; that all he had was a renouncer's fire and a handful of ash. Mahasu was really in a fix, but in the end he chose the soil. He accepted Raja Karan's gift of permission to travel through his territory, and his supporters agreed that, henceforth, Raja Kharan and Shalya could take their traditional route to Khanyasini village via Pujeli, which had been closed to them for generations because it lay in Mahasu's territory. The boy who went mad was suddenly cured, and the following memorandum was duly written and signed:

> Today, 15 Māgh 2053, at the holy place of Devara, the council of leaders of Singtur and the council of leaders of Bangan have ended the ancient dispute between Raja Karan and Mahasu Devata concerning ingress and egress, to wit: when Mahasu Devata went to Fateh Parvat, he was prohibited from setting foot in Naitwar in Raja Karan's territory. With the agreement of both deities, and the help of the local population, Raja Karan has, as a gift, lifted that prohibition. It has been firmly resolved that if Raja Karan or King Shalya wishes to go anywhere in Mahasu Devata's territory, he will not be disturbed by any of its residents, nor will he have any other trouble. Moreover, if Mahasu Devata wishes to enter Raja Karan's territory, there will be no trouble from either the residents or the god. If Raja Karan or Raja

Shalya wishes to go to Kanyasini in the future via the village of Pujeli, then the residents of Fateh Parvat will not be angry, and they will cause no trouble. Mahasu Devata, the dwellers in our territory have no objection to your taking whichever of Raja Karan's roads seems easiest to you. This has been written by Shri ___, chief of the headmens' council, on behalf of the deputation of the advocate Shri ___, in the presence of the *vazīr* of Raja Karan and of the *ṣāṭhīs* [Kauravas] Shri ___, Shri ___, the *vazīr* of the Pamsai subregion Shri ___, representatives of the *ṣāṭhī* [Kaurava] and *pāṃsāī* [Pandava] warriors, Shri ____ , Shri ____, and the *vazīr* Mahasu Devata Shri ____.

In addition to the above-mentioned conditions, it has also been determined that local residents will make no difficulties if the god Sherkudiya wishes to travel through Raja Karan's territory, or if Raja Karan or Raja Shalya wishes to travel in Kiranu Bangan.[41]

Therefore has it been written, and we have troubled Shri ___, Shri ____, and Shri _____, by giving each of them a copy for safekeeping, so that this agreement may last forever.[42]

This most recent confrontation between Raja Karan and Mahasu Devata echoes the contest at Dyojani long ago. In both cases, the principal matter in dispute was the right of gods to move through each other's territory; in both cases, Raja Karan achieved his final victory by virtue of being

41. Shalya's warriors from Dargan village in Singtur have relatives living in Kiranu. But Kiranu is located in Bangan, so that until now, they were unable to invite Raja Karan to visit them.

42. ham ke pāñc gāṃv māl guzār siṅgtūr paṭṭī, ham ke pāñc gāṃv fateh parvat evam baṅgāṇ kā āj dināṅk 28.01.97 arthāt 15 gati Māgh 2053 ko devasthal devaṛā meṃ prācīn kāl se karaṇ mahārāj tathā mahāsu devatā ke bīc āne-jāne ke rāste kā vivād samāpt kiyā gayā hai, jo ki mahāsu devatā jab fateh parvat ko jāte the, us meṃ karaṇ mahārāj ke kṣetra naiṭwāṛ se pāv-bandhī thī. Vah pāv-bandhī donoṃ devatāoṃ kī ām-sahamati se janatā ke sahayog se karaṇ mahārāj dvārā dān svarūp haṭhā dī gaī hai. Yah pūraṇ tay huā hai ki karaṇ mahārāj evam śalyā mahārāj mahāsu devatā ke kṣetra meṃ kahīṃ jānā cāheṃ, to kṣetravāsiyoṃ tathā devatāoṃ kī or se kisī bhī prakār kī āpatti nahīṃ hogī.

Is ke sāth-sāth karaṇ mahārāj ke kṣetra meṃ yadi mahāsu devatā ānā cāheṃ to kṣetravāsiyoṃ evam devatāoṃ kī or se koī āpatti nahīṃ hogī. Yadi karaṇ mahārāj, śalyā mahārāj bhaviṣya meṃ kanyāsinī jānā cāheṃ to rāstā pujelī hokar jāne meṃ fateh parvat ke logoṃ kī koī āpattī nahīṃ itrāj nahīṃ hogā.

āp mahāsu devatā karaṇ mahārāj ke jis rāste se bhī suvidhā-janak samajhe, hamārā kṣetravāsiyoṃ kā vah devatāoṃ kā koī etrāz nahīṃ hogā. Yah likhit karaṇ ke vazir śrī ___ ___ ___, sāṭhī bazir, tathā śrī ___ ___ ___ evam ___ ___ bazir, pāṃsāī thok, sri ___ ___, ___ ___, sāṭhī pāṃsāī khūnd vah mahāsū devatā ke vazīr śrī ___ ___ ki upasthiti meṃ mujh ___ ___ ___ blāk pramukh dvārā śrī ___ ___ ___ advokeṭ ke ḍipṭeśaṇ meṃ likhī gaī hai. Ukt śartoṃ ke atirikt yah bhī nirṇay liyā gayā hai ki śerkuḍiyā devatā ko rājā karaṇ mahārāj ke kṣetra meṃ tathā rājā karaṇ mahārāj yā śalyā mahārāj ko kirāṇū baṅgāṇ meṃ āne-jāne meṃ kṣetravāsiyoṃ kī koī āpatti nahīṃ hogī.

Is prakār yah likh dī tāki bhaviṣya meṃ sānand rahe, likhit kī ek prati śrī ___ ___ ___Bhitri, ek prati śrī ___ ___bazir Baṅkwāṛ, tathā ek prati bazir śrī ___ ___ ___, gaicāṇ gāṃv ko surakṣit rakhne ki tū pariśrit kī gaī hai.

a renouncer, with the magical powers believed to be possessed by such persons; and in both cases (at least, according to Raja Karan's followers), the dispute ended with Raja Karan giving a gift to Mahasu Devata.

In other respects, however, both the dispute and the manner of its resolution illustrate just how much times have changed. Such quarrels were formerly resolved through violence, and victory went to the group that was most effective in killing or terrorizing its enemies. But this time the dispute was settled through negotiation; each god opened his territory to the other, ending generations of closed borders; and the joint memorandum was seen by both sides as a new and better way of doing things. Such changes are partly a result of the fact that these formerly isolated valleys are being integrated with the rest of India at unprecedented speed. A generation ago, there was virtually no public education, but the signatories of the joint memorandum included prominent men with university degrees and much experience of the outside world. They could see that no one's interest would be served by violence, and that it was to the advantage of both parties to settle the dispute peacefully.

There is no doubt that Mahasu Devata's followers were in a difficult position. They could either continue to take the difficult path along the cliffs on the right bank of the river on their periodic visits to Bhitari, or they could risk traveling through hostile territory, with the likely risk of attack by Karna's followers, who vastly outnumbered them. So it was in their interest to negotiate passage through Raja Karan's territory, in return for which Karna gained the right to travel throughout Mahasu's territory.[43] It was also in Karan's interest to settle. Even though customary precedent is strong, still Karan could not legally prohibit Mahasu Devata or his followers from processing on a public road, and with the growing influence of the government of India, such legal considerations are of increasing importance. In return for his concession, Karan reestablished his old right to process through *paṭṭī* Fateh Parvat to Kanyasini village. Most interesting of all is the way in which Karan adroitly defined this concession as a gift, as yet another instance of his kingly generosity. As described in chapter 5, generosity and gift giving are strongly associated with Rajputs and especially kings. While such gifts sometimes involve the passing on of negatives (see Raheja 1988b), in this case Karan's gift to Mahasu is more Maussian. It creates a relation of obligation (Chalda Mahasu is now in Karan's debt), while at the same time establishing the moral superiority of Raja Karan in terms of the pervasive Hindu transactional calculus according to which givers rank higher than receivers (Marriott 1976). Raja Karan is kinglike because he is the linchpin of the numerous material and symbolic exchanges that occur in his domain. Only he, as complex agent for the entire territory, has the authority to grant ingress to and egress from Singtur. At the

43. In view of the Mahasu brothers' history of territorial expansion over the past hundred years and more (see Ibbetson and Maclagan 1919), this concession by Raja Karan might ultimately prove to be a strategic mistake.

same time, he is a yogi who has nothing and keeps nothing, and this, too, establishes his moral superiority to the godling Mahasu. In this most recent dispute with Mahasu, the complex agency of the village was confounded by rapid social change. The whole *paṭṭī* was in need of the cool detachment of a yogi, and Karna manifested himself in that form. Once again, his manifest identity was not a matter of essence but of action, and more especially of requisite actions for particular situations, a kind of strategic relationality.

So Karna is constituted as both king and renouncer by his own actions, but in certain important respects his actions also make him a Brahman. He promotes a number of reforms that are at odds with the traditional, Kshatriya-dominated culture of the area and are instead based on Brahmanical values. For example, the peoples of the western Himalayas, and of these valleys in particular, are notorious for their drinking. Members of the musician caste commonly distill country liquor to sell to their high-caste neighbors, and drinking is an integral part of many local festivals. Karna and his priests oppose these well-established practices, discourage the use of alcohol at any time, and resolutely forbid it on temple premises. Miscreants are fined or publicly scolded by temple officers. Similarly, Karna and his officers have introduced what can only be called "Brahmanical" changes in the temple rituals. Karna does not accept animal sacrifice, and he encourages vegetarianism among his followers. Such reforms of drinking and diet serve to distinguish Karna and his cult quite clearly from other local deities, most of whom tolerate drinking and accept animal sacrifice, and to distinguish his devoted followers from the mass of the population who, in this pastoral society, are overwhelmingly nonvegetarian.

Furthermore, Karna actively promotes reform of marriage customs, seeking to bring them into line with Brahmanical values. In the upper reaches of the Tons River, various types of marriage are found, including marriage by capture and fraternal polyandry (Majumdar 1963), but by far the most common form is bride-price, where the groom pays a cash price to the parents of the bride (Sax 1990b, 1991a). All these forms are known to, and are more or less disapproved by, the classical tradition, which has always regarded *kanyādāna*, "the gift of a virgin," as the highest form of marriage (Fruzetti 1982; Inden and Nicholas 1977). However, it is this very form that is actively promoted by King Karna and his priests, who feel somewhat disadvantaged because, alone among their compatriots, they are compelled by the god to practice *kanyādāna*, thus forgoing the income they might otherwise have received from the marriage of their daughters (but also saving the costs associated with the marriage of sons).

It might be objected that the promotion of Brahmanical reforms such as teetotaling, vegetarianism, and *kanyādāna* marriage hardly makes Karna a Brahman. And such an objection would indeed be valid if the only evidence for Karna's Brahmanhood was in terms of values (shades of Dumont!). But values are never purely abstract: along with religion, gender, politics, language, and the other objects of the human sciences, they are always embodied. This insistence on the embodiedness of culture is one of the leitmotifs of contemporary social analysis, and perhaps the most persuasive evidence of Karna's Brahmanical identity is that the person with whom he is most closely identified—the oracle whose body he temporarily inhabits—must be a Brahman. This is particularly striking because the oracles of the nearby deities Duryodhana/Someshwar, Pokkhu, and Mahasu are all Rajputs. This is of course no surprise, since Duryodhana and the others have passionate and aggressive personalities, but Karna was also a warlike Kshatriya in the *Mahābhārata*, so why is his oracle a Brahman and not a Rajput? How are we to explain this further anomaly in the increasingly complex constitution of Karna's "self"?

An adequate answer to this question brings us back to a description of the way in which Karna is constituted by his actions, which implicate him in a web of strategic relationality. It is not only the oracles but also the priests of Duryodhana, Pokkhu, and Mahasu who are Rajputs, while King Karna's priests are Nautiyals, Brahmans of the highest caste. It would seem that if the deity's priests are Brahmans, then the oracle must also be a Brahman, and the final result is to raise the esteem in which the cult is popularly held. As I argued in chapter 4, Brahmans are ideologically hegemonic, even in these remote valleys famous for their antipathy to Brahmans and renouncers, and even though Rajputs are so overwhelmingly dominant in both economic and political terms. Karna's reforms, like his use of a Brahman as oracle, serve to give his cult a moral and symbolic edge over the cults of his rivals; they guarantee that when comparisons are made, he will emerge as the most "dharmic" of all. Applying Bourdieu's language, we could say that the material capital Karna expends—the gifts he gives when on procession, the rights of egress he granted to Mahasu—is actually an investment with highly profitable symbolic returns. From a traditional perspective, Karna's reforms, along with his employment of Brahman priests and oracles, might be considered disadvantageous, since they serve to distance him and his cult from the local culture and social structure. But they can also be understood as a prudent strategy for integrating Karna's cult with the wider Indian society that is impinging on this remote valley as never before, and even with the global culture that is beginning to appear on the horizon. In the new millennium, resources and opportunities will flow to those who are integrated with these new forms of culture and society, and not to those who are perceived as pugnacious and backward hillbillies.

Toward an Ontology of Action

It is all well and good to claim that a god is simultaneously king, Brahman, and renouncer, but what does the ethnography of King Karna tell us about human persons? Can they accomplish the same feat? Indian literature and history suggest that they can. The identity of Brahman and renouncer, for example, has been discussed at length by Heesterman, for whom "the ideal Brahman is the renouncer" (1985, 43). There are many examples of Brahmans who were also kings and/or warriors, beginning with the Vedic period and its "apparent fusion of the warrior and the priest in the king" (Heesterman 1990, 99). Arguing from the centrality of raiding and raiding episodes in the structure of the *rājasūya* sacrifice, Heesterman asserts that the *rājan* "is not a god nor a mere man, neither is he a priest in the usual sense nor a 'simple' ruler. He is a consecrated warrior."[44] In the *Mahābhārata* story, we have the example of Drona, the famous Brahman general, and Karna's guru Rama Jamadagnya, the exterminator of the Kshatriyas.[45] India offers numerous historical instances of martial Brahmans, from Pushyamitra Shunga, the Brahman general who assassinated the last of the Mauryan emperors in 184 B.C., to powerful ruling Brahmans like the Peshwas of Pune in the seventeenth and eighteenth centuries, or the Joshi clan of Kumaon in the same period.[46]

What about the fusion of raja and yogi? It might strike some as contradictory that Raja Karan is regarded as both king and renouncer at the same time. After all, kings are associated in the Indian tradition with passionate action and renouncers with passionless nonaction; kings control great wealth, while renouncers have a bare minimum of possessions. But as it turns out, the Indian tradition connects kings and renouncers in numerous and often profound ways. In north India, renouncers are customarily addressed as "Great King" (*mahārāj*), and there are numerous historical examples of kingly renouncers like Shankaracharya and his successors, along with other prominent monastic leaders,[47] as well as renunciant kings like Siddhartha Gautama, Gopichand, and Harishchandra (Gold 1992). The royal sage (*rājaṛṣi*) is a familiar figure in Indian literature from the Upanishads onward. Garhwal's kings and its national deity, Badrinath, were both traditionally considered to be "warriors" as well as "renouncers," having to renounce the world in order to protect it (Galey 1990, 170). Renouncers, it is said, are the greatest of kings because they have conquered the most difficult of opponents, the Self. That is why the Sanskrit poet Kalidasa wrote that King Raghu "set out by land to conquer the Persians: thus the ascetic sets out by way of true knowledge to conquer his enemies, the senses" (*Raghuvaṃśa* IV.60; Antoine's translation).

That Karna can simultaneously be king, Brahman, and renouncer is perhaps not as problematic as it might at first have seemed. Indian history and literature provide a great many examples of persons with similarly multiple selves. This should come as no surprise because, according to Hindu thought, selves are not constituted by mysterious and/or transcendent

44. Note that in Heesterman's discussion, the *rājan* is distinguished from the *kṣatriya*, "the ruler, the holder of *kṣatra*" (1990, 105–6).

45. MBh 12.18, 12.321; Goldman 1977.

46. For the Joshis of Kumaon, see Atkinson 1974 [1882]. For martial Brahmans generally, see Bharati 1983, 245; Heesterman 1962; Kolff 1990, 185.

47. Lorenzen 1976; Orr 1940; Sax 1987, 2000a; Tambiah 1976.

essences but rather by action: as one acts, so does one become. And one normally acts in accord with interests that are contextually (i.e., relationally) determined, employing pragmatically effective strategies. Thus Karna's roles, like the roles employed by any other person, may be regarded as relational strategies: he is a king in relation to his territory because he defends it when it is threatened, and this strategy has particular rewards (e.g., territorial dominance) vis-à-vis his subjects as well as his opponents. He is a renouncer in relation to his petitioners because only a renouncer has the detachment that guarantees impartiality, and this strategy, too, has its payoff, especially because it bolsters his reputation as an impartial arbiter. And he is a Brahman not only during the brief time that he inhabits the body of his oracle but also because he advocates cultural changes that will lead his people in the direction of hegemonic Brahmanical values: yet another rewarding strategy in the context of the wider culture and economy into which both Karna and his subjects are inexorably being drawn.

7

The Hall of Mirrors

Orientalism, Anthropology, and the "Other"

The Dialectics of Sameness and Difference

Anthropologists specialize in human difference. As merchants of the exotic, we have confronted the problem of representing the Other[1] since long before that word was spelled with a capital O. Both as scholars and as persons, we cannot escape from the dialectics of sameness and difference,[2] and this gives rise to an epistemological-cum-moral problem: How should we represent exotic cultures in our teaching and research?

The usual strategy is to make the exotic familiar, and the familiar exotic. An initial object of study—a religious cult, a political movement, an Other kinship system—at first seems strange and puzzling, but in the process of learning (and later teaching) about it in its own context, it comes to seem less exotic and more familiar. Conversely, when we look closely at more familiar cultures, or at parts of those cultures that have previously been ignored, they begin to look rather exotic, less natural, more conventional.

Because anthropologists specialize in difference, we are heir to a double legacy of relativism. We are powerfully attracted to human diversity, and for most of us the glittering array of cultures and forms of life is something to be treasured, proof of the vast range of human potential. And so we are enamored of cultural particulars and suspicious of human universals, and whenever a claim is advanced for the latter, the anthropologist leaps to her feet and says, "Not among the Inuit!" "Not among the Kwaio!" Or, as we South Asianists say, "Not in the South!" This is not the ontological relativism that is the bogeyman of the philosophers,[3] but merely a decent re-

1. This chapter is slightly adapted from Sax 1998.
2. See Narayan 1993.
3. Though see Quine 1968; and Geertz 1984.

spect for human difference, a relativism of the culturally particular, with certain methodological implications (Marcus and Fischer 1986, 180).

Anthropology is, then, the discipline par excellence that is immersed in the study of difference, of the Other. And yet, as is well known, studying Others has been the object of a moral and epistemological attack in recent years, most notably by Edward Said, who led the charge in *Orientalism*, first published in 1978. It is difficult these days to find a book by a historian or anthropologist of non-"Western" culture that does not include some gesture of obeisance to Said: his influence has been immense. Said argues that Western students of Oriental civilization—the Orientalists—did not study an empirical Orient existing "out there" somewhere east of the Bosporus. It would be more accurate to say that they studied an object that they themselves had invented. The Orient, along with its inhabitants, was not so much a place and a set of people as it was a state of mind, an artifact of the scholar's study. As Disraeli put it, "The Orient is a career."

So far, so good. We can only profit from being warned against reifying our objects of study, from the "Religion" of religious studies to the "Politics" of political science and the "Culture" of cultural anthropology. But Said does not let the matter rest there. He goes on to say that the so-called Orientals were compelled to live in this constructed Orient, that Europe "produced the Orient politically, sociologically, militarily, ideologically, scientifically, and imaginatively during the post-Enlightenment period. . . . In brief, because of Orientalism the Orient was not (and is not) a free subject of thought or action" (1978, 3).

Now this is not only silly; it is profoundly dismissive of those "Orientals" with whom Said self-consciously identifies. As van der Veer (1993) and others have argued, in order to show the power of Orientalism, Said denies autonomy, agency, and even thought to the Orientals. He even denies them the possibility of resisting their colonial oppressors, which flies in the face of historical fact. More crucially for my argument, Said sees the mere postulation of difference as dangerous, ominous: "Can one divide human reality, as indeed human reality seems to be genuinely divided, into clearly different cultures, histories, traditions, societies, even races, and survive the consequences humanly? By surviving the consequences humanly, I mean to ask whether there is any way of avoiding the hostility expressed by the division, say, of men into 'us' (Westerners) and 'they' (Orientals)" (1978, 45).

Said is right to call attention to the risks of studying difference, and his rhetorical question is one with which every anthropologist must eventually come to terms. It is a question that forces us to confront the dark side of our methodological relativism, the danger that lurks in our suspicion of universals. In my view, the danger is that in celebrating the culturally particular, we may lose sight of the universally human. Understanding other cultures would be impossible were there not, at some level, a universal human nature underlying differences of religion, language, race, and so on. More important, to ignore or deny this shared humanity has horrific consequences, as the history of the twentieth century so clearly illustrates. In the age of ethnic cleansing, a concern for human universals looks more and more like a moral necessity.

Nevertheless, we do in practice make distinctions among cultures, and this brings us back to the dialectics of sameness and difference. According to Said, any division of humanity into "us" and "them" leads to "hostility," and this hostility may be unavoidable, so that the division of humanity into different cultures is (perhaps inevitably) a dehumanizing activity. Later in the same chapter, Said points to the universal propensity of human groups to differentiate themselves from others—Westerner versus Oriental, civilized versus barbarian, black versus white, and so on. He says that all these divisions are synonyms, more or less value-laden, for the fundamental difference between "us" and "them," and he persuasively argues that no matter how much we increase our positive knowledge of Oriental languages, geography, and culture, our perceptions of Orientals will still be structured by this fundamental dichotomy.[4] Said thus resolves the dialectics of sameness and difference into a transcendent hostility.

It is partly due to the influence of such ideas that anthropologists seem recently to have become rather embarrassed by cultural difference. For example, in a thoughtful essay, Abu-Lughod has argued that the central concept of American anthropology—the culture concept—should be written "against." The culture concept is problematic, says Abu-Lughod, because it focuses on difference, and in doing so it "operates to enforce separations that inevitably carry a sense of hierarchy"; culture is thus "the essential tool for making other" (1991, 137–38, 143). According to Said, Abu-Lughod, and others, focusing on difference "otherizes" the objects of our research, fetishizes their exotic features, and inevitably creates a hierarchical difference between "us" and "them." In the same vein, Appadurai writes of "the unruly body of the colonial subject (fasting, feasting, hookswinging, abluting, burning, and bleeding)" as a body that is created by the "exoticizing gaze" of Orientalism (1993, 333–34).

And yet, as Said himself acknowledges, significant differences among human beings appear to us as so many self-evident facts, and it is not possible (nor would it be desirable) to abolish them. Whether explicitly or implicitly, they continue to be the primary data for anthropologists. Moreover, it is far from evident that anthropological writing must necessarily inferiorize the Others that are its objects. On the contrary, such writing often inverts regnant hierarchies, holding up the exotic Other as worthy of emulation rather than scorn. Said is certainly correct when he says that human beings have a universal propensity to distinguish themselves from others and to rank the difference. What he fails to note is the frequency with which anthropologists, and even the dread Orientalists, play this game in reverse

4. Kakar 1990 makes many of the same points about the universality of otherizing processes, from a psychoanalytic (mostly Kleinian) point of view.

by valorizing the Other and implicitly criticizing the Self. When Margaret Mead wrote that Samoan adolescence was trouble-free, she was holding up Samoan culture as a mirror to show Western culture its own warts. She was praising the Samoans, not disparaging them.[5] When Mircea Eliade wrote about the pervasiveness of the sacred in "primordial" societies, he was praising them by appealing to Western primitivism (Eliade 1959 [1957]). And the granddaddies of English Orientalism in India, Sir William Jones and Sir Warren Hastings, were in many respects apologists and publicists in England for Indian civilization (Rocher 1993).

I would not, however, wish to justify a scholarly interest in exotic cultures simply by claiming that it often inverts the hierarchy of Self and Other: this would merely be the substitution of one ideology for another. Instead, I seek to defend anthropology's focus on the exotic by arguing, first of all, that focusing on human differences is itself a human universal, and for anthropologists a methodological necessity; second, that perceived differences are often matters of sheer convention, and the anthropologist from afar, himself an exotic Other to those being studied, is particularly well placed to perceive this; and third, that the recognition of difference, whether by anthropologists or natives, does not always or necessarily involve an inferiorization of the Other.

I think it will be granted that difference-making is a human universal, and the burden of the rest of this chapter will be to illustrate how this works in one particular case. But why do I say that difference-making is a methodological necessity? Because there is and always will be at least one difference between the scholar and her object of study, and that is the difference between subject and object, the old dichotomy between thought and action, which cannot be avoided in academic life, no matter how much our political agenda or mystical inclinations might inspire us to try (Bell 1992). Now, a sophisticated ontology may well require us to see ourselves in an interactive relationship with our objects of study: such a relational ontology is certainly encouraged by the method of participant observation that is at the heart of sociocultural anthropology, and recent experiments with new forms of ethnographic writing can be seen as attempts to embody it. Still, it is difficult to imagine how academic anthropology could proceed without an object of study, however loosely defined, because the dichotomy of subject and object is a condition of disciplinary knowledge. It is necessary for any theoretical project whatsoever, in the human as well as the physical sciences. Neither the physicist nor the anthropologist nor the literary critic can pursue her study without objectifying its object, and to make of this an ethical dilemma is like questioning the morality of gravity. Anthropologists certainly have their share of ethical dilemmas, but these stem from economic and political asymmetries, not from cultural difference (Keesing 1989).

5. This theme, and especially the Margaret Mead example, have been skillfully developed by Marcus and Fischer 1986. For criticisms of Mead's findings, see Freeman 1983. For a recent contribution to this debate, see Grant 1995.

Why do I claim a special anthropological ability to perceive the conventionality of cultural difference? Because there are differences and differences, and the anthropologist's disciplined analysis of difference is itself different than the uncritical perception of difference by one whose personal interests are at stake. If it is true that human beings have a universal propensity to construct hierarchies based on perceived differences among themselves, then the scholar from afar, the student of the exotic, is especially well placed to understand and describe those hierarchies, as well as the presumed differences from which they are constructed. Since she is from another culture (which may well be the culture of the university down the road), she can recognize the arbitrariness of the locally salient differences and hence grasp the "constructed-ness" of the hierarchies based on them. As a relatively (though of course never completely) disinterested observer, she can more clearly see that difference is often a matter of convention. It is not that the anthropologist is purely "objective"—in a relational ontology this would be an empty term—but rather that in certain situations such as the mutual stereotyping that is the subject of this chapter, she is relatively neutral, "above the fray," and thus able to show that what is understood as a "natural" difference is in fact conventional.

My final claim is that difference-making does not always or necessarily involve the inferiorization of the Other. It could be argued that, in recent decades at least, anthropologists have been more guilty of romanticizing than of denigrating the Other. But my point is more subtle than that. I contend that difference-making involves a double movement, where the Other is simultaneously emulated and repudiated, admired and despised, and that the source of this ambivalence is the recognition of Self in Other.[6] That is to say, the Other represents a kind of screen upon which both the despised and the desired aspects of the Self can be projected, so that the dialectics of sameness and difference is resolved into a kind of difference *in* sameness, the culturally particular apprehended only against the background of the generically human. But to illustrate these points, we must enter a veritable hall of mirrors.

An Evil Empire?

The people of Garhwal have long been regarded as distinctive and backward Others by Hindus from the Gangetic Plain, which has been a major center of Indic civilization for over 3,000 years. To them, the mountain dwellers are thought of as poverty-stricken and backward hillbillies. They violate the dietary rules of orthodox Hinduism by consuming meat and liquor, they violate the rules of caste endogamy by practicing intercaste marriage, and they violate Hindu norms of marriage by practicing bride-

6. See Nandy's (1988 [1983]) brilliant study of colonialism. The idea of "self-in-other" pervades the work of Nandy, to whom I owe a profound intellectual debt.

price and widow remarriage (Berreman 1972 [1963]). The classical lawbooks called them fallen Hindus, and the orthodox still regard them as degenerate and impure (Joshi 1990; Sax 1994b).

But to catalog these stereotypes is to enter a hall of mirrors, because all the customs for which the Garhwalis are denigrated—eating meat, drinking liquor, and unorthodox marriage—are practiced by at least some Hindus in virtually every village, and certainly in every town and city in the north. This is the hidden face of Hindu society, and so when fingers are pointed, one has to ask: Are they pointing at the Garhwali Other or at the repressed Self? Moreover, the mountain people are also renowned for their courage and god-fearing honesty, and thus they are in great demand as domestic servants in the plains, and disproportionately represented in the Indian military. For Garhwalis, too, Hindus from the plains are Other, and in an equally ambivalent fashion. On the one hand, Garhwalis seek to emulate them by reforming their religious, dietary, and marriage customs so as to conform more closely to those of the plains.[7] On the other hand, both Garhwalis and Kumaonis regard these Hindus as political oppressors, and over the last several years a separatist movement has gathered momentum (Dhoundiyal, Dhoundiyal, and Sharma 1993), finally resulting in the creation of India's twenty-seventh state, Uttaranchal, in November 2000. So the first point to be made is that, although Garhwal is geographically and culturally marginal, and its people are Other to the mainstream culture of the north Indian plains, this relationship is neither simple nor straightforward. The Other is also a reflection of the self, at times resented, at other times emulated.

Within Garhwal as well, there is a mainstream culture and a peripheral, Other culture. The mainstream culture is that located in the former British Garhwal. Partly because of the effects of colonialism, but mostly because of the presence of major pilgrimage routes, the people in the Alakananda and Mandakini basins have been exposed to mainstream Hinduism, and to the cultural conventions of the north Indian plains, more intensively and for a longer time than those living in the former princely state of Tehri Garhwal. Moreover, because of geographic (and consequently economic and political) isolation, the westernmost districts of Tehri Garhwal bordering on Himachal Pradesh (especially in the Tons River basin) are themselves culturally peripheral to Tehri state. According to one local historian, the people of this region were notoriously "turbulent and refractory" (Sakalani 1987, 44, 174ff.), and this reputation persists to the present day. Local history is punctuated with riots, rebellions, and resistance to the king, to the colonialists, and in fact to any external authority. Pity the poor civil servant who is posted to these remote valleys, giving new meaning to the local term "punishment posting."

7. This is an immediately recognizable and fairly common process in India, still best referred to by Srinivas's (1966 [1955]) term "Sanskritization," despite extensive debate over the usefulness of this term (e.g., Staal 1963).

The people from the upper Tons basin are not considered Other merely because they are a rough bunch. More important, the area is associated with a number of unusual customs, especially the worship of demons and the practice of fraternal polyandry (Majumdar 1963; Rawat 1991; Zoller 1988). Villagers in the eastern districts of Garhwal are virtually unanimous in their suspicion and distrust of those from the west. When my village friends heard that I was planning to travel to the Tons basin, they did their best to dissuade me. I was warned that men did not return from valleys of the Rupin and Supin Rivers: local women enslaved them, turning them into goats or frogs by day, and back into men at night "for their pleasure." There were rumors of poison cults, and once again it was the women of the area who were to be feared: they were said to worship supernatural beings who demanded one human sacrifice per year, and woe to the unfortunate guest who darkened the door on the designated day. A village healer went so far as to empower some salt with special magical spells and give it to me. He said that if any local woman were to offer me food, I should sprinkle this salt on it, and if it turned blood-red, I should not eat it. I assured him that if the food turned red, I certainly would not eat it! In fact, only one of my friends from the east had actually been to the Tons basin. He was a retired government officer from Nauti who had toured the area in the 1920s, and he told me that whenever he was offered food, it would first be tasted by a prepubescent girl, to demonstrate that it was not poisoned.

Despite (or perhaps because of) these warnings, I was eager to journey to the Tons basin. And I had a definite goal: for many years I had heard rumors and read reports of a local cult in which the Kauravas, villains of *Mahābhārata*, were worshiped (Munshi 1962 [1954], ix–x; Nautiyal 1971, 133–34; Ravat 1993; Sharma 1977, 79; Thukral and Thukral 1987, 41). Given my interest in *pāṇḍav līlā*, this was clearly something that I should investigate. But I seriously doubted that there was an actual Kaurava cult. I reasoned that because people from the Tons basin practiced polyandry and other unusual customs, Garhwalis elsewhere were willing to believe that local women were sexually aggressive, and that the local culture was inverted and strange. And nothing seemed more implausible, to me or to my friends elsewhere in India, than the outlandish suggestion that these people worshiped the Kauravas.

But we were wrong. Soon after arriving in the area for the first time in the winter of 1991, I was directed to the large, imposing temple of King Karna, the presiding deity of Singtur *paṭṭī* at the confluence of the Rupin and Supin Rivers, where social and religious life centers on the god. Here was a prime example of Otherness: a temple devoted to Karna of the *Mahābhārata*, the illegitimate elder brother of the Pandavas who fought on the side of the villain Duryodhana and his allies the Kauravas, and was killed by Arjuna at the urging of his divine ally, Krishna. Karna is strongly associated with death and defeat. He is such a dark and inauspicious figure that elsewhere in Garhwal (and in India), people do not even open the "Book of Karna" from the *Mahābhārata* without first performing a goat sacrifice.

They believe that if they do not perform a sacrifice, catastrophe will strike. For my friends in British Garhwal, this cult devoted to the tragic figure of Karna was quintessentially Other.

But as it turned out, the people of Singtur did not regard Karna as tragic or inauspicious at all. King Karna is regarded by the local population as a ruler. He is served by numerous lineages of priests, musicians, carpenters, and watchmen; he is the subject of a rich folklore; and he is often called upon to settle local disputes, which he does through his oracle. Like other kings, he travels frequently, sometimes in royal processions to the villages under his rule, sometimes to drive away other gods encroaching on his domains, and sometimes on pilgrimage to local sacred places. He is perceived as a real king who acts for the good of his subjects (see chapter 6).

That Karna is a virtuous and progressive ruler is shown by his enthusiastic promotion of certain social and religious reforms. Nearly all of these have the effect of reducing the cultural distinctiveness of the local population, by conforming more closely to the customs of the north Indian plains. For example, Karna and his priests are fierce prohibitionists, opposed to drinking in general and especially on religious occasions. They are opposed to animal sacrifice within the temple compound, and they seek to reform local marriage customs. In fact, what I had heard about polyandrous marriage was incorrect, for it occurs but rarely in the area.[8] However, the locally prevalent form of marriage—by bride-price—is also regarded by the orthodox as backward. As a reformer, King Karna also objects to this form of marriage and will not allow his priests to accept the bride-price for their daughters. His priests explain that Karna was famous for his generosity—in fact, one of the most popular epithets for him is the "generous king" (*dānī rājā*)—and so they, like him, refuse to accept the bride-price and even give a dowry along with their daughters. In doing so, they conform to the orthodox form of marriage among north Indian Hindus.[9]

It was beginning to look as though the local culture was not so radically Other as I had been told. Many of the customs I was curious about—polyandry, poison cults, and the like—were nowhere to be found. None of the women had tried to turn me into a sex slave. Nearly everyone but the god's priests practiced bride-price, but I knew from previous research that this custom was still practiced in eastern Garhwal and in some areas had been normative as recently as the previous generation (Sax 1991a). The idea of worshiping the tragic antihero Karna had shocked me at first, but he was actually a benevolent and rather orthodox god. And when I thought about it, I realized that in eastern Garhwal as well, I had met many deities who had been demons of one kind or another in their previous lives and had only later been converted

8. Polyandry is still found—albeit increasingly rarely—in the Jaunsar and Jaunpur regions, a few hours' journey away. See Majumdar 1963.

9. For normative marriage associated with dowry, see Fruzetti 1982; and Tambiah 1973. For a discussion of bride-price in general, see Goody and Tambiah 1973; for bride-price in the central Himalayan region, see Berreman 1972 [1963]; Fanger 1987; and Sax 1991a.

to the good side.[10] In fact, nearly all the strange customs of these remote valleys were echoed in the mainstream culture of eastern Garhwal. For example, when I translated the oral epic of the goddess Nanda Devi in 1984, some of the words in it had puzzled me; in the end, they could be explained only by very old persons who remembered these things from their youth. The songs had mentioned items of dress and adornment—golden earrings worn by men, for example—that were nowhere to be seen. They had also told of architectural details like four- and five-story houses, but no one's house was taller than two stories: a lower one for the animals and an upper one for the people. Once again, it was the old people who explained that multistory houses had disappeared long ago, when the population grew, the forest was cut down, and peasant landholdings shrunk to a fraction of what they had previously been. So these images from the old songs never came alive for me unjtil I reached the Tons River basin and found myself staying in a five-story house: first floor for the cows, second floor for the goats, third floor for the grain, fourth floor for the people, fifth floor for the family goddess and the visiting anthropologist. Not only that, but I was surrounded by men wearing golden earrings. And then I realized what was happening: the "turbulent and refractory" people of the western valleys were feared and despised by other Garhwalis not because they were intrinsically Other but because their Otherness was itself a reflection of those other Garhwalis' own past. I had entered a few steps further into the hall of mirrors and could not be sure whose reflection I was seeing.

Meanwhile, Karna's subjects from Singtur assured me that their customs were not different from those in other parts of Garhwal. But they insisted that higher up the valley dwelled a god and his subjects who were truly Other, uneducated and barbaric. That god, they said, was Duryodhana, archvillain of the *Mahābhārata* and, for most Hindus, a symbol of evil. They insisted that, although some people might deny it, the god really was Duryodhana: "Just as people everywhere are changing their caste these days, so they are trying to change their deity from a demon [*rākṣas yonī*] to a god [*deva yonī*]." King Karna's subjects assured me that there were several temples of Duryodhana higher up in the valley, and they even whispered of a shrine to the most despicable of the Kauravas, Duhsasana, who dragged the Pandavas' wife Draupadi into the assembly hall by her hair and attempted to strip her naked.[11] They said that the oracle of Duryodhana, whenever he was possessed, had to lean on a crutch for support, since Duryodhana's thighs had been broken in his final combat with Bhima.[12] I was told that

10. Sax 1991a, 47–49, 52; cf. Hiltebeitel 1989.

11. According to one of Duryodhana's priests in Jakhol, there are a total of fourteen temples dedicated to the god in the immediate vicinity. I have not found any evidence of a Duhshasana temple.

12. There is a Duryodhana temple in Kerala with a priest who, when possessed by Duryodhana, dances on one leg for several hours (Tarabout 1986, 223, 483, cited in Hiltebeitel 1991, 178).

Duryodhana went on royal tours throughout the region, and that wherever he halted, the people of that village were obliged to offer their finest animals and grain, their milk and butter, to the god and his priests. So frightened were they of his curse that they would do so without complaint. Once, it was said, villagers had not given the god his due, and he had responded by ordering that the breasts of a nursing mother be hacked off. King Karna's subjects assured me that they had suffered a great deal at the hands of Duryodhana and his minions. For years their high-altitude herdsmen were forced to offer the finest of their flocks as annual tribute, until one year five brothers defeated Duryodhana's followers even though they were vastly outnumbered, thereby ending the custom (see chapter 1).

Now I was well and truly puzzled. Was this cult of Duryodhana a collective fantasy, as I had previously assumed? Was it an example of an "otherizing" discourse based on an arbitrary difference? Was it perhaps true that this exotic Himalayan valley harbored an equally exotic religious cult, in which the most notorious villains of Hindu mythology were adored by the local population? I pondered these questions while trying to arrange a visit to the god's chief cult center, in the village of Jakhol. This was not easy to do because it was winter and the mountain trails were buried in snow and often impassable. One evening I was explaining my interest in Duryodhana to a fellow patron of the tiny inn where I took my meals, when a small group of men sitting next to us fell silent. One of them angrily called out, "Who says our god is Duryodhana? His name is Someshvara!" and I realized that my opportunity had arrived. The situation was very delicate, so I asked the man to come outside with me where we could not be overheard. I apologized to him for causing offense and said that I was only repeating what I had been told by the local people. Perhaps he would be willing to take me to Jakhol and show me the truth. The man, whose name was Kula Singh, said that he would be willing to take me there, but not now; it was midwinter, and the paths were too dangerous. But if I would come for the god's spring festival, I could stay with him, and he would help me in my research.

Later that spring I spent several days in Kula Singh's house, observing and participating in the god's festival, and three years later I returned to Jakhol. During these two trips I began to lose my way in the hall of mirrors. First of all, I discovered that within the god's village there was a dispute between two factions over the identity of the god and the rituals appropriate to him. Each faction was, in effect, Other to the other. One faction—I will call them the "traditionalists"—tacitly acknowledged that their god was Duryodhana, and they supported old customs such as demanding sheep and goats as tribute and sacrificing them in front of the deity. Meanwhile, a second faction—I will call them the "reformers"—insisted that their god was not Duryodhana but rather Someshvara, a form of the great Hindu god Shiva, and regarded the appropriation of livestock as a kind of theft, unsuitable for a religious institution. As the god's priest put it:

> Look, if we steal someone's sheep and bring it here, then people will accuse us of all sorts of things. This is theft, and the god's name will be sullied—they'll say he promotes thievery. Now a god's works are these: do meritorious action, sponsor scriptural readings, go on pilgrimage. It is not a god's task to steal things from people and bring them, sacrifice sheep and eat them, and put the blame on the god. The god isn't eating those sheep: men are.

There was also a dispute over the way in which the god makes his appearance during festivals. Traditionally, he is carried outside the temple on a "chariot" (*rath*), actually a kind of palanquin made of freshly cut pine saplings, and young men have great fun leaping on the saplings, jumping up and down on them, and trying to break them. The reformers felt that this custom demeaned the deity by failing to show him the proper respect; moreover, people were allowed to wear shoes when they approached the "chariot," and low-caste persons could pollute the deity by coming in contact with him during the melee.

Several years ago the reformers managed to convince their rivals to take Duryodhana/Someshvara on a pilgrimage to the famous, nearby temple of Kedarnath. They felt that after completing such a virtuous act, he would be likely to go along with their vegetarian and teetotaling reforms. But in the end he did not, and tensions continued. When I visited during the spring festival in 1991, there was an altercation between the reformers and the traditionalists, and that evening, members of the reformist faction sought me out and begged me to bring my camera the next day. They were certain that their rivals were going to gun them down, and they wanted me to document the massacre for posterity.

Even the god was ambivalent about his own identity. In 1994, during my second visit to Jakhol, he returned from a brief tour to some nearby villages and was ritually welcomed home, at which time he possessed his oracle, as is customary. It was the end of winter, and there had been a prolonged dry spell, but as we stood in the flagstone square before the temple, dark storm clouds whirled around us, and we were briefly pelted with hail, while the slopes above the village were blanketed with fresh snow. After possessing his oracle, the god demonstrated his power and ferocity—and simultaneously drew together the collective masculine force of the assembly—by taking the mens' ritual battle-axes in his mouth (plate 12). He removed the axes and began to speak, calling upon the two factions to settle their dispute and unite. People were becoming educated, he said: times were changing, and he would change with them. But he also commanded his subjects to maintain their old traditions. During much of his speech, the oracle supported himself by leaning on what looked rather like a long metal sword with an unusually short hilt. Was it not the crutch about which I had already been told, required by Duryodhana since his thighs were broken by Bhima in their final combat? His speech was punctuated by frequent interjections: "Ak! ak!" Was this not an expression of pain from his broken

Plate 12. Duryodhana/Someshvara possessing his oracle in Jakhol village. Photo by William S. Sax.

thigh? After the trance had ended, the oracle leaped to a standing position, obviously relieved that the trance was complete. Was he also relieved of Duryodhana's pain?

Now I had reached a place of radical Otherness at the center of the hall of mirrors. When I tell my north Indian friends about the possession and the crutch, I invariably elicit a shudder of dread. And yet in a fundamental sense, Duryodhana's subjects are not so different from people elsewhere in Garhwal. They do not worship Duryodhana because he is evil but because he is powerful, like the other deities that are worshiped throughout the area. Specifically, he has the power to bring rain or to withhold it, something that is obviously of crucial importance to local farmers (see chapter 6, note 33). There are other reasons, too, for worshiping the Kauravas, and these are hardly different than the reasons people elsewhere in Garhwal give for worshiping the Pandavas. Both sets of reasons have to do with people's ideas about who they are, about their identity and how they acquired it. The belligerence of the Kauravas and their eagerness to do battle fit in well with local men's images of themselves as courageous and warlike. People sometimes say that their ancestors fought on the side of the Kauravas, so that Duryodhana is king of his subjects in the Rupin and Supin valleys, just as he was king of their ancestors. In worshiping him they are remaining loyal to their ancestral traditions—to do otherwise would be dishonorable. Throughout the region, gods have been and still are among the most prominent political actors, and the boundaries of their domains are the subject of continual and lively dispute.[13] Devotion to the ancestral god is, therefore, a kind of protonationalism, in which loyalties to one's lineage, caste, and region are all mutually reinforced in the cult of the deity. To its neighbors, Duryodhana's domain might look like an "evil empire," but to those within it, loyalty to the cult is an appropriate and honorable attitude.[14]

So in the end, the subjects of Duryodhana were not so very different from Garhwalis elsewhere. And at all levels, elements of the Self could be detected in stereotypes of the Other. The very things that marked King Karna's subjects as different in the eyes of eastern Garhwalis—their style of dress, their architecture, their marriage customs—were elements of those eastern Garhwalis' own past.[15] Similarly, the aspects of Duryodhana's cult to which Karna's people derisively pointed had been practiced within living memory by Karna and his priests.[16] Animals were formerly sacrificed in front of King Karna, and he, too, used to be taken out during festivals on a "chariot" of pine saplings, which the village youths would joyfully try to break. Now, however, when he leaves the inner sanctum, he is placed on a tiger skin, symbol of royalty, and the faction of reformers in Jakhol wished to follow suit, just as they wished to adopt the vegetarian and teetotaling customs of Karna and his priests. Even in Duryodhana's capital, elements of the Self could be detected in characterizations of the Other. The reformers themselves had previously practiced many of the customs for which they castigated the traditionalists, while many of the traditionalists clearly felt that the reformers occupied the high moral ground.

So who exactly is this deity in the upper reaches of the Tons River basin? In one sense, the answer to this question is a matter of perspective, of social position. For King Karna and his subjects, the god is clearly and unambiguously Duryodhana, which shows that the residents higher up the valley are barbaric demon-worshipers. For reformers within the cult, the god is just as clearly Someshvara, and those who call him Duryodhana are ignorant and uneducated.[17]

But in another sense, the issue of the god's identity can be clarified by employing an anthropological perspective. In my view, the tensions and

13. Ibbetson and Maclagan 1919; Raha 1979; Rosser 1955; Sax 1991a; Sutherland 1998.

14. One cannot help but be reminded of W. C. Smith's seminal demonstration of the way that discrete "religions" arise in situations of cultural confrontation and conflict.

15. One of the minor, humorous *līlās* in Sutol village in 1993 involved a couple of wild men (*ban mānus*): first they ran around with little sticks and baskets, picking up grains and roots and eating them. Arjuna explained to the wild men that the Pandavas had been exiled to the forest, and in the end the "wild men" shared their food with them. This burlesque, accompanied by much horseplay, went on for a long time, and people thought it was uproariously funny. After it was over, Padam Singh, the master of ceremonies, explained that we are like the wild men and can only progress by using our intelligence.

16. As Csordas has observed, demonology "is a mirror image of the culturally ideal self, representing the range of its negative attributes" (1990, 15). Cf. O'Flaherty 1976.

17. In March 2001, I visited Jakhol again, and found that some people have begun to refer to him as "Mahashiva."

inconsistencies surrounding the god's identity stem from the fact that he and his cult are undergoing a profound transformation, one that is linked to wider socioeconomic processes. These formerly isolated valleys are being integrated with the rest of India as they never have been before. A generation ago, there were no roads into the area, there were few visitors from outside, and there was virtually no public education. But now domestic and international tourism is rapidly expanding, government and private schools are everywhere, and the transportation network is burgeoning. The area has been declared a wildlife refuge, and there are alarming plans to relocate the inhabitants. In 1991, I had to walk more than ten kilometers and ford a major river to reach Jakhol from the trailhead at Sankari, but in 1994 I took the twice-daily taxi service. However, these changes do not, in and of themselves, account for changes in the cult. The most important issues in this regard have to do with how the people of Rawain represent themselves to each other and to the outside world, and how they in turn are represented. As communications with the north Indian plains have expanded, reformers have become aware that other Hindus regard them as perverse and backward Others because they worship Duryodhana the notorious villain, and that is the main reason that they are in the process of reinventing their deity as Someshvara. One youth obtained a law degree in Delhi several years ago and returned to become an influential proponent of the view that the god is Someshvara and not Duryodhana. A rule of thumb seems to be that the more contact a person has had with the plains, the more likely he is to insist that the god is Someshvara. Such contact will only increase in the coming years, and as it does so, the reformers' self-representation will continue to gain ground against that of the traditionalists. Eventually, the god's metamorphosis from Duryodhana to Someshvara will be complete.

As an outsider with little personal stake in this controversy, I was to some extent able to situate myself above the fray, from where I could see that while the deity was probably called Duryodhana by his subjects in previous times, he is undergoing a transformation. Such an anthropological explanation, cobbled together from historical inference, ethnographic observation, and sociological analysis, is not generally available to local persons. For them, the question of the god's identity is, in principle, a black-and-white issue. Religious belief cannot accommodate a shifting or contextually based divine identity: either the god is Duryodhana or he is Someshvara. He cannot be both at once: his followers are not postmodernists.

Conclusion

Where does this leave us? In an important sense, I think it leaves us stranded in the hall of mirrors, with no way out. Paradoxically, our tendency to focus on that which divides human beings from each other, to focus on difference, is a universal that we all we share. We cannot help noticing that other people speak different languages, observe different customs, and are, well, *different*, Other. Yet these differences, though they are believed to be essential,[18] are largely matters of perspective. My own anthropological journey provides an illustration. I went to India because I was curious about another culture, another form of life. But when I got there, I discovered that as far as most north Indians were concerned, the truly Other form of life, one that was strange and backward, was in Garhwal. After spending some time there, I discovered that local people thought of the residents of western Garhwal as Other in all sorts of ways: religious, cultural, and sexual. When I traveled to western Garhwal, I found that similar things were said of those Others who lived higher up the valley. And when I finally reached the end of the valley, the last human habitation, I found that even within that village, there were two factions, each of which was Other to its twin.

All of which clearly illustrates Said's first point, that people everywhere create distinctions between Self and Other. But his second point—that the self is always valorized and the Other always vilified—is simply not true, or at least not so simple. It is not true, for example, of those who hold up the Other as a model to be emulated, or as a mirror of the shadow side of the self. In fact, the situation is always much more complex than Said implies, with selfhood and otherness, virtue and vice, subject to ceaseless negotiation and reinterpretation. To many of my students, India is a land of poverty and suffering but also one of ancient wisdom, while to my friends in Garhwal, the places I have lived in North America, the South Pacific, and Europe are lands of material wealth alongside spiritual degradation. To the higher castes and upper classes of the plains, the mountain dwellers of Garhwal are ignorant hillbillies, but also and at the same time they are admired for their courage and honesty. To the Garhwalis, people from the plains are political oppressors, but simultaneously they are the objects of envy and desire, and their customs are the model for the religious reforms I have described. To the subjects of King Karna, Duryodhana's followers are barbaric but admirably strong and warlike, while Duryodhana's followers see Karna's subjects subjects as physically weak but morally superior and worthy of emulation. In this hall of mirrors, Self and Other cannot be neatly distinguished.

18. "As recent critiques and revisions of post-colonialist approaches have pointed out, essentialist categories were current in south Asia prior to colonialism, and Indian categories were adapted and reified by Europeans in complex ways, not all of which were essentializing" (Titus n.d., 2).

Bibliography

Abu-Lughod, Lila. 1991. Writing against culture. In *Recapturing anthropology: Working in the present*, edited by Richard G. Fox. Santa Fe: School of American Research Press.

Agastya, Sannyasi. 1928. Aśvamedha. All India Oriental Conference V.

Agnew, Jean-Christophe. 1986. *Worlds apart: The market and the theater in Anglo-American thought, 1550–1750*. Cambridge: Cambridge University Press.

———. 1990. History and anthropology: Scenes from a marriage. *Yale Journal of Criticism* 3 (2): 29–50.

Agnew, John A. 1989. The devaluation of place in social science. In *The power of place: Bringing together geographical and sociological imaginations*, edited by John A. Agnew and James S. Duncan. Boston: Unwin Hyman.

Anderson, Mary M. 1971. *The festivals of Nepal*. London: Allen and Unwin.

Antoine, Robert, trans. 1972. *The dynasty of Raghu (Kalidas's Raghuvamsa)*. Calcutta: Writer's Workshop.

Appadurai, Arjun. 1993. Number in the colonial imagination. In *Orientalism and the postcolonial predicament: Perspectives on South Asia*, edited by Carol A. Breckenridge and Peter van der Veer. Philadelphia: University of Pennsylvania Press.

Aronoff, Myron J. 1977. *Power and ritual in the Israel Labor Party*. Assen: Van Gorcum.

Artaud, Antonin. 1958 [1938]. *The theatre and its double*. Translated from the French by Mary Caroline Richards. New York: Grove Press.

Asad, Talal. 1993. *Geneaologies of religion: Discipline and reasons of power in Christianity and Islam*. Baltimore: Johns Hopkins University Press.

Atkinson, Edwin T. 1974 [1882]. *Kumaon Hills: Its history, geography and anthropology with reference to Garhwal and Nepal*. Delhi: Cosmo Publications.

Atkinson, Jane Monnig. 1987. The effectiveness of shamans in an Indonesian ritual. *American Anthropologist* 89:342–55.

Austin, J. L. 1962. *How to do things with words*. 2d ed. Cambridge, Mass.: Harvard University Press.

Awasthi, Induja. 1979. Rāmlīlā: Tradition and styles. *Quarterly Journal for the National Centre for the Performing Arts* 8 (3): 23–26.

Babb, Lawrence A. 1976. *The divine hierarchy*. New York: Columbia University Press.

Bacchetta, Paola. 1993. All our goddesses are armed: Religion, resistance, and revenge in the life of a militant Hindu nationalist woman. *Bulletin of Concerned Asian Scholars* 25 (4): 38–52.

Bahadur, Rai Pati Ram. 1916. *Garhwal ancient and modern*. Simla: Army Press.

Bandhu, C. M. 1997. Nepali oral epic: Ramayana. Paper presented at the conference Katha Vachana or Katha Vachak: Exploring India's Chanted Narratives. Indira Gandhi National Centre for the Arts, New Delhi, February 3–7.

Bauman, Richard. 1977. *Verbal art as performance*. Prospect Heights, Ill.: Waveland.

Bauman, Richard, and C. L. Briggs. 1990. Poetics and performance as critical perspectives on language and social life. *Annual Review of Anthropology* 19:59–88.

Bautze, Joachim. 1983. The problem of the Khaḍga (*Rhinoceros unicornis*) in the light of archaeological finds and art. *South Asian Archaeology* 1983:405–33.

Beals, Alan R. 1955. Change in the leadership of a Mysore village. In *India's villages*, edited by M. N. Srinivas. Bombay: Asia Publishing House.

Beck, Brenda E. F. 1980. The role of women in a Tamil folk epic. *Canadian Folklore Canadien* 2:7–29.

———. 1982. *The three twins: The telling of a south Indian folk epic*. Bloomington: Indiana University Press.

Beeman, William O. 1993. The Anthropology of Theater and Spectacle. *Annual Review of Anthropology:* 22:369–93.

Bell, Catherine. 1992. *Ritual theory, ritual practice*. New York: Oxford University Press.

Bennett, Lynn. 1983. *Dangerous wives and sacred sisters: Social and symbolic roles of high-caste women in Nepal*. New York: Columbia University Press.

Berreman, Gerald D. 1972 [1963]. *Hindus of the Himalayas: Ethnography and change*. Berkeley: University of California Press.

———. 1964. Brahmins and Shamans in Pahari Religion. *Journal of Asian Studies* 23 (1): 53–69.

Bhartati, Agehananda. 1983. India: South Asian perspectives on aggression. In *Aggression in global perspective*, edited by Arnold P. Goldstein and Marshall H. Segall. New York: Pergamon Press.

———. 1985. The self in Hindu thought and action. In *Culture and self: Asian and Western perspectives*, edited by Anthony J. Marsella, George DeVos, and Francis L. K. Hsu. New York: Tavistock.

Bhardwaj, Surinder Mohan. 1973. *Hindu places of pilgrimage in India: A study in cultural geography*. Berkeley: University of California Press.

Biardeau, Madeleine. 1976. Etudes de mythologie hindoue: 4. Bhakti et avatāra. *Bulletin de l'Ecole Française d'Extrême Orient* 63:87–237.

———. 1978. Etudes de mythologie hindoue: 5. Bhakti et avatāra. *Bulletin de l'Ecole Française d'Extrême Orient* 65:111–263.

———. 1981. *L'Hindouisme: Anthropologie d'une civilisation*. Paris: Flammarion.

———. 1989. *Histoires de poteaux: Variations védiques autour de la déesse hindoue.* Paris: Ecole Française d'Extrême Orient.

Blackburn, Stuart H. 1988. *Singing of birth and death: Texts in performance.* Philadelphia: University of Pennsylvania Press.

Blackburn, Stuart H. and A. K. Ramanajan. 1986. *Another harmony: New essays on the folklore of India.* Berkeley: University of California Press.

Blackburn, Stuart H., Peter J. Claus, Joyce B. Flueckiger, and Susan S. Wadley, eds. 1989. *Oral epics in India.* Berkeley: University of California Press.

Bloch, Maurice. 1974. Symbols, song, dance and features of articulation: Is religion an extreme form of traditional authority? *European Journal of Sociology* 15:55–81.

———. 1986. *From blessing to violence: History and ideology in the circumcision ritual of the Merina of Madagascar.* Cambridge: Cambridge University Press.

———. 1987. The ritual of the royal bath in Madagascar. In *Rituals of royalty: Power and ceremonial in traditional societies*, edited by David Cannadine and Simon Price. Cambridge: Cambridge University Press.

Bocock, Robert. 1986. *Hegemony.* London: Tavistock.

Bora, R. S. 1996. *Himalayan migration: A study of the hill region of Uttar Pradesh.* Institute of Economic Growth, Studies in Economic Development and Planning, no. 62. New Delhi: Sage.

Bourdieu, Pierre. 1977. *Outline of a theory of practice.* Translated by Richard Nice. Cambridge: Cambridge University Press.

———. 1984. *Distinctions: A social critique of the judgement of taste.* Translated by Richard Nice. Cambridge, Mass.: Harvard University Press.

———. 1990. *The logic of practice.* Translated by Richard Nice. Cambridge: Polity.

Bratman, M. 1992. Shared cooperative activity. *Philosophical Review* 101:327–41.

Brown, Charles W. 1992. "What we call 'Bhotias' are in reality not Bhotias": Perspectives of British colonial conceptions. In *Himalaya: Past and present*, vol. 2, edited by Maheshwar P. Joshi, Allen C. Fanger, and Charles W. Brown. Almora, India: Shree Almora Book Depot.

Buck-Morss, S. 1977. *The origin of negative dialectics.* New York: Free Press.

Burghart, Richard. 1978. Hierarchical models of the Hindu social system. *Man*, n.s., 13:519–26.

Butler, Judith. 1993. *Bodies that matter: On the discursive limits of "sex."* New York: Routledge.

Caland, W. 1932. A note on the Śatapatha Brāhmaṇa. *Acta Orientalia* 10:126–34.

Cannadine, David. 1984. The context, performance and meaning of ritual: The British monarchy and the "invention of tradition," c. 1820–1977. In *The invention of tradition*, edited by Eric Hobsbawn and Terence Ranger. Cambridge: Cambridge University Press.

Carrithers, Michael, Steven Collins, and Steven Lukes, eds. 1985. *The category of the person: Anthropology, philosophy, history.* Cambridge: Cambridge University Press.

Carstairs, G. Morris. 1957. *The twice-born: A study of a community of high-caste Hindus.* London: Hogarth Press.

Chandola, Anoop. 1977. *Folk drumming in the Himalayas: A linguistic approach to music.* New York: AMS Press.

Chandra, Lokesh. 1990. The Mahābhārata in Asian literature and arts. In *The Mahabharata revisited*, edited by R. N. Dandekar. New Delhi: Sahitya Akademi.

Chetwode, Penelope. 1981. Western Himalayan Hindu architecture and sculpture. In *The arts of India*, edited by Basil Gray. Ithaca, N.Y.: Cornell University Press.

Coward, R., and J. Ellis. 1977. *Language and materialism*. London: Routledge and Kegan Paul.

Crews, Frederick. 1994. The revenge of the repressed. *New York Review of Books*, November 17.

Csordas, Thomas J. 1990. Embodiment as a paradigm for anthropology. *Ethos* 18 (1): 5–47.

Cunningham, Alexander. 1970. *Report of a tour in the Punjab in 1878–79*. Vol. 14 of *Archeological survey of India*. Varanasi: Indological Book House.

Dabaral, Shivaprasad. 1965–78 [2022–2035 Vikrama]. *Uttarākhaṇḍ kā Itihās* (The history of Uttarakhand). 8 vols. Dogaḍā, Garhwal: Vīr Gāthā Prakāśan.

Daniel, E. Valentine. 1984. *Fluid signs: Being a person the Tamil way*. Berkeley: University of California Press.

Das, Veena. 1976. Indian women: Work, power, and status. In *Indian women from purdah to modernity*, edited by B. R. Nanda. Delhi: Vikas.

———. 1977. *Structure and cognition: Aspects of Hindu caste and ritual*. Delhi: Oxford University Press.

Davies, Charlotte Aull. 1998. "A oes heddwch?" Contesting meanings and identities in the Welsh National Eisteddfod. In *Ritual, performance, media*, edited by Felicia Hughes-Freeland. Association of Social Anthropologists Monographs no. 35. London: Routledge.

de Bruin, Hanne M. 1998. Studying performance in south India: A synthesis of theories. *South Asia Research* 18 (1): 12–38. Special issue, The Performing Arts of South India; guest editor, Stuart Blackburn.

de Jong, J. W. 1975. Recent Russian publications on the Indian epic. *Adyar Library Bulletin* 39:1–42.

Deliége, Robert. 1992. Replication and consensus: Untouchability, caste and ideology in India. *Man* 27:155–73.

Dennett, Daniel. 1991. *Consciousness explained*. Boston: Little, Brown.

———. 1995. Consciousness: More like fame than television. Unpublished manuscript.

Dennis, Ken, ed. 1998. *Rationality in economics: Alternative perspectives*. Boston: Kluwer Academic Publishers.

Dern, Steven. 1995. *Culture in action*. Buffalo: State University of New York Press.

Derrida, J. 1978. *Writing and difference*. Chicago: University of Chicago Press.

Desai, Santosh N. 1970. Ramayana—an instrument of historical contact and cultural transmission between India and Asia. *Journal of Asian Studies* 30 (1): 5–20.

Devahuti, D. 1970. *Harsha, a political study*. Oxford: Clarendon Press.

Dhoundiyal, N. C., Vijaya R. Dhoundiyal, and S. K. Sharma, eds. 1993. *The separate hill state*. Almora, India: Shree Almora Book Depot.

Dirks, Nicholas B. 1987. *The hollow crown: Ethnohistory of an Indian kingdom*. Cambridge: Cambridge University Press.

———. 1989. The original caste: Power, history and hierarchy in South Asia. *Contributions to Indian Sociology*, n.s. 23 (1, special issue): 59–78. Reprinted in McKim Marriott, ed., *India through Hindu categories* (New Delhi: Sage, 1990).

——— 1992a. Castes of mind. *Representations* 37:56–78.

——— 1992b. Ritual and resistance: Subversion as social fact. In *Contesting power: Resistance and everyday social relations in South Asia*, edited by Douglas Haynes and Gyan Prakash. Berkeley: Universiy of California Press.

Doniger, Wendy. 1988. Jewels of rejection and recognition in Ancient India. *Journal of Indian Philosophy* 26:435–53.

———. *The implied spider: Politics and theology in myth*. New York: Columbia University Press.

———. 1999. *Splitting the difference: Gender and myth in ancient Greece and India.* Chicago: University of Chicago Press.

Dowding, Keith, and Desmond King, eds. 1995. *Preferences, institutions, and rational choice*. Oxford: Clarendon Press.

Dumont, Louis. 1960. World renunciation in Indian religions. *Contributions to Indian Sociology* 4:33–62.

———. 1962. The conception of kingship in ancient India. *Contributions to Indian Sociology* 6:48–77.

———. 1970 [1966]. *Homo hierarchicus: The caste system and its implications.* Chicago: University of Chicago Press.

———. 1975. Terminology and prestations revisited. *Contributions to Indian Sociology*, n.s., 9:197–215.

Dumont, P.-E. 1927. *L'Aśvamedha: Description du sacrifice solonnel du cheval dans le culte védique d'après les textes du Yajurveda blanc*. Paris: Paul Geuthner.

Durkheim, Emil. 1898. L'Individualisme et les intellectuals. *Revue Bleue*, ser. 4, 10:12n. English translation by S. Lukes and J. Lukes, Individualism and the intellectuals, *Political Studies* 17 (1969): 28.

Eliade, Mircea. 1959 [1957]. *The sacred and the profane: The nature of religion.* New York: Harcourt Brace Jovanovich.

Erndl, Kathleen M. 1993. *Victory to the mother: The Hindu goddess of northwest India in myth, ritual, and symbol.* New York: Oxford University Press.

Evans-Pritchard, E. E. 1940. *The Nuer*. Oxford: Oxford University Press.

———. 1948. *The divine kingship of the Shilluk of the Nilotic Sudan*. Cambridge: Cambridge University Press.

Fabian, Johannes. 1990. *Power and performance*. Madison, Wisconsin: University of Wisconsin Press.

Fanger, Alan C. 1987. Brideprice, dowry, and diverted bridewealth among the Rajputs of Kumaon. In *The Himalayan heritage*, edited by Manis Kumar Raha. Delhi: Gian Publishing House.

Feeley-Harnik, Gillian. 1985. Issues in divine kingship. *Annual Review of Anthropology* 14:273–313.

Fitzgerald, James L. 1980. The Mokṣa anthology of the Great Bhārata: An initial survey of structural issues, themes, and rhetorical strategies. Ph.D. diss., University of Chicago.

———. 1991. India's Fifth Veda: The *Mahābhārata*'s Presentation of Itself. In *Essays on the Mahābhārata*, edited by Arvind Sharma. Leiden: E. J. Brill.

Flueckiger, Joyce Burkhalter. 1989. Caste and regional variants in an oral epic tradition. In *Oral epics in India*, edited by Stuart H. Blackburn, Peter J.

Claus, Joyce B. Flueckiger, Susan S. Wadley. Berkeley: University of California Press.
———. 1996. *Gender and genre in the folklore of middle India.* Ithaca, N.Y.: Cornell University Press.
Fogelson, Raymond G. 1982. Person, self, and identity: Some anthropological retrospects, circumspects, and prospects. In *Psychosocial theories of the self*, edited by Benjamin Lee. New York: Plenum Press.
Foley, William A. 1997. *Anthropological linguistics: An introduction.* Oxford: Blackwell.
Foucault, Michel. 1977. *Discipline and punish.* London: Allen Lane.
Foucault, Michel. 1980. *Power/knowledge: Selected interviews and other writings, 1972–1977.* Brighton: Harvester Press.
Fox, Richard G. 1971. *Kin, clan, raja and rule: State-hinterland relations in preindustrial India.* Berkeley: University of California Press.
———. 1991. *Recapturing anthropology: Working in the present.* Santa Fe: School of American Research Press.
Frasca, Richard A. 1990. *The theater of the Mahabharata: Terukuttu performances in south India.* Honolulu: University of Hawaii Press.
Freeman, John Derek. 1983. *Margaret Mead and Samoa: The making and unmaking of an anthropological myth.* Canberra: Australian National University Press.
Freud, Sigmund. 1923. The ego and the id. In *The Standard Edition of the Complete Psychological Works of Sigmund Freud*, 24 volumes, translated by James Strachey. London: Hogarth Press. Volume 19, pp. 12–59.
Fruzetti, Lina M. 1982. *The gift of a virgin: Women, marriage, and ritual in a Bengali society.* New Brunswick, N.J.: Rutgers University Press.
Fruzetti, Lina, and Akos Ostor. 1982. Bad blood in Bengal: Category and affect in the study of kinship, caste, and marriage. In *Concepts of person: Kinship, caste, and marriage in India*, edited by Akos Ostor, Lina Fruzetti, and Steve Barnett. Cambridge, Mass.: Harvard University Press.
Fuller, Christopher J. 1992. *The camphor flame: Popular Hinduism and society in India.* Princeton, N.J.: Princeton University Press.
Gaborieau, Marc, 1977. Introduction. In *Himalayan folklore, Kumaon and West Nepal*, by E. S. Oakley and Tara Dutt Gairola. Edited by H. K. Kuloy. Bibliotheca Himalayica, series 11, vol. 10. Kathmandu: Ratna Pustak Bhandar.
Gadamer, Hans-Georg. 1960. *Truth and method.* New York: Crossroad.
Galey, Jean-Claude. 1983. Creditors, kings and death: Determination and implications of bondage in Tehri-Garhwal. In *Debts and debtors*, edited by Charles Malamoud. Delhi: Vikas.
———. 1984. Souveraineté et justice dans le Haut-Gange. La fonction royale au-delà des codes brahmaniques et du Droit coutumier. In *Différences, Valeurs, Hiérarchie*, edited by Jean-Claude Galey. Paris: l'École des Hautes Études en Sciences Sociales.
———. 1986. Totalité et hiérarchie dans les sanctuaires royaux du Tehri-Garhwal. *Purusartha* 10:55–95.
———. 1990. Reconsidering kingship in India: An ethnological perspective. In *Kingship and the kings*, edited by Jean-Claude Galey. Chur: Harwood.
———. Forthcoming. The absented throne: Royal houses and tutelary sanctuaries in the former kingdom of Garhwal. In *Autorita e Potere in nel subcontinente indiano*, edited by E. Fasana. Trieste.

Ganguli, K. M. 1981–82. *The Mahābhārata of Krishna-Dwaipayana Vyasa*. 12 vols. 4th ed. New Delhi: Manshiram Manoharlal.

Geertz, Clifford. 1973. *The interpretation of cultures*. New York: Basic Books.

———. 1983. "From the native's point of view": On the nature of anthropological understanding. In *Local knowledge: Further essays in interpretive anthropology*. New York: Basic Books.

———. 1984. Anti-anti-relativism. *American Anthropologist* 86:263–78.

Gell, Alfred. 1998. *Art and agency: An anthropological theory*. Oxford: Clarendon Press.

Gergen, Kenneth J. 1991. *The saturated self: Dilemmas of identity in contemporary life*. New York: BasicBooks.

Gerholm, Tomas. 1988. On ritual: A postmodernist view. *Ethnos* 3–4:190–203.

Gerow, Edwin. 1994. Abhinavagupta's aesthetics as a speculative paradigm. *Journal of the American Oriental Society* 114:186–208.

Gesick, L., ed. 1983. *Centers, symbols and hierarchies: Essays on the classical states of Southeast Asia*. Southeast Asian Monograph no. 26. New Haven, Conn.: Yale University Press.

Ghosh, Gautam. 1998. "God is a refugee": Nationalism, morality and history in the 1947 partition of India. In *Partition, unification, nation: Imagined moral communities in modernity*, edited by Gautam Ghosh. Social Analysis 42 (1).

Ghoshal, Upendra Nath. 1966 [1959]. *A history of Indian political ideas*. London: Oxford University Press.

Gilbert, Margaret. 1989. *On social facts*. London: Routledge.

Gitomer, David. 1992. King Duryodhana: The Mahābhārata discourse of sinning and virtue in epic and drama. *Journal of the American Oriental Society* 112:222–32.

Gluckman, Max. 1965. *Politics, law, and ritual in tribal society*. Oxford: Blackwell.

Gnoli, Raniero. 1985. *The aesthetic experience according to Abhinavagupta*. Chowkhamba Sanskrit Series, vol. 62. Varanasi: Chowkhamba Sanskrit Series Office.

Goddard, C., and A. Wierzbicka. 1995. Key words, culture and cognition. *Philosophica* 55:37–67.

Goffman, Erving. 1959. *The presentation of self in everyday life*. New York: Doubleday.

Gold, Ann G. 1992. *A carnival of parting: The tales of King Bartrhari and King Gopi Chand as sung and told by Madhu Natisar Nath of Ghatiyali, Rajasthan*. Berkeley: University of California Press.

———. 1994. Sexuality, fertility, and erotic imagination in Rajasthani women's songs. In *Listen to the heron's words: Reimagining gender and kinship in north India*, edited by Gloria G. Raheja and Ann G. Gold. Berkeley: University of California Press.

Goldman, Robert P. 1977. *Gods, priests, and warriors: The Bhrgus of the Mahabharata*. Studies in Oriental Culture no. 12. New York: Columbia University Press.

———. 1978. Fathers, sons and gurus: Oedipal conflict in the Sanskrit epics. *Journal of Indian Philosophy* 6:325–92.

———. 1986. Structure, substance, and function in the great Sanskrit epics (1). Paper presented at the Festival of India Conference on Indian Literatures, University of Chicago, April.

Gonda, Jan. 1969. *Ancient Indian kingship from the religious point of view*. Leiden: E. J. Brill.

Good, Byron J. 1994. *Medicine, rationality and experience: An anthropological perspective*. Cambridge: Cambridge University Press.

Goody, Jack. 1977. Against "ritual": Loosely structured thoughts on a loosely defined topic. In *Secular ritual*, edited by Sally Falk Moore and Barbara Myerhoff. Amsterdam: Van Goreum.

Goody, Jack, and S. J. Tambiah. 1973. *Bridewealth and dowry*. Cambridge Papers in Social Anthropology no. 7. Cambridge: Cambridge University Press.

Gramsci, Antonio. 1971. *Selections from the prison notebooks*. Edited and translated by Quentin Hoare and Geoffrey Nowell Smith. New York: International Publishers.

Grant, Nicole J. 1995. From Margaret Mead's field notes: What counted as "sex" in Samoa? *American Anthropologist* 97:678–82.

Grintser, P. A. 1974. *Drevneindiiskii epos: Genezis i typologia*. Moscow.

Grodin, D., and T. R. Lindlof, eds. 1996. *Constructing the self in a mediated world*. Thousand Oaks; London; New Delhi: SAGE Press.

Gross, Philip H. 1982. *Birth, death and migration in the Himalayas: A study in social demography and community intervention*. New Delhi: Bahri Publications.

Guha, Ramachandra. 1991. *The unquiet woods: Ecological change and peasant resistance in the Himalaya*. Delhi: Oxford University Press.

Guha, Ranajit. 1997. *Dominance without hegemony*. Cambridge, Mass.: Harvard University Press.

Gupte, Balakrshna Atmarama. 1994. *Hindu holidays*. New Delhi: Asian Educational Service.

Haberman, David. 1988. *Acting as a way of salvation: A study of Rāgānugā Bhakti Sādhana*. New York: Oxford University Press.

Hannu, Nurmi. 1998. *Rational behaviour and the design of institutions: Concepts, theories and models*. Cheltenham, England: Edward Elgar.

Hansen, Kathryn. 1988. The Virangana in north Indian history, myth, and popular culture. *Economic and Political Weekly* 23 (18): 25–33.

Harlan, Lindsey. 1992. *Religion and Rajput women: The ethic of protection in contemporary narratives*. Berkeley: University of California Press.

Harrè, Rom. 1998. *The singular self: An introduction to the psychology of personhood*. London: Sage.

Harris, G. 1989. Concepts of individual, self and person in description and analysis. *American Anthropologist* 91:599–612.

Heesterman, J. C. 1962. Vrātya and sacrifice. *Indo-Iranian Journal* 6:1–37.

———. 1964. Brahmin, ritual and renouncer. *Wiener Zeitschrift für die Kunde Süd- und Ostasiens* 8:1–31.

Heesterman, J. C. 1985. *The inner conflict of tradition: Essays in Indian ritual, kingship, and society*. Chicago: University of Chicago Press.

———. The king's order. *Contributions to Indian Sociology* 20:1–13.

———. 1990. King and warrior. In *Kingship and the Kings*, edited by Jean-Claude Galey. Chur: Harwood.

Hein, Norvin. 1972. *The miracle plays of Mathura*. New Haven, Connecticut: Yale University Press.

Herath, H. M. D. R. 1977. Princess Sita and the historically, geographically and anthropologically important locations (villages) and associated verbal narratives in the central hills of Sri Lanka. Paper presented at the confer-

ence Katha Vachana or Katha Vachak: Exploring India's Chanted Narratives. Indira Gandhi National Centre for the Arts, New Delhi, February 3–7.
Hillman, James. 1991 [1987]. Oedipus revisited. In *Oedipus variations*, edited by Karl Kerenyi and James Hillman. Dallas: Spring Publications.
Hiltebeitel, Alf. 1976. *The ritual of battle: Krishna in the Mahābhārata*. Ithaca, N.Y.: Cornell University Press.
———. 1980. Śiva, the Goddess, and the Disguises of the Pāṇḍavas and Draupadī. *History of Religions* 19 (1): 147–74.
———. 1981. Draupadī's hair. *Puruṣārtha* 5:179–214.
———. 1982. Sexuality and sacrifice: Convergent subcurrents in the firewalking cult of Draupadī. In *Images of man: Religion and historical process in South Asia*, edited by Fred. W. Clothey. Madras: New Era Publications.
———. 1988. *The cult of Draupadi*. Vol. 1, *Mythologies, ritual and the goddess*. Chicago: University of Chicago Press.
———. 1991. *The cult of Draupadi*. Vol. 2, *On Hindu ritual and the goddess*. Chicago: University of Chicago Press.
———. 1995a. *Draupadī cult lilas*. In *The gods at play: Lila in South Asia*, edited by William S. Sax. New York: Oxford University Press.
———. 1995b. Dying before the Mahābhārata war: Martial and transsexual body-building for Aravāṉ. *Journal of Asian Studies* 54:447–473.
———. 1999. *Rethinking India's oral and classical epics: Draupadī among Rajputs, Muslims, and Dalits*. Chicago: University of Chicago Press.
———, ed. 1989. *Criminal gods and demon devotees: Essays on the guardians of popular Hinduism*. Albany, New York: State University of New York Press.
Höfer, Andràs. 1992. On the poetics of healing in Tamang shamanism. In *Aspects of Nepalese traditions*, edited by Bernhard Kölver. Stuttgart: Franz Steiner Verlag.
Hocart, Arthur M. 1968 [1950]. *Caste: A comparative study*. London: Methuen.
Holmes, David S. 1990. The evidence for repression: An examination of sixty years of research. In *Repression and dissociation: Implications for personality theory, psychopathology, and health*, edited by Jerome L. Singer. Chicago: University of Chicago Press.
Hoon, Vineeta . 1996. *Living on the move: Bhotiyas of the Kumaon Himalaya*. New Delhi: Sage.
Hubert, Henri, and Marcel Mauss. 1967 [1898]. *Sacrifice: Its nature and function*. (Translated from the French by W. D. Halls.) Chicago and London: The University of Chicago Press.
Humphrey, Caroline, and James Laidlaw. 1994. *The archetypal actions of ritual*. Oxford: Clarendon Press.
Huntington, Samuel P. 1996. *The clash of civilizations and the remaking of world order*. New York: Simon and Schuster.
Hutton, Patrick H. 1988. Foucault, Freud, and the technologies of the self. In *Technologies of the self*, edited by Luther H. Martin, Huck Gutman, and Patrick H. Hutton. London: Tavistock.
Ibbetson, D., and E. Maclagan. 1919. The cult of Mahasu in the Simla Hills. In *A glossary of the tribes and castes of the Punjab and Northwest Frontier Province*, edited by D. Ibbetson and E. Maclagan. Vol. 15. Lahore: Superintendent of Government Printing.
Inden, Ronald. 1990. *Imagining India*. Oxford: Basil Blackwell.

Inden, Ronald B., and Ralph W. Nicholas. 1977. *Kinship in Bengali culture*. Chicago: University of Chicago Press.

Jacobson, Doranne. 1977. The women of north and central India: Goddesses and wives. In *Women in India: Two perspectives*, by Doranne Jacobson and Susan Wadley. New Delhi: Manohar.

———. 1978. The chaste wife: Cultural norm and individual experience. In *American studies in the anthropology of India*, edited by Sylvia Vatuk. New Delhi: Manohar.

Johnson, B. 1981. Translator's introduction to *Dissemination*, by J. Derrida, Chicago: University of Chicago Press.

Joshi, M. C. 1990. The Khasas in the history of Uttarākhaṇḍ. In *Himalaya: Past and present*, edited by Maheshwar P. Joshi, Allen C. Fanger, and Charles W. Brown. Almora, India: Shree Almora Book Depot.

Joshi, M. P. 1990. Kumāonī Vaṃśāvalīs: Myth and reality. In *Himalaya: Past and present*, edited by Maheshwar P. Joshi, Allen C. Fanger, and Charles W. Brown. Almora, India: Shree Almora Book Depot.

Kakar, Sudhir. 1979. A case of depression. *Samiksa* 33 (3): 61–71.

———. 1980. Observations on the "oedipal alliance" in a patient with a narcissistic personality disorder. *Samiksa* 34 (2): 47–53.

———. 1982. *Shamans, mystics and doctors*. Delhi: Oxford University Press.

———. 1990. Some unconscious aspects of ethnic violence in India. In *Mirrors of violence: Communities, riots and survivors in South Asia*, edited by Veena Das. Delhi: Oxford University Press.

Kapferer, Bruce. 1983. *A celebration of demons: Exorcism and the aesthetics of healing in Sri Lanka*. Bloomington: Indiana University Press.

———. 1997. *The feast of the sorcerer: Practices of consciousness and power*. Chicago: University of Chicago Press.

Kaushal, Molly. 1997. Saveen: Singers and performances. Paper presented at the conference Katha Vachana aur Katha Vachak: Exploring India's Chanted Narratives, Indira Gandhi National Centre for the Arts, New Delhi, February 3–7.

Keesing, Roger. 1987. Anthropology as interpretive quest. *Current Anthropology* 28:161–69

———. 1989. Creating the past: Custom and identity in the contemporary Pacific. *Contemporary Pacific* 1 (1 and 2): 19–42.

Keith, Arthur Barriedale. 1925. *The religion and philosophy of the Veda and Upaniṣads*. Cambridge, Mass.: Harvard University Press.

Kertzer, David. 1988. *Ritual, politics, and power*. New Haven, Conn.: Yale University Press.

Kinsley, David R. 1979. *The divine player (A study of Kṛṣṇa Līlā)*. Delhi: Motilal Banarsidass.

Kolff, Dirk H. A. 1990. *Naukar, Rajput and Sepoy: The ethnohistory of the military labour market in Hindustan, 1450–1850*. Cambridge: Cambridge University Press.

Kondo, Dorinne K. 1990. *Crafting selves: Power, gender, and discourses of identity in a Japanese workplace*. Chicago: University of Chicago Press.

Kondos, Vivienne. 1986. Images of the fierce goddess and portrayals of Hindu women. *Contributions to Indian Sociology* 20:173–97.

Köpping, Klaus-Peter, and Ursual Rao, eds. 2000. *Im Rausch des Rituals*. Münster: Lit-Verlag.

Kunjunni Raja, K. 1990. Architectonics of the Mahābhārata and the place of legends in its structure. In *The Mahabharata revisited*, edited by R. N. Dandekar. New Delhi: Sahitya Akademi.

Kurtz, Stanley M. 1992. *All the mothers are one: Hindu India and the cultural reshaping of psychoanalysis*. New York: Columbia University Press.

Larson, Gerald James. 1993. Āyurveda and the Hindu philosophical systems. In *Self as body in Asian theory and practice*, edited by Thomas P. Kasulis with Roger T. Ames and Wimal Dissanayake. Albany: State University of New York Press.

Laver, Michael. 1997. *Private desires, political action: An invitation to the politics of rational choice*. London: Sage.

Lawless, Elaine J. 1992. "*I was afraid someone like . . .*" *Journal of American Folklore* 195/417:302–14.

Lears, T. Jackson. 1985. The concept of cultural hegemony: Problems and possibilities. *American Historical Review* 90:567–93.

Leavitt, John. 1988. A Mahabharata story from the Kumaon hills. *Himalayan Research Bulletin* 8 (2): 1–12.

———. 1991. Himalayan variations on an epic theme. In *Essays on the Mahabharata*, edited by Arvind Sharma. Leiden: E. J. Brill.

Levi, Isaac. 1997. *The covenant of reason: Rationality and the commitments of thought*. Cambridge: Cambridge University Press.

Liddle, Joanne, and Rama Joshi. 1986. *Daughters of independence: Gender, caste and class in India*. London: Zed Books.

Lincoln, Bruce. 1981. *Priests, warriors, and cattle: A study in the ecology of religions*. Berkeley: University of California Press.

———. 1991. *Death, war, and sacrifice: Studies in ideology and practice*. Chicago: University of Chicago Press.

Lingat, Robert. 1973. *The classical law of India*. Translated from the French with additions by J. Duncan M. Derrett. Berkeley: University of California Press.

Lorenzen, David N. 1976. The life of Sankaracarya. In *The biographical process: Studies in the history and psychology of religion*, edited by Frank E. Reynolds and Donald Capps. The Hague: Mouton.

Lukes, Steven. 1975. Political ritual and social integration. *Sociology* 9:289–308.

———. 1985. Conclusion. In *The category of the person: Anthropology, philosophy, history*, edited by Michael Carrithers, Steven Collins, and Steven Lukes. Cambridge: Cambridge University Press.

Lutgendorf, Phillip. 1991. *The life of a text*. Berkeley: University of California Press.

Lutz, Catherine. 1988. *Unnatural emotions: Everyday sentiments of a Micronesian atoll and their challenge to Western theory*. Chicago: University of Chicago Press.

Lutz, Catherine, and Lila Abu-Lughod, eds. 1990. *Language and the politics of emotion*. Cambridge: Cambridge University Press.

Mabbett, I. W. 1969. Devarāja. *Journal of Southeast Asian History* 10:202–23.

Madan, T. N. 1965. *Family and kinship: A study* of the Pandits of rural Kashmir. London: Asia Publishing House.

———. 1987. *Non-renunciation: Themes and interpretations of Hindu culture*. Delhi: Oxford University Press.

Majumdar, D. N. 1963. *Himalayan polyandry: Structure, functioning and culture change. A case-study of Jaunsar Bawar*. New York: Asia Publishing House.

Malik, Aditya. 1999. Divine testimony: The Rajasthani oral narrative of Devnārāyaṇ. Habilitation Thesis, University of Heidelberg.

Marcus, George E., and Michael M. J. Fischer. 1986. *Anthropology as cultural critique: An experimental moment in the human sciences*. Chicago: University of Chicago Press.

Marriott, McKim. 1968. Caste ranking and food transactions: a matrix analysis. In *Structure and change in Indian society*, edited by Milton B. Singer and Bernard S. Cohn. Chicago: Aldine Publishers.

———. 1976. Hindu transactions: Diversity without dualism. In *Transaction and meaning*, edited by Bruce Kapferer. Philadelphia: Institute for the Study of Human Issues.

———. 1988. The open Hindu person and interpersonal fluidity. Unpublished manuscript.

———, ed. 1990. *India through Hindu categories*. New Delhi: Sage.

Marsella, Anthony J., George DeVos, and Francis L. K. Hsu, eds. 1985. *Culture and self: Asian and Western perspectives*. New York: Tavistock.

Mauss, Marcel. 1966. *The gift*. London: Cohen and West.

Mayer, Adrian C. 1960. *Caste and kinship in central India: A village and its region*. Berkeley: University of California Press.

Menon, Dilip. 1988. The moral community of the Teyyattam: Popular culture in late colonial Malabar. Unpublished manuscript.

Mihirachandra, Pandit Shri. 1984 [sambat 2041]. *Dharmasindhuḥ*. Bombay: Shrivenkateshvara Steam Press.

Mishra, Mahendra Kumar. 1993. Influence of the Ramayana tradition on the folklore of central India. In *Tribal and folk traditions of India*, edited by K. S. Singh. Calcutta: Anthropological Survey of India.

Moffatt, Michael. 1979. *An untouchable community in south India*. Princeton, N.J.: Princeton University Press.

Monier-Williams, Monier. 1976. *A Sanskrit-English dictionary*. Berkeley: Shambhala.

Moore, David Chioni. 1994. Anthropology is dead, long live anthro(a)apology: Poststructuralism, literary studies, and anthropology's "nervous present." *Journal of Anthropological Research* 50:345–66.

Moore, Melinda A. 1990. The Kerala house as a Hindu cosmos. In *India through Hindu categories*, edited by McKim Marriott. New Delhi: Sage.

Munshi, K. M. 1962 [1954]. Foreword to the first edition. In *Social economy of a polyandrous people*, edited by R. N. Saksena. 2d rev. London: Asia Publishing House.

Murray, D. W. 1993. What is the Western concept of the self? On forgetting David Hume. *Ethos* 21 (1): 3–23.

Nandy, Ashis. 1988 [1983]. *The intimate enemy: Loss and recovery of self under colonialism*. Delhi: Oxford University Press.

Narasimhan, Chakravarthi V. 1965. *The Mahabharata: An English version based on selected verses*. New York: Columbia University Press.

Narayan, Kirin. 1993. How native is a "native" anthropologist? *American Anthropologist* 95:671–85.

Narayana Rao, Velcheru. 1991. A Rāmāyaṇa of their own: Women's oral tradition in Telugu. In *Many Rāmāyaṇas: The diversity of a narrative tradition in South Asia*, edited by Paula Richman. Berkeley: University of California Press.

Nasr, Sayeed Hossein Nasr. *Islam and the plight of modern man*. London: Longmans.

Nautiyal, Shivanand. 1971 [1902 Śaka]. *Gaḍhwāl ke Lokanṛtya Gīt* (Folk songs and dances of Garhwal). Prayag: Hindi Sahitya Sammelan.

Newell, William. 1955. *A "hermit" village in Kulu*. In *India's villages*, edited by M. N. Srinivas. Bombay: Asia Publishing House.

Nicholas, Ralph W. 1982. The village mother in Bengal. In *Mother worship: Theme and variations*, edited by J. J. Preston. Chapel Hill: University of North Carolina Press.

Oakley, E. S. 1991. *Holy Himalaya: The religion, traditions, and scenery of a Himalayan province (Kumaon and Garhwal)*. Edinburgh: Oliphant, Anderson, and Ferrier.

Obeyesekere, Gananath. 1981. *Medusa's hair: An essay on personal symbols and religious experience*. Chicago: University of Chicago Press.

———. 1990. *The work of culture: Symbolic transformation in psychoanalysis and anthropology*. Chicago: University of Chicago Press.

O'Flaherty, Wendy Doniger. 1976. *The origins of evil in Hindu mythology*. Berkeley: University of California Press.

———. 1978. *Religious Studies Review* 4 (1): 19–28.

———. 1980. *Women, androgynes, and other mythical beasts*. Chicago: University of Chicago Press.

O'Hanlon, Rosalind. 1985. *Caste, conflict and ideology: Mahatma Jotirao Phule and low caste protest in nineteenth-century western India*. Cambridge: Cambridge University Press.

———. 1988. Recovering the subject: Subaltern studies and histories of resistance in colonial South Asia. *Modern Asian Studies* 22:189–224.

Oldenberg, Hermann. 1988. *The religion of the Veda*. Delhi: Motilal Banarsidass.

Olivelle, Patrick. 1986–87. *Renunciation in Hinduism: A medieval debate*. 2 vols. Vienna: Gerold.

———. 1992. *Samnyasa Upanisads: Hindu scriptures on asceticism and renunciation*. New York: Oxford University Press.

Orr, W. G. 1940. Armed religious ascetics in northern India. *Bulletin of the John Rylands Library* 24:81–100.

Pande, Raj Bali. 1969. *Hindū Saṃskāras* (Socio-religious study of the Hindu sacraments). Delhi: Motilal Banarsidass.

Pandey, Gyanendra. 1992. In defense of the fragment: Writing about Hindu-Muslim riots in India today. *Representations* 37:27–55.

Pandeya, Pandit Śrī Matrprasad. N.d. *Gāyā Māhātmya Bhāṣā Ṭīkā*. Varanasi: Thakurprasad and Sons Bookseller.

Parish, Steven. 1994. *Moral knowing in a sacred city*. New York: Columbia University Press.

Parker, Ian. 1989. Discourse and power. In *Texts of identity*, edited by John Shotter and Kenneth J. Gergen. London: Sage.

Patel, Bhagvandas. 1997. *Bhīlo nuṇ Bharatha* (The Mahabharata of the Bhils). Khedbrahinā, Gujarat: K.T. High School.

Patnaik, Nityananda. 1972. The recent rajas of Puri: A study in secularization. In *Aspects of Indian culture and society: Essays in felicitation of Professor Nirmal Kumar Bose*, edited by Surajit Sinha. Calcutta: Eka Press, for the Indian Anthropological Society.

Pletsch, Carl E. 1981. The three worlds, or the division of social scientific labor, circa 1950–1975. *Comparative Studies in Society and History* 23 (4): 565–90.

Pollock, Sheldon I. 1986. *The Rāmāyaṇa of Vālmīki: An epic of ancient India.* Vol. 2, *Ayodhyākāṇḍa.* Introduction, translation, and annotation by Sheldon I. Pollock. Edited by Robert P. Goldman. Princeton, N.J.: Princeton University Press.

———. 1991. *The Rāmāyaṇa of Vālmīki: An epic of ancient India.* Vol. 3, *Araṇyakāṇḍa.* Introduction, translation, and annotation by Sheldon I. Pollock. Edited by Robert P. Goldman. Princeton, N.J.: Princeton University Press.

Prasad, G. N.d. *Gayā Māhātmya or the religious significance of Gayā.* Gayā: Gītā Pustak Kendra.

Proudfoot, Ian. 1987. *Ahiṃsā and a Mahābhārata story.* Asian Studies Monographs, n.s., no. 9. Canberra: Australian National University.

Puhvel, Jaan. 1955. Vedic Aśvamedha and gaulish Epumeduos. *Language* 31:353–54.

Purohit, Data Ram. 1993. Medieval English folk drama and Garhwali folk theatre: A comparative study. Ph.D. thesis, Garhwal University.

Quigley, Declan. 1993. *The interpretation of caste.* Oxford: Clarendon Press.

Quine, W. V. O. 1968. Ontological relativity. *Journal of Philosophy* 65:185–212.

Raha, Manis Kumar, 1979. Stratification and religion in a Himalayan society. In *Himalayan anthropology*, edited by James F. Fisher. The Hague: Mouton.

Raheja, Gloria G. 1988a. India: Caste, kingship, and dominance reconsidered. *Annual Review of Anthropology* 17:497–522.

———. 1988b. *The poison in the gift: Ritual, prestation, and the dominant caste in a north Indian village.* Chicago: University of Chicago Press.

———. 1989. Centrality, mutuality and hierarchy: Shifting aspects of intercaste relationships in north India. *Contributions to Indian Sociology*, n.s., 23 (1, special issue): 79–102. Reprinted in McKim Marriott, ed., *India through Hindu categories* (New Delhi: Sage, 1990).

Raheja, Gloria G., and Ann G. Gold, eds. 1994. *Listen to the heron's words: Reimagining gender and kinship in north India.* Berkeley: University of California Press.

Ramachandran, T. N. 1951. Asvamedha site near Kalsi. *Journal of Oriental Research* 21:3–31.

Ramanujam, B. K. 1986. Social change and personal practice: A view from an Indian practice. In *The cultural transition*, edited by Merry I. White and Susan Pollak. Boston: Routledge and Kegan Paul.

———. N.d. The importance of fathers: An overview of Indian cases. Unpublished manuscript.

Ramanujan, A. K. 1983. The Indian Oedipus. In *Oedipus: A folklore Casebook*, edited by Lowell Edmunds and Alan Dundes. New York: Garland.

———. 1986. Two realms of Kannada folklore. In *Another harmony: New essays on the folklore of India*, edited by Stuart A. Blackburn and A. K. Ramanujan. Berkeley: University of California Press.

Rao, Bhuvana. 1992. From sharing husbands to being a co-wife: Women's views on family and economic change. Paper presented to the panel New Research from the Central Himalayas, 91st annual meetings of the American Anthropological Association, San Francisco, California.

Rassers, W. H. 1959. *Pañji, the culture hero: A structural study of religion in Java* (trans.). The Hague: Martinus Nijhoff.

Ratuḍī, Pt. Harikṛṣṇa. 1980 [1928]. *Gaḍhwāl kā Itihās* (History of Garhwal). Ṭiharī: Bhāgīrathī Prakāśan Gṛha.

Rawat, Prahlad Singh. 1991. Gaḍhvāl Himālaya kī Saṃskṛti, tīrthayātrā evam nayā paryaṭan (The culture, pilgrimage places, and new tourism of the Garhwal Himalayas). Ph.D. thesis, Garhwal University.

Rawat, Vijendra. 1993. Jahāṃ āj bhī prakaṭ hote haiṃ Duryodhan (Where Duryodhan is found even today). *Hindustān Ravivāsarīya*, New Delhi, October 3.

Rawat, Ajay Singh. 1983. *Garhwal Himalayas: A historical survey*. Delhi: Eastern Book Linkers.

Richman, Paula, ed. 1991. *Many* Rāmāyaṇas: *The diversity of a narrative tradition in South Asia*. Berkeley: University of California Press.

Robinson, Sandra. 1985. Hindu paradigms of women. In *Women, religion, and social change*, edited by Y. Y. Haddad and E. B. Findly. Albany: State University of New York Press.

Rocher, Rosane. 1993. British Orientalism in the eighteenth century: The dialectics of knowledge and government. In *Orientalism and the postcolonial predicament: Perspectives on South Asia*, edited by Carol A. Breckenridge and Peter van der Veer. Philadelphia: University of Pennsylvania Press.

Roghair, Gene H. 1982. *The epic of Palnāḍu: A study and translation of Palnāṭī Vīrula Katha, a Telugu oral tradition from Andhra Pradesh, India*. Oxford: Clarendon Press.

Rosaldo, Michelle. 1984. Toward an anthropology of self and feeling. In *Culture theory: Essays on mind, self, and emotion*, edited by Richard Shweder and Robert LeVine. Cambridge: Cambridge University Press.

Rosser, Colin. 1955. A "hermit" village in Kulu. In *India's villages*, edited by M. N. Srinivas. Bombay: Asia Publishing House.

Royce, Anya Peterson. 1977. *The anthropology of dance*. Bloomington: Indiana University Press.

Rule, James B. 1997. *Theory and progress in social science*. Cambridge: Cambridge University Press.

Sadananda, Yogindra. 1968. *Vedantasara of Sadananda*. Translated by Swami Nikhilananda. Calcutta: Advaita Ashram.

Sahlins, Marshall. 1976. *Culture and practical reason*. Chicago: University of Chicago Press.

Said, Edward W. 1978. *Orientalism*. New York: Random House.

Sakalani, Atul. 1987. *The history of a Himalayan princely state*. Delhi: Durga Publications.

Sampson, Edward E. 1989. The deconstruction of the self. In *Texts of identity*, edited by John Shotter and Kenneth J. Gergen. London: Sage.

Sax, William S. 1987. Kumbha Mela. In *Encyclopedia of religion*, edited by Mircea Eliade et al. New York: Macmillan.

———. 1990a. The Ramnagar Ramlila: Text, pilgrimage, performance. *History of Religions* 29:129–53.

———. 1990b. Village daughter, village goddess: Residence, gender, and politics in a Himalayan pilgrimage. *American Ethnologist* 17:491–512.

———. 1991a. *Mountain goddess: Gender and politics in a Himalayan pilgrimage.* New York: Oxford University Press.

———. 1991b. Ritual and performance in the Pāṇḍavalīlā of Uttarākhaṇḍ. In *Essays on the Mahābhārata*, edited by Arvind Sharma. Leiden: E. J. Brill.

———. 1993. Goddess or goddesses? Politics and theology in the study of Hinduism. *Sites: A Journal for Radical Perspectives on Culture* 25:105–17.

———. 1994. Gender and politics in Garhwal. In *Women as subjects: South Asian histories*, edited by Nita Kumar. Calcutta: Stree.

———. 1995a. Introduction: Playful religion. In *The gods at play: Lila in South Asia*, edited by William S. Sax. New York: Oxford University Press.

———. 1995b. Who's who in pāṇḍav līlā? In *The gods at play: Līlā in South Asia*, edited by William S. Sax. New York: Oxford University Press.

———. 1996. Draupadi and Kuntī in the pāṇḍav līlā. In *The wild goddess in South Asia*, edited by Axel Michaels and Cornelia Vogelsanger. Studia Religiosa Helvetica, vol. 2. Zurich: Peter Lang.

———. 1997. Fathers, songs, and gurus: Masculinity and violence in the pandav lila of Garhwal. *Journal of the American Oriental Society* 117 (2): 278–94.

———. 1998. The hall of mirrors: Anthropology, Orientalism, and the "Other." *American Anthropologist* 100 (2): 22–31.

———. 1999. Worshiping epic villains: A Kaurava cult in the central Himalayas. In *Epic traditions in the contemporary world*, edited by Margaret Beissinger et al. Berkeley: University of California Press.

———. 2000a. Conquering the quarters: Religion and politics in Hinduism. *International Journal of Hindu* Studies 4 (1): 39–60.

———. 2000b. In Karna's realm: An ontology of action. *Journal of Asian Philosophy* 28 (3): 295–324.

———. Forthcoming a. Divine kingdoms in the western Himalaya. In Sacred Landscapes of the Himalaya. Proceedings of an International Conference at Heidelberg, Germany, 25–27 May 1998, edited by Axel Michaels, Niels Gutschow, Charles Ramble and Ernst Steinkellner. Vienna: Österreichischen Akademie der Wissenschaft.

———. Forthcoming b. Gender and the representation of violence in pāṇḍav līlā. In *Gender and social position in South Asian religions*, edited by I. Julia Leslie. Delhi: Motilal Banarsidass.

———. Forthcoming c. Pāṇḍav līlā. In *South Asian folklore: An encyclopedia*, edited by Peter J. Claus and Margaret A. Mills. New York: Garland.

Schechner, Richard. 1977. *Essays on performance theory*. New York: Drama Books Specialists.

———. 1983. *Performative circumstances, from the avant garde to Ramlila.* Calcutta: Seagull Books.

———. 1985. *Between theatre and anthropology*. Philadelphia: University of Pennsylvania Press.

———. 1990. Magnitudes of performance. In *By means of performance: Intercultural studies of theatre and ritual*, edited by Richard Schechner with Willa Appel. Cambridge: Cambridge University Press.

———. 1993. *The future of ritual: Writings on culture and performance*. London: Routledge.

Schechner, Richard, with Willa Appel, eds. 1990. *By means of performance: Intercultural studies of theatre and ritual.* Cambridge: Cambridge University Press.

Schechner, Richard, and Linda Hess. 1977. The Ramlila of Ramnagar. *Drama Review* 21 (3): 51–82.

Schieffelin, Edward L. 1985. Performance and the cultural construction of reality. *American Ethnologist* 12:707–24.

———. 1998. Problematizing performance. In *Ritual, performance, media*, edited by Felicia Hughes-Freeland. ASA Monographs no. 35. London: Routledge.

Schnepel, Burkhard. 1995. Durga and the king: Ethnohistorical aspects of politico-ritual life in a south Orissan jungle kingdom. *Journal of the Royal Anthropological Institute*, n.s., 1:145–66.

———. 1997. *Die Dschungelkönige: Ethnohistorische Aspekte Von Politik und Ritual in Südorissa/Indien.* Beiträge zur Südasienforschung Südasien-Institut, Universität Hedelberg, no. 177. Stuttgart: Franz Steiner Verlag.

Schomer, Karine. 1989. Paradigms for the Kali Yuga: The heroes of the Alha epic and their fate. In *Oral epics in India*, edited by Stuart Blackburn, Peter J. Claus, Joyce B. Flueckiger, Susan S. Wadley. Berkeley: University of California Press.

Searle, John R. 1995. *The construction of social reality*. New York: Free Press.

Seneviratne, H. L. 1978. *Rituals of the Kandyan state*. Cambridge: Cambridge University Press.

Sethi, Sqn. Ldr. Anup S. 1968. Mahasu: The moving god of Jaunsaries. *Vanyajati*, January, 21–24.

Sharma, Man Mohan. 1977. *Through the valley of gods: Travels in the central Himalayas*. New Delhi: Vision.

Shulman, David. 1985. *The king and the clown in South Indian myth and poetry*. Princeton, N.J.: Princeton University Press.

———. 1993. *The hungry god: Hindu tales of filicide and devotion*. Chicago: University of Chicago Press.

Shweder, Richard, and E. Bourne. 1984. Does the concept of the person vary cross-culturally? In *Culture theory: Essays on mind, self, and emotion*, edited by Richard Shweder and Robert LeVine. Cambridge: Cambridge University Press.

Simon, Herbert Alexander. 1997. *An empirically based microeconomics*. Cambridge: Cambridge University Press.

Singer, Milton. 1955. The cultural pattern of Indian civilization. *Far Eastern Quarterly* 15:23–36.

Skorupski, John. 1976. *Symbol and theory: A philosophical study of theories of religion in social anthropology*. Cambridge: Cambridge University Press.

Smith, Donald Eugene. 1963. *India as a secular state*. Bombay: Oxford University Press.

Smith, John D. 1989. Scapegoats of the gods: The ideology of the Indian epics. In *Oral epics in India*, edited by Stuart H. Blackburn, Peter J. Claus, Joyce B. Flueckiger, and Susan S. Wadley. Berkeley: University of California Press.

———. 1990. Worlds apart: Orality, literacy, and the Rajasthani folk-Mahābhārata. *Oral Tradition* 5 (1): 3–19.

———. 1991. *The epic of Pābūjī: A study, transcription and translation*. Cambridge: Cambridge University Press.

———. n.d. The Rajasthani folk-Mahābhārata. Unpublished manuscript.

Smith, Jonathan Z. 1987. *To take place: Toward theory in ritual*. Chicago: University of Chicago Press.

Smith, Wilfred Cantwell. 1964 [1962]. *The meaning and end of religion*. New York: New American Library.

Sorensen, Soren. 1978. *An index to the names in the Mahābhārata: With short explanations and a concordance to the Bombay and Calcutta editions and P. C. Roy's translation*. Delhi: Motilal Banarsidass.

Spencer, Paul, ed. 1985. *Society and the dance*. Cambridge: Cambridge University Press.

Sperber, Dan. 1975. *Rethinking symbolism*. Cambridge: Cambridge University Press.

Spiro, Melford E. 1982. *Oedipus in the Trobriands*. Chicago and London: The University of Chicago Press.

———. 1993. Is the Western conception of the self "peculiar" within the context of the world cultures? *Ethos* 21 (2): 107–53.

Spratt, P. 1966. *Hindu culture and personality: A psycho-analytic study*. Bombay: Manaktala.

Srinivas, M. N. 1966. *Social change in modern India*. Berkeley: University of California Press.

———. 1969 [1955]. *Religion and society among the Coorgs of South India*. Bombay: Asia Publishing House.

———. 1994 [1959]. The dominant caste in Rampura. In *The dominant caste and other essays*. Delhi: Oxford University Press.

Srivastava, Ram P. 1979. Tribe-caste mobility in India and the case of the Kumaon Bhotias. In *Caste and kin in Nepal, India and Ceylon: Anthropological studies in Hindu-Buddhist contact zones*, edited by Christoph von Furer-Haimendorff. New Delhi: Sterling.

Staal, J. F. 1963. Sanskrit and Sanskritization. *Journal of Asian Studies* 22:261–76.

———. 1975. The meaninglessness of ritual. *Numen* 26 (1): 2–22.

———. 1983–84. Indian Concepts of the Body. *Somatics* Autumn-Winter 1983–84: 31–41.

Stallybrass, Peter, and Allon White. 1986. *The politics and poetics of transgression*. London: Methuen.

Stein, Burton. 1977. The segmentary state in South Indian history. In *Realm and region in traditional India*, edited by Richard G. Fox. Durham, N.C.: Duke University, Program in Comparative Studies in Southern Asia.

———. 1980. *Peasant state and society in medieval South India*. Delhi: Oxford University Press.

———. 1985. Politics, peasants and the deconstruction of feudalism in medieval India. *Journal of Peasant Studies* 12 (2–3): 54–86.

Subba Rao, T. V. 1976. Telugu folk additions to the Mahabharatha. *Folklore* (Calcutta) 17:269–75.

Sukthankar, Vishnu S., et al., eds. 1933–59. *The Mahābhārata, for the first time critically edited*. 37 fascicules. Pune: Bhandarkar Oriental Research Institute.

Sullivan, Bruce M. 1995. The religious significance of Kūṭiyāṭṭam drama. In *The sun god's daughter and King Saṃvaraṇa: Tapatī-Saṃvaraṇam and the Kūṭiyāṭṭam drama tradition*, by N. P. Unni and Bruce M. Sullivan. Text with Vivaraṇa commentary. Delhi: Nag Publishers.

Sutherland, Peter. 1988. The travelling deities of the western Himalaya. Unpublished manuscript.

———. 1998. Travelling gods and government by deity: An ethnohistory of power, representation and agency in west Himalayan polity. Ph.D. diss., Oxford University.

Tambiah, Stanley J. 1973. Dowry and bridewealth and the property rights of women in South Asia. In *Bridewealth and dowry*, edited by Stanley J. Tambiah and Jack Goody. Cambridge Papers in Social Anthropology no. 7. Cambridge: Cambridge University Press.

———. 1976. *World conqueror and world renouncer*. Cambridge: Cambridge University Press.

———. 1979. A performative approach to ritual. *Proceedings of the British Academy* 65:113–69.

Thukral, Gurmeet, and Elizabeth Thukral. 1987. *Garhwal Himalaya*. Singapore: Frank Bros.

Titus, Paul. N.d. Honor the Baloch, buy the Pushtun: Stereotypes, history, and social organization in western Pakistan. *Modern Asian Studies* 32 (3): 657–687.

Todorov, Tzvetan. 1993. *On human diversity: Nationalism, racism, and exoticism in French thought*. Translated by Catherine Porter. Cambridge, Mass.: Harvard University Press.

Traill, George William, esq. 1828. Statistical sketch of Kumaon. *Asiatic Researches* 16. Reprint, Delhi: Cosmo Publications, 1979.

Trautmann, T. R. 1981. *Dravidian kinship*. Cambridge: Cambridge University Press.

Tuomela, Raimo. 1995. *The importance of us: A philosophical study of basic social notions*. Stanford, Calif.: Stanford University Press.

Tuomela, Raimo, and K. Miller. 1988. We-intentions. *Philosophical Studies* 53:367–89.

Turner, Victor. 1974. *Dramas, fields and metaphors*. Ithaca, N.Y.: Cornell University Press.

———. 1981 [1968]. *The drums of affliction: A study of religious processes among the Ndembu of Zambia*. Ithaca: Cornell University Press.

———. 1982. *From ritual to theatre: The human seriousness of play*. New York: PAJ Publications.

———. 1986. *The anthropology of performance*. New York: PAJ Publications.

Ulbricht, H. 1970. *Wayang purwa, shadows of the past*. Kuala Lumpur: Oxford University Press.

Underhill, Muriel Marion. 1921. *The Hindu religious year*. Calcutta: Association Press.

van Buitenen, J. A. B. 1973–78. *The Mahābhārata*. Vol. 1, *The book of beginnings*. Vol. 2, *The book of the assembly hall* and *The book of the forest*. Vol. 3, *The book of Virāṭa* and *The book of the effort*. Chicago: University of Chicago Press.

van der Veer, Peter. 1993. The foreign hand: Orientalist discourse in sociology and communalism. In *Orientalism and the postcolonial predicament: Perspectives on South Asia*, edited by Carol A. Breckenridge and Peter van der Veer. Philadelphia: University of Pennsylvania Press.

Vidal, Denis. 1982. Le culte des divinités locales dans une région de l'Himachal Pradesh. These de IIIe cycle. Laboratoire d'Ethnologie et de sociologie Comparative. Université de Paris X, Nanterre.

Wadley, Susan S. 1975. *Shakti: Power in the conceptual structure of Karimpur religion*. Studies in Anthropology, Series in Social, Cultural and Linguistic Anthropology, no. 2. Chicago: University of Chicago, Department of Anthropology.

———. 1977. Women and the Hindu tradition. In *Women in India: Two Perspectives*, by Doranne Jacobson and Susan S. Wadley. New Delhi: Manohar.

Warnke, Georgia. 1987. *Gadamer: Hermeneutics, tradition and reason*. Cambridge: Polity.

Werbner, Pnina. 1996. The fusion of identities: Political passion and the poetics of cultural performance among British Pakistanis. In *The politics of cultural performance*, edited by David Parkin, Lionel Caplan, and Humphrey Fisher. Oxford: Berghahn.

Witzel, Michael. 1995. Rgvedic history: Poets, chieftains and politics. In *Language, material culture and ethnicity: The Indo-Aryans of ancient South Asia*, edited by G. Erdosy (Indian Philology and South Asian Studies, vol. 1, edited by Albrecht Wezler and Michael Witzel). Berlin and New York: de Gruyter.

———. 1997. Early Sanskritization: Origins and development of the Kuru state. In *Recht, Staat und Verwaltung im klassischen Indien* (The state, the Law, and Administration in Classical India), edited by B. Kölver. Munich: R. Oldenbourg.

Wulff, Donna M. 1984. *Drama as a mode of religious realization: The Vidagdhamādhava of Rūpa Gosvāmin*. Chico, Cal.: Scholars Press.

Yalman, Nur. 1967. On the purity of women in the castes of Ceylon and Malabar. *Journal of the Royal Anthropological Institute of Great Britain and Ireland* 93:25–58.

———. 1989. On royalty, caste and temples in Sri Lanka and south India. *Social Analysis* 25:142–49.

Zey, Mary. 1998. *Rational choice theory and organizational theory: A critique*. Thousand Oaks, Calif.: Sage.

Zoller, Claus Peter. 1988. Bericht uber besondere Archaismen im Bangani, einer Western Pahari-Sprache. (Report on certain archaisms in Bangani, a western Pahari: language) *Munchener Studien zur Sprachwissenschaft* 49:173–200.

———. 1993. On Himalayan ball games, head-hunting, and related matters. In *Flags of fame: Studies in South Asian folk culture*, edited by Heidrum Brückner, Lothar Lutze, and Aditya Malik. Delhi: Manohar.

———. 1996. *Heroic ballads and the biography of a woman: On coping with conflicts in the western Garhwal Himalayas*. In Proceedings-Band Mainz (Occasional Papers 3), edited by I. Stellrecht. Reinbek bei Hamburg: Verlag für Orientalistische Fachpubliketionen.

———. 1997. Die Paṇḍuaṇ: Ein mündliches Mahābhārata-Epos aus dem Garhwal-Himalaya. (The Paṇḍuāṇ: an oral Mahābhārata epic from the Garhwal-Himalaya). Habilitation Thesis, University of Heidelberg.

Index